A Word
from
the Wise

A Word
from
the Wise

A sufficiency of quotes &
images to brighten your day

OTTO L. BETTMANN

H·A·R·M·O·N·Y B·O·O·K·S

All pictures in this book are from
The Bettmann Archive, Inc., New York,
with the exception of those listed below.

p. 36 *Madame X*, John Singer Sargent.
  Metropolitan Museum of Art, New York
  Arthur H. Hearn Fund, 1916

p. 74 *The Collectors*, Honoré Daumier.
  Victoria and Albert Museum, London

p. 87 *Mark Twain*, Max Beerbohm.
  National Portrait Gallery, London

p. 109 *Youth in Landscape*, Moritz von Schwind.
  Schack Gallery, Munich

Inquiries should be addressed to:

HARMONY BOOKS, a Division of CROWN PUBLISHERS, Inc.
One Park Avenue
New York, New York 10016

Published simultaneously in Canada by
General Publishing Company Limited

Printed in the United States of America

•

Book and Cover Design: Fred Czufin

•

Library of Congress Cataloging in Publication Data
Main entry under title:
A Word from the Wise

　1. Quotations, English.　I.　Bettmann, Otto,
1903-
PN6081.W59　1977　808.88′2　76-54849
ISBN 0-517-52932-7 pbk.
ISBN 0-517-52922-X

Second Printing

Alice was beginning
to get very tired of sitting
by her sister on the bank,
and of having nothing to
do: once or twice she had
peeped into the book her
sister was reading, but it
had no pictures or conversations in it, and where is the
use of a book, thought Alice, without pictures or con-
-versations?

Contents

Introduction

Whatever it be — love or money, lox or medicine — you may be certain that someone, somewhere, has said something memorable on the subject.

The salty wisdom you'll find in this book springs from a great variety of sources, some quite unexpected. They range from Socrates to Aristotle Onassis, including Johann Sebastian Bach, James Baldwin, John F. Kennedy, and Gloria Steinem. Their words alone are worth remembering, and worthy of graphic expression to give them a new dimension.

It is a fact that words and pictures work well together. One enhances the other. This I know from experience. As an obsessive picture sleuth from way back, I started with a cigar box full of old photographs — and wound up with an Archive of some 3,000,000 pictures. And in a lifetime of reading, I have culled with equal avidity picturesque sayings and words of wisdom. To team these up with illustrations I have often thought might double the pleasure they can give.

This book is the result: An illustrated alphabet of quotations, a sampling of great thoughts with pictures from the Bettmann Archive. May they join in tandem to provide you with solace and guidance, an occasional uplift, or a wry smile . . . "a sufficiency to brighten your day."

Otto Ludwig Bettmann

Advice

Wise men don't need advice.
Fools won't take it.

Benjamin Franklin

When a man comes to me for advice,
I find out what kind of advice he wants
and I give it to him.

Josh Billings

A good SCARE is worth more
to a man than good advice.

E.W. ("Ed") Howe

Air

Morning Air!
If men will not drink of this
at the fountainhead of the day,
why then,
we must even bottle up some
and sell it in the shops,
for those who have lost
their subscription ticket
to morning time in this world.

Henry David Thoreau

Animals

I think I could turn and live with animals,
   they are so placid and self-contained,
They do not sweat and whine
   about their condition,
They do not lie awake in the dark
   and weep for their sins,
Not one is dissatisfied,
   not one is demented with the mania of owning things.

Walt Whitman

14

HIPPOPOTAMUS

The skin of the hippopotamus is two inches thick. With a face like that he needs it.

Herbert V. Prochnow

Behold the turtle.

HE ONLY MAKES PROGRESS WHEN HE STICKS HIS NECK OUT

James B. Conant

Every horse thinks his pack heavy.

German saying

15

Applause: *that which makes good men better and bad men worse.*

Thomas Fuller

The deepest principle of Human Nature is the *craving to be appreciated.**

William James

*James made this remark when a class of young ladies who had studied with him at Radcliffe College in 1896 presented him with a potted azalea. Touched by this gesture of appreciation, he vowed to cherish the plant for the rest of his life. "If it dies, I will die too . . . and it shall be planted on my grave." Elizabeth Hardwick, ed., *The Selected Letters of Williams James*, (New York: Farrar, Straus, 1961), p. 152.

When someone does something good, applaud! You will make two people happy.

Sam Goldwyn

If you achieve success, you will get applause. Enjoy it — but never quite believe it.

Robert Montgomery

16

Arrogance

He was like a cock who thought the sun had risen to hear him crow.

George Eliot

Small man gets arrogant riding big horse.

German saying

The greatest of faults,
I should say,
is to be conscious of none.

Thomas Carlyle

Boasting and arrogance
are a compensation
for self-distrust.

Ralph Barton Perry

Books

The multitude of books is making us ignorant.

Voltaire

For books are not absolutely dead things, but do
contain a potency of life . . . as that soul was whose
progeny they are; they do preserve . . . the . . . extraction
of that living intellect that bred them.

John Milton

*A book so rich, intellectually — I had to put it down once in a while
to give my intellect a chance to burp.*

Anatole Broyard, *New York Times, 1973*

You think your pain and your heartbreak
are unprecedented in the history of the
world, but then you read. It was books
that taught me that the things that
tormented me most were the very things that
connected me with all the people who were
alive, or who had ever been alive.

James Baldwin

*A book must be
an ice - axe
to break the seas
frozen inside
our soul.* Franz Kafka

All good and true book-lovers
practice the pleasure
and improving avocation
of reading in bed.

Eugene Field

19

Business

If... the profession you have chosen has some unexpected inconveniences, console yourself that no profession is without them... and that all the perplexities of business are softness compared with the vacancy... of idleness.

Samuel Johnson

The secret of business is to know something that nobody else knows.
Aristotle Onassis

BUSINESS IS LIKE A WHEELBARROW. NOTHING EVER HAPPENS UNTIL YOU START PUSHING.
Popular saying

If you deal with a fox, think of his tricks.
Jean de La Fontaine

YOU NEED A PIG

TO FIND TRUFFLES.
French saying

21

Character

Do not free a camel of the burden of his hump.
You may be freeing him from being a camel. G. K. Chesterton

Be not angry that you cannot make
others as you wish them to be,
since you cannot make yourself
as you wish to be. Thomas à Kempis

The porcupine, whom one must handle, gloved,
May be respected, but is never loved. Arthur Guiterman

Chastity

Of all sexual aberrations,
the strangest perhaps is chastity.

Rémy de Gourmont

*A woman's chastity
consists like an onion
of a series of coats.*

Nathaniel Hawthorne

Children

When the Hen calls her
Chickens,
They follow straight-
way ;
So Children should always
Their Parents obey.

*The more you love your childen
the more care you should take
to neglect them occasionally.
The web of affection
can be drawn too tight.*

D. Sutten

First you teach a child to talk; then you have to teach it to keep quiet.

Anonymous

Men are but children of a larger growth.

John Dryden

Committees

Call no council —
it is proverbial that
councils of war never fight.

General H. W. Halleck

A committee is a group of men who
individually can do nothing,
but collectively can meet and decide
that nothing can be done.

Anonymous

If Moses had been a committee
the Israelites would still be in Egypt.

J. B. Hughes

Courage

- The essence of courage is not that your heart
  should not quake, but that
  nobody else knows that it does. E. B. Benson

- They conquer who believe they can.
  He has not learned the first lesson of life
  who does not every
  day surmount a fear. Ralph Waldo Emerson

- That's a valiant flea who dares eat his breakfast
  on the lips of a lion. Shakespeare

Discovery

Discovery consists in seeing what
everybody has seen
and thinking what nobody has thought.

Albert Szent-Györgyi

Dreams

... excursions to the limbo of things,
a semi-deliverance of the human prison.

Henri F. Amiel

*Dreaming permits each and every one of us
to be safely insane every night of the week.*

Dr. William Charles Dement

Drinking

Wine makes a man better pleased
with himself. I don't say
that it makes him more
pleasing to others.

Samuel Johnson

"For dust thou art, and unto dust thou shalt return"
— in between, can a little drink hurt?

Talmudic comment

It's all right
to drink like a fish
— if you drink what a fish drinks.

Mary Pettibone Poole

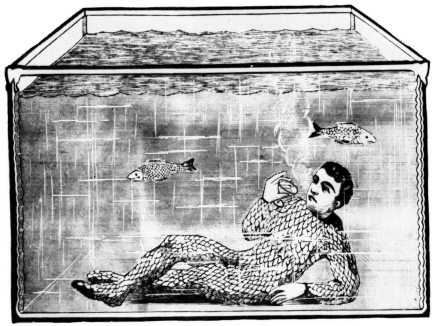

Eating

In general, mankind, since the improvement of cookery, eats twice as much as nature requires.

Benjamin Franklin

All human history attests
That happiness for man the hungry sinner
Since Eve ate apples
Much depends on dinner!

George Gordon, Lord Byron

No man is lonely
while eating spaghetti;
it requires so much attention.

Christopher Morley

**There is no love
sincerer
than the love
of food.** George Bernard Shaw

*Indigestion is charged by
God with enforcing
morality on the stomach.*

Victor Hugo

Editors

"A person
who knows
precisely
what he wants
but isn't
quite sure."

Walter Davenport

Your manuscript is both
good and original; but the
part that is good is not
original, and the part that
is original is not good.

Samuel Johnson

*The true function of art is to . . . edit
nature and so to make it coherent and
lovely. The artist is a sort of
impassioned proofreader, blue-pencilling
the bad spelling of God.*   H. L. Mencken

34

Education

What school, college or lecture bring to men depends on what men bring to carry it home in.

Ralph Waldo Emerson

Hegel in Berlin, 1828

Some men are graduated from college cum laude, some are graduated summa cum laude and some are graduated mirabile dictu.

William Howard Taft

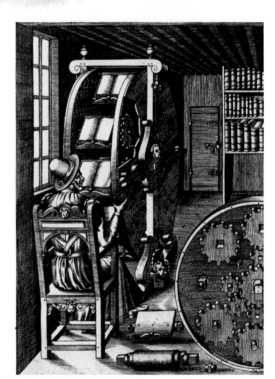

He is educated who knows how to find out what he doesn't know.

Georg Simmel

35

Elegance

The sense of being
perfectly well-dressed
gives a feeling of inward
tranquility which religion
is powerless to bestow.

Ralph Waldo Emerson

*Judge a man not by his clothes
but by his wife's clothes.*

Thomas R. Dewar

Those who think that in order to dress well
it is necessary to dress extravagantly or grandly,
make a great mistake.
Nothing so well becomes true feminine beauty as simplicity.

George Denison Prentice

Experience

Experience is a
good school,
but the
fees are high.

Heinrich Heine

Finance

Don't try to buy at the bottom
and sell at the top.
This can't be done
— except by liars.

Bernard M. Baruch

THERE ARE TWO TIMES IN A MAN'S LIFE WHEN HE SHOULDN'T SPECULATE — WHEN HE CAN'T AFFORD IT AND WHEN HE CAN.

Mark Twain

Always live within your income,
even if you have to
borrow money to do so.

Josh Billings

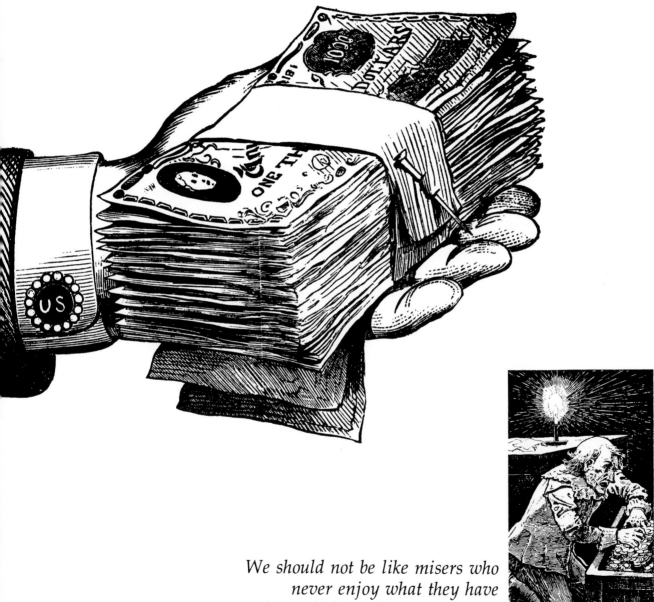

*We should not be like misers who
never enjoy what they have
but only bewail what they lose.*

Plutarch

39

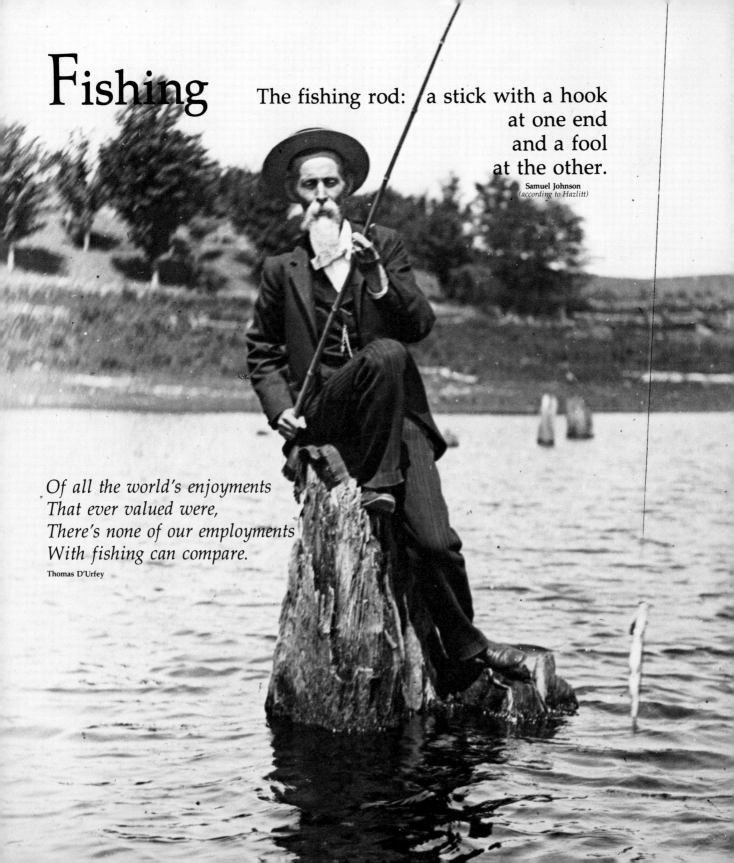

Fishing

The fishing rod: a stick with a hook
at one end and a fool
at the other.

Samuel Johnson
(according to Hazlitt)

*Of all the world's enjoyments
That ever valued were,
There's none of our employments
With fishing can compare.*

Thomas D'Urfey

Fools

**A fool takes two steps
where a wise man takes none.**

Jewish saying

*Every man is a damn fool
for at least five minutes
every day;
wisdom consists in
not exceeding the limit.*

Elbert Hubbard

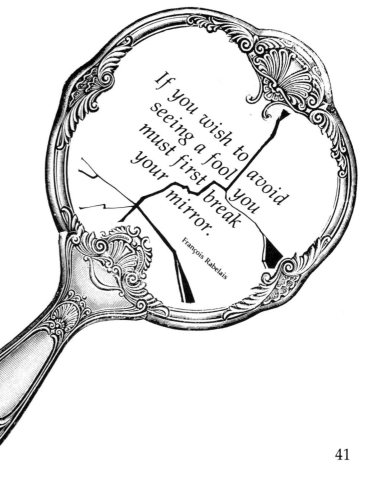

If you wish to avoid
seeing a fool you
must first break
your mirror.

François Rabelais

Gambling

> The safest way to double your money is to fold it over once and put it in your pocket.
>
> Kin Hubbard

*The best throw of the dice
is to throw them away.*

Austin O'Malley

Why they call a feller who keeps
losing all the time a good sport,
gits me.

Kin Hubbard

Games

BASEBALL:
*A game which consists of
tapping a ball with a piece
of wood, then running like
a lunatic.*

H. J. Dubiel

Men tire themselves in pursuit of rest.

Laurence Sterne

A stereotyped but unconscious despair is concealed even under what are called the games and amusements of mankind.

Henry David Thoreau

43

Genius

If children grew up
according to early indications,
we should have nothing
but geniuses.

Johann Wolfgang Goethe

*Genius is one percent inspiration
and ninety-nine percent perspiration.*

Thomas Edison

Gossip

What none claims to like but everybody enjoys.
Joseph Conrad

I have the most perfect confidence in your indiscretion.
Sydney Smith

Do not concern yourself with the ill fame of others . . . the more one grubs about in such matters the more one befouls oneself. Gracian

45

Hair

Better a bald head than none at all.

Austin O'Malley

Hats

If you are going to wear a hat at all,
be decisive and go the whole hat.
In making a courageous choice of millinery,
you have nothing to lose but your head.

The Bedside Guardian, *1962*

Infidelity

I pray that I may not be married
but if I am to be married
that I may not be a cuckold
but if I am to be a cuckold
that I may not know it
but if I am to know
that I may not mind.

The Bachelor's Prayer, *1650*

A jealous man always finds more than he looks for.

Magdeleine de Scudéry

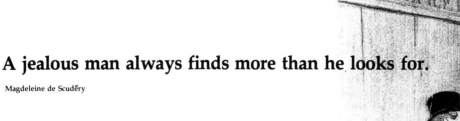

Joy

To get the full value of a joy you must have somebody to divide it with.

Mark Twain

People are constantly
clamoring for the
joy of life . . .
As for me I find
the joy of life
in the hard and cruel
battle of life . . .
to learn something
is joy to me.

August Strindberg

If you're going to do
something wrong,
at least enjoy it.

Leo Rosten

49

Kindness

Stretch a hand to one unfriended
And thy loneliness is ended

John Oxenham

Three things in human life are important:
The first is to be kind
The second is to be kind
And the third is to be kind.

Henry James

Kissing

When a rogue kisses you,
Count your teeth. Hebrew saying

Kisses kept are wasted;
Love is to be tasted.

Edmund Vance Cooke

Stolen kisses
are always sweeter.

Leigh Hunt

Law

We are in bondage to the law
so that we may be free.

Cicero

I was never ruined but twice —
Once when I lost a lawsuit,
Once when I won one. Voltaire

Ignorance of the law excuses
no man. Not because all men
know the law, but because 'tis
an excuse every man will
plead, and no man can
tell how to refute him.

John Selden

Laziness

Never learn to do anything.
If you don't learn, you will always
find someone else to do it for you.

Mark Twain

Work is the greatest thing
in the world. So we should
save some of it for tomorrow.

Don Herold

*The world is full of
willing people, some
willing to work, the rest
willing to let them.*

Robert Frost

53

Learning

Ignorance is the curse of God
Knowledge the wing
wherewith we fly to heaven.

Shakespeare, *Henry VI*

He has the facts but not the
phosphorescence of learning.

Emily Dickinson

*I have always
thought the reputation
of learning a misfortune
to a woman.*

Lady Mary Wortley Montagu

Love

'Tis sweet to court,
but, oh how bitter
To court a girl
and then not git her.

Album verse, *1850s*

**Breathes there a man with
soul so tough
Who says two sexes
aren't enough?**

Samuel Hoffenstein

There's nothing half so sweet
in life as love's young dream.

Thomas Moore

To speak of love
is to make love.

Honoré de Balzac

55

Love

Love consists in this:
that two
solitudes protect
and touch
and greet
each other.

Rainer Maria Rilke

Love is the drama of completion

Henry Miller

*It doesn't matter what you do
in the bedroom as long as
you don't do it in the
street and frighten
the horses.*

Mrs. Patrick Campbell

Luck

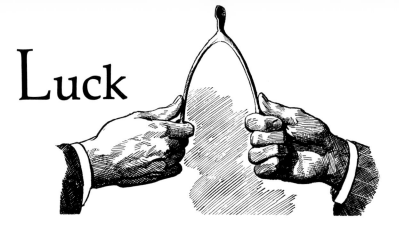

He that waits upon fortune is never sure of a dinner.

Benjamin Franklin

I am a great believer in luck and the harder I work the more I have of it.

Stephen Leacock

The wheel goes round and round
And some are up and some are down
And still the wheel goes round.

Josephine Pollard

Lying

It is aways the best policy
to speak the truth unless
you are of course an
exceptionally good liar.

Jerome Jerome

**A lie stands
on one leg,
truth on two.**

Benjamin Franklin

Marriage

Grave authors say and witty poets sing
That honest wedlock is a glorious thing.
Alexander Pope

Love — an affliction
curable by marriage.

Ambrose Bierce

"His House She Enters, There to be a Light"

10 Cents a Copy

A happy marriage has in it all
the pleasures of friendships,
all the enjoyments of sense
and reason — and indeed
all the sweets of life.

Joseph Addison, *Spectator*

While he is snoring in a trembling bed she wonders
– is
this
all
I am
going
to
get?

Adapted from Daumier

61

Money

*No man's credit
is ever as good
as his money.*

E.W. ("Ed") Howe

When a fellow says, "It ain't the money
but the principle of the thing,"
it's the money.

Elbert Hubbard

Music

There's music in all things
If man had ears;
The earth is but an echo
Of the spheres.

George Gordon, Lord Byron

If we were all determined to play
the first violin we should never
have a full ensemble. Therefore
respect every musician in his
proper place.

Robert Schumann

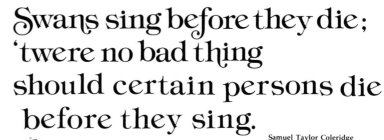

Swans sing before they die;
'twere no bad thing
should certain persons die
before they sing.

Samuel Taylor Coleridge

Who hears music
feels his solitude
peopled at once.

Robert Browning

Music is the moonlight in the gloomy night of life.

Jean Paul Richter

65

News

Scarcely anything awakens attention
like a tale of cruelty.
The writer of news never fails to
tell how the enemy murdered children
and ravaged virgins.

Samuel Johnson

To the press alone, checkered
as it is with abuses, the world
is indebted for all the triumphs
which have been gained by
reason and humanity over
error and oppression.
Th Jefferson

66

New York

A BEAUTIFUL CATASTROPHE

Charles E. Jeanneret

The straphanger's complaint is one of long standing.

El Paso Times

New York has always been an absurd city to live in but in a perverse sense this is one of its delights.

John Corry, *New York Times*, 1973

Noise

I DO NOT LIKE NOISE

UNLESS
I MAKE IT
MYSELF.

French proverb

*How the ear of man is tortured in this terrestrial planet!
Go where you will, the melody of jackasses,
wooden clogs and loud voiced men
breaks upon the hapless brain.*

Thomas Carlyle

Nonsense

A little nonsense now and then

Is relished by the wisest men.
Anonymous

Old Age

GEORGE CRUIKSHANK AT 79.—DRAWN BY HIMSELF IN 1871.

Growing old is no more than
a bad habit which a busy
man has no time to form.

André Maurois

The years teach what
the days never know.

Ralph Waldo Emerson

If a man does not make new acquaintances
as he advances through life he will find
himself left alone. Man, sir, should
keep his acquaintances in constant repair.

Samuel Johnson

Optimism

*Why do birds sing in the morning?
It's the triumphant shout: "We got
through another night."*

Enid Bagnold

*Had he been captain of the Titanic
he would have announced on impact:
"One moment please, we have just
stopped to take on ice."*

Anonymous

'Twixt the optimist and pessimist
The difference is droll:
The optimist sees the doughnut,
But the pessimist sees the hole.

McLandburgh Wilson

*An optimist is a person
who sees a green light everywhere
... while the pessimist sees only
the red stop light ...
But the truly wise person is color blind.*

Albert Schweitzer

71

Physicians

Some patients, though conscious
that their condition is perilous,
recover their health through
their contentment with the
goodness of the physician.

Hippocrates

Dame Nature gives long credit,
but never forgets to send in her bill.

William Osler

*This is where the strength of the
physician lies: He supplies the perennial
demand for comfort, the craving for
sympathy that every human sufferer feels.*

Leo Tolstoi

℞ It is part of the cure
to want to be cured.
Seneca

Half of the modern drugs could well be thrown out of the window, except that the birds might eat them.

Dr. Martin Henry Fischer

Diseases desperate grown
By desperate appliance are relieved,
Or not at all.

Shakespeare, *Hamlet*

*Being asked by his doctor if he had followed
his prescription, Beau Nash replied,
"If I had, I should have broken my neck;
for I threw it out of the second story window."*

Pictures

Pictures are loopholes of escape to the soul leading it to other scenes and spheres, where the fancy for a moment may revel, refreshed and delighted. Sir John Gilbert

Politics

A politician thinks
of the next election
– a statesman
of the next generation.

James Freeman Clarke

THE POLITICIAN.

You hear politics until you wish
that both parties were
smothered in their own gas.

Woodrow Wilson

The marvel of all history
is the patience with which
men and women submit to
burdens unnecessarily
laid upon them
by their governments.

William E. Borah

75

Presidents

I know that when things don't go well, they like to blame the President, and that is one of the things Presidents are paid for.

John F. Kennedy

Prophecy

Don't ever prophesy;
for if you prophesy wrong,
nobody will forget it
and if you prophesy right,
nobody will remember it.

Josh Billings

Quarrel

The time to win a fight is before it starts.

Frederick W. Lewis

Those who in quarrels interpose
Must often wipe a bloody nose. John Gay

Quote

Shakespeare was a dramatist of note. He lived by writing things to quote.

H. C. Bunner

"A quotation,
like a pun,
should come unsought,
and then be welcomed
only for some propriety or felicity
justifying the intrusion."

Robert W. Chapman

PATCH GRIEFS WITH PROVERBS

Shakespeare

79

Reading

Read diligently.
They who do not read
can have nothing to think
and little to say.

Samuel Johnson

Books have to be read. It is the only way of
discovering what they contain. A few savage tribes
eat them, but reading is the only method
of assimilation revealed to the West.

E. M. Forster

Reading is the greatest gift with which man has endowed himself, by whose means we may soar on unlimited voyages.

Barbara Tuchman

We read to say that we have read.

Charles Lamb

I never read a book before reviewing it. It prejudices one so.

Sydney Smith

Risk

Only those who will risk going too far can possibly find out how far one can go.

go.

T.S. Eliot

Rush

A first rate organizer
is never in a hurry.
He is never late.
He always keeps up his sleeve
a margin for the unexpected.

Arnold Bennett

To hurry is useless. The thing to do is to set out in time.

Jean de La Fontaine

Unquiet meals make ill digestions.

Shakespeare, *The Comedy of Errors*

Silence

A wise old owl sat on an oak,
The more he saw the less he spoke;
The less he spoke the more he heard;
Why aren't we like that wise old bird?

E. H. Richards

Be silent as a politician
for talking may beget suspicion.

Jonathan Swift

Better to remain silent
and be thought a fool
than to speak out
and remove all doubt.

Abraham Lincoln

Solitude

I never found the companion that was so companionable as solitude. **Joseph Addison**, *Spectator*

Smoking

Tobacco is the only excuse
for Columbus's misadventure
of discovering America.

Sigmund Freud

Tobacco is a dirty weed: I like it.
It satisfies no normal need: I like it.
It makes you thin, it makes you lean,
It takes the hair right off your bean,
It's the worst darn stuff I've ever seen.
I like it.

Graham Lee Heminger

To cease smoking is the
easiest thing I ever did;
I ought to know
for I have done it
a thousand times.

Mark Twain

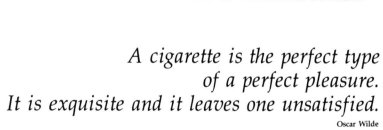

A cigarette is the perfect type
of a perfect pleasure.
It is exquisite and it leaves one unsatisfied.

Oscar Wilde

Speakers

Here comes the orator
with his flood of words
and his drop of reason.

Benjamin Franklin

Even when I am reading my lectures,
I often think to myself, 'What a
humbug you are.' And I wonder
the people don't find it out.

William Makepeace Thackeray

Now I lay me back to sleep,
The speaker's dull – the subject deep;
If he should stop before I wake,
Give me a nudge for goodness sake.

Anonymous

It's a great art to know how to sell wind.

Confucius

No speech can be entirely bad if it is short.

Popular saying

"He made a bow and that was all he said."

Newspaper report on President Grant's Lexington speech

89

Temper

Anger is never without a reason,
but seldom with a good one.

Benjamin Franklin

Anger is an expensive luxury
in which only men of a
certain income can indulge.

George William Curtis

**WHEN ANGRY, COUNT TEN BEFORE
YOU SPEAK; IF VERY ANGRY,
AN HUNDRED**

Thomas Jefferson

Theatre

Theatre adds to living
by being
more than life.

John Mason Brown

Not to go to the theatre
is like making
one's toilet
without a mirror.

Arthur Schopenhauer

Time

Doest thou
love life?
Then do not
squander time,
for that
is
the stuff
life is
made of.

Benjamin Franklin

Hell, by the time a man scratches his ass,
clears his throat,
and tells me how smart he is,
we've already wasted fifteen minutes.
Lyndon B. Johnson

Lose an hour in the morning, and you will be all day hunting for it.

Richard Whately

SIT DOWN, LINCOLN, YOUR TIME IS UP.
Douglas to Lincoln during
Great Debate of 1858

I have made this letter longer
because I lack the time to make
it shorter. Blaise Pascal

Travel

We would not take a voyage
for the sole pleasure of seeing,
without hope of ever telling.

Blaise Pascal

*The soul of a journey is liberty,
perfect liberty .... We go on a
journey to be free of all
impediments; to leave ourselves
behind, much more than to get
rid of others.* William Hazlitt

Travelling by Steam Prediction, 1820

*We are not travelling –
we are just
rushing around a lot.*

Marshall McLuhan

If an ass goes travelling,
he will not come home a horse.

Thomas Fuller

Trees

I like trees because they seem more resigned to the way they have to live than other things do.

Willa Cather

Universe

Why assume so glibly that the God who presumably created the universe is still running it?
It is certainly conceivable that He may have finished it and then turned it over to lesser gods to operate.

H.L. Mencken

Had I been present at the creation,
I would have given some useful hints
for a better ordering of the universe.

Alfonso the Wise

96

Nature and Nature's laws
lay hid in night:
God said, Let Newton be!
And all was light.

Alexander Pope

*For the world was
built in order
and the atoms
march in tune.*

Ralph Waldo Emerson

The most incomprehensible
thing about the world
is that it is comprehensible.

Albert Einstein

Visiting

For I, who hold sage Homer's rule the best,
Welcome the coming, speed the going guest.

Alexander Pope

*Unbidden guests
Are often welcomest
when they are gone.*

Shakespeare, *Henry VI*

Some people can stay longer in an hour than others can in a week.

William Dean Howells

Voting

**Bad officials are the ones elected by
good citizens who do not vote.**

George Jean Nathan

Vote!

Weight

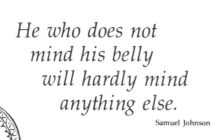

THE ONLY THING THAT CONTINUES TO GIVE US MORE FOR OUR MONEY IS THE WEIGHING MACHINE
George Clark

He who does not mind his belly will hardly mind anything else.

Samuel Johnson

100

Women

The proper study of mankind
is woman.

Henry Adams

Women

Whilst Adam slept
  Eve from his side arose;
Strange his first sleep
  would be his last repose.

Anonymous

The society of women
is the foundation of good manners.

Johann Wolfgang Goethe

The errors of women spring,
almost always,
from their faith in the good
or their confidence in the true.

Honoré de Balzac

The great fault in women is the desire to be like men.

Joseph Marie de Maistre

MADONNA OF THE TRAIL

If I were asked to what the singular prosperity of the American people ought to be mainly attributed, I should reply: to the superiority of their women.

Alexis de Tocqueville

Women are strange and incomprehensible . . . invented by Providence to keep the wit of men well sharpened by constant employment.

Arnold Bennett

Work

Make hay while the sun shines.

Cervantes

The busier we are the more acutely we feel that we live. The more conscious we are of life.

Immanuel Kant

I was made to work; if you are equally industrious you will be equally successful.

Johann Sebastian Bach.
Dir: Musices v Cantor.

*This Bachian understatement appears in Johann Nicolaus Firkel's biography of Bach (1802). Philipp Spitta, the famous Bach biographer, tells a similar story: To someone who praised his skill at the organ Bach said: "There is nothing wonderful about it. You merely strike the right note at the right time and the organ does the rest." Phillip Spitta, *Johann Sebastian Bach*, 3 vols. (New York: Dover Publications, Inc.).

**My father taught me to work;
he did not teach me to love it.**

Abraham Lincoln

Make it a point to do something every day that you
don't want to DO. THIs is the golden rule for
acquiring thE habit of doing your duty without paIN.

Mark Twain

Labor, if it were not
necessary for the existence,
would be indispensable
for the happiness of man.

Samuel Johnson

MEN HAVE BECOME THE TOOLS OF THEIR TOOLS

Henry David Thoreau

105

Writing

If you wish to be a writer, **write.**

Epictetus

When Stephen Vincent Benét was asked how it felt to write John Brown's Body, *he answered: "Just about like giving birth to a grand piano."*

The art of writing is the art of applying the seat of the pants to the seat of the chair.

Vorse M. Heaton

In composing, as a general rule, run your pen through every other word you have written; you have no idea what vigor it will give your style. Sydney Smith

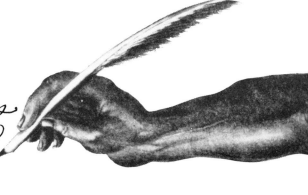

When once the itch of literature comes over a man, nothing can cure him but the scratching of a pen

Samuel Lover

I do not like to write, but I like to have written. Gloria Steinem

Xantippe*

The calmest husbands make the stormiest wives.

Anonymous

As to marriage or celibacy let a man take which course he may — he will be sure to repent.

Socrates

* *The shrewish wife of Socrates. Medieval legend represented the great philosopher as henpecked.*

Youth

I
loafe
and
invite
my
soul.

Walt Whitman

Nonconformity is self-discovery,
not puerile defiance.

Ralph Waldo Emerson

I do not own an inch of land,
But all I see
is mine.

Lucy Larcom

109

Zodiac

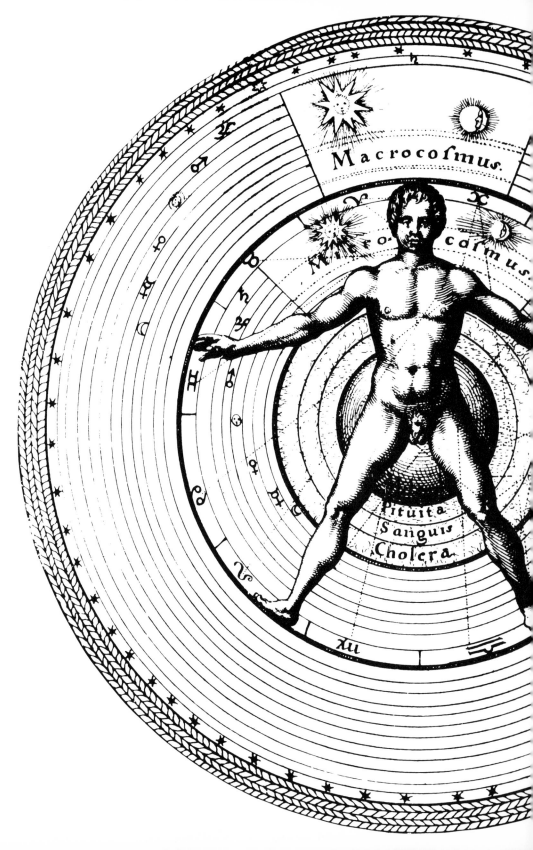

*Do you know that your bodies
are made of some of the same
substances that are found in the
stars and other stars? You are a sample
of the great Universe. So don't let little
things trouble you but think and act as if you
were a part of a bigger world than the little earth
upon which you live.*

Edwin Brant Frost

111

Acknowledgments

Most of the quotes in this book are by writers whose work is now considered in the public domain. The few sayings of a more recent vintage fall, to my best understanding, within the definition of fair use. Still, as a matter of courtesy, I have applied to writers still living and have been given permission to use their sayings — for which I extend my thanks.

James Baldwin		Books p. 19
Anatole Broyard	*The New York Times*	Books p. 19
John Corry	*The New York Times*	New York p. 67
Grove Press	Henry Miller quote	Love p. 56
Dr. John Gardner	D. Sutten quote	Children p. 24
Manchester Guardian		Hats p. 47
Herbert Mayes		Zodiac p. 111
Herbert V. Prochnow		Animals p. 15
Leo Rosten		Infidelity p. 49
Dr. Szent-Györgyi		Discovery p. 28
Gloria Steinem		Writing p. 106
Barbara Tuchman		Reading p. 81

The Bernard Baruch quote on page 38 is courtesy Holt, Rinehart & Winston. Copyright © 1952. The Henry Miller quote on page 56 is courtesy of Grove Press, New York.

The quotes in this book have been collected over many years. At times, in the excitement of the chase, I may not have taken the time required for complete authentication. If any holders of rights have been inadvertently overlooked, I offer my apologies and the promise of adjustment.

All pictures, except those listed on the Copyright page, are the property of the Bettmann Archive in New York and have been copyrighted in its name. © 1977 by the Bettmann Archive.

I would like to express my gratitude to Ms. Linda Sunshine, my editor at Harmony Books, and to Ms. Nancy Jennens for her unflagging help in the preparation of the manuscript.

— O.L.B.

Index of Authors

Index of Artists

Haircutting

Haircutting

2nd Edition

by Jeryl E. Spear

for
dummies®
A Wiley Brand

Haircutting For Dummies®, 2nd Edition

Published by: John Wiley & Sons, Inc., 111 River Street, Hoboken, NJ 07030-5774, www.wiley.com

Copyright © 2022 by John Wiley & Sons, Inc., Hoboken, New Jersey

Published simultaneously in Canada

For general information on our other products and services, please contact our Customer Care Department within the U.S. at 877-762-2974, outside the U.S. at 317-572-3993, or fax 317-572-4002. For technical support, please visit https://hub.wiley.com/community/support/dummies.

Wiley publishes in a variety of print and electronic formats and by print-on-demand. Some material included with standard print versions of this book may not be included in e-books or in print-on-demand. If this book refers to media such as a CD or DVD that is not included in the version you purchased, you may download this material at http://booksupport.wiley.com. For more information about Wiley products, visit www.wiley.com.

Library of Congress Control Number: 2021950999

ISBN 978-1-119-79049-5 (pbk); ISBN 978-1-119-79051-8 (ebk); ISBN 978-1-119-79052-5 (ebk)

SKY10031905_121021

Contents at a Glance

Table of Contents

PART 5: MAKING YOUR HAIRCUTS SHINE 231

Introduction

I f you've ever dreamed of becoming a painter, a sculptor, or a home decorator, you have a talent for cutting hair. The same holds true if you love designing, drawing, or helping your kids with their art projects. *Haircutting For Dummies,* 2nd Edition is designed to help you discover your inner artist — and put this artist to good use! With this book at your side, you can easily enhance your loved ones' haircuts while trimming big bucks off your family's grooming budget.

About This Book

I wrote this book for people like you who want to cut their family and friends' hair at home in order to save time and money, be creative, and do something nice for those who trust you with their good looks. *Haircutting For Dummies,* 2nd Edition offers good advice on how to do simple trims and styles, while giving your own creative spirit plenty of room to roam.

Haircutting For Dummies, 2nd Edition is the most comprehensive yet free-spirited book written for the home haircutter. It lives up to its name by giving step-by-step instructions for the latest short, medium, and long hairstyles, as well as more advanced haircutting techniques like slicing, notching, and texturing the hair. To help you achieve these creative looks, this snip-and-tell guide provides insider information about the tools you need to support your handiwork, ways to follow lengths and angles, and above all, how to have fun while you're creating your show-stopping styles!

Anytime you find yourself hungry for even more haircutting knowledge, this book also contains a wealth of information about how to style your masterpieces, tips on maintaining your own haircut, and countless ways to shamelessly bribe young children into behaving like angels while you cut their hair. You should also be on the lookout for tips on ways to judge texture, strength, and the health of the hair, and how to find out what people really want their hair to look like before taking a single snip.

Conventions Used in This Book

Before I throw you into the step-by-steps of any haircut in this book, I let you know how difficult the cut will be to do. I have based my ratings on a scale from the easiest cuts to the most difficult ones:

>> Easiest

>> Easy

>> Moderate

>> Advanced

>> Most advanced

Your current ability to cut hair — coordination with handling scissors, ability to judge length, and a knack for creating the correct shapes — should dictate the degree of difficulty you undertake. If creating accurate haircutting lines challenges you, for instance, or your hair sections still tend to drift to one side or the other, avoid anything higher than a Moderate rating until these basic skills become second nature to you.

The illustrations in this book give you a good idea of what steps to take while cutting hair. Keep in mind that a solid line means that this is where hair should be parted. A broken line indicates where you should cut the hair.

And finally, an *italicized* word means that a beauty-pro term is heading your way.

Foolish Assumptions

Having been a home haircutter many times in my life, I've experienced most of the motivations behind trimming your little beauty queen's hair, crisping the lines of a man's haircut, or extending the life of your own haircut by taking a few strategic snips off the ends. All that was missing in my household was a fun, friendly book on haircutting. While writing this book, I assumed that you've found yourself in similar situations (and without a lively, straightforward book). I also made a few other assumptions about you.

If one or more of the following statements describes you, *Haircutting For Dummies*, 2nd Edition is probably your kind of book.

- You feel the urge to express your creativity and haircutting is an attractive outlet.

- You're happy saving hundreds of dollars each year in haircutting costs simply by maintaining your family's hair at home.

- You want to extend the time between your own visits to the salon.

- You love pleasing people by making them feel good about the way they look.

- You want to have better control over your personal time by limiting your salon visits.

- You buy every book on the market with a yellow and black cover.

- You're considering a career in haircutting and want a taste of what it's like to be a successful hairdresser.

Icons Used in This Book

Throughout this book you find a collection of handy icons in the margins. These icons perform useful functions to maximize your use of *Haircutting For Dummies.*

AUTHOR SAYS

You want anecdotes? I got anecdotes. After years of experience cutting hair and knowing people who cut hair, I get to share with you some of my funniest stories.

TIP

This icon makes your life easier by marking special hair-related tidbits throughout the book. These bits of information signal an activity that saves you time or useful knowledge born of experience.

WARNING

Think danger! This icon warns you to tread carefully. Although nothing in this book puts the hair or scalp in mortal peril, this icon tells you to pay close attention to what you're doing and how to avoid common pitfalls. Your health or hair could turn out worse for the wear if you don't follow this advice.

REMEMBER

I use this important icon to call out basic rules and information that you can file away for future reference whenever you encounter related situations.

Beyond the Book

The Cheat Sheet is an awesome way to explore bite-sized information on some of the most important points about cutting and caring for hair. Are you curious about how to slide cut? How about hair plopping or 10 different ways to create fringes and curtain bangs? If you're excited — even passionate — about hair, simply go to www.dummies.com and type "Haircutting For Dummies Cheat Sheet" in the Search box.

Where to Go from Here

Like all *For Dummies* books, *Haircutting For Dummies,* 2nd Edition is divided into easy, manageable sections that allow you to start anywhere that addresses your needs or questions. Diving into the middle of the book works just as well as starting at the beginning. In a nutshell, how you read this book is up to you. You can go from front to back, back to front (a little more difficult, but still manageable), or start with the basics chapters and then head to a step-by-step haircut that strikes your fancy.

Now, here's one final note before you dive in: Please remember that haircutting is a subjective art. My haircutting instructions represent just one method to doing the fun haircutting designs in this book. After you become more skilled with haircutting, feel free to experiment with different approaches to these same styles. What you're really doing is honing your personal style of cutting — something everyone needs to do in order to produce one-of-a-kind works of art.

1

Shopping, Talking, and Acting Like a Pro

Get up close and personal with how to set up a cutting area.

Select the tools you need to get cutting.

Become a beauty sleuth and typecast hair –– two major skills that seriously contribute to your cutting success.

Chapter 1

Setting Up Shop: Kitchen Beauticians

When my friend Ling Moon first arrived in the United States, she was overwhelmed by all the different hair colors and textures that dotted the American landscape. Although I didn't have the heart to tell her until much later that many of the hair colors she saw were chemically created, I did identify with how she felt about the diversity of hair all around us.

Everyone's hair texture, growth patterns, and length are different, making every haircut a unique cutting experience. And because you'll always have an endless supply of the stuff — rain or shine, hair grows about ½ inch (1.3 centimeters) per month — haircutting is also one of the few artful activities where saving money is a sure thing. If you cut your family's hair just sometimes, you can shave dollars off your grooming budget. And if you find yourself falling in love with haircutting, becoming a licensed stylist could give you the chance to make an above-average wage.

Discovering Your Inner Artist: Do You Have What It Takes?

Haircutting is a three-dimensional art form consisting of different lengths, angles, and elevations. While haircutting is a simple science, it only produces exceptional results when you also draw on your unique talents. If you think that you don't have any talents worth considering, think again. It certainly helps to be a sculptor, a painter, or an all-around artistic fellow, but talents needed for haircutting also come from other areas that may surprise you.

>> Do you love to paint, draw, or sculpt?

>> Do you love to work with software graphics?

>> Are you mechanically inclined?

>> Do you have carpentry or handyman skills?

>> Do you know how to sew?

>> Do you have a strong sense of symmetry?

>> Are you methodical by nature?

Knowing how to sew, for instance, means that you're adept at putting pattern pieces together — a skill that you can apply to creating the various sections of your haircuts. If you have drafting or carpentry skills, the precision of your angles can make your haircuts look exceptional. And if you have the gift of symmetry, or you're extremely methodical, your haircuts will be straight and true — two of the major challenges for real artistic types who intuitively cut hair.

This list makes up just a smattering of the talents you can draw from to create exceptional haircuts. For instance, I personally don't draw, paint, sew, fix houses, or assemble my child's toys, but I do apply my own unique sense of balance that brings a signature quality to all my haircuts. Someone else may apply a keen sense of integration so that every haircut moves and styles perfectly. And others . . . well, you can see my point.

Setting the Scene

Assuming that you're not preparing to build a salon business in your home — that's illegal unless you're a licensed cosmetologist and have a business (establishment) license — here are some things you need to set up an informal shop:

>> **Stool and beanbag:** Get a swivel stool that's tall enough for you to comfortably cut the hair without having to stoop down and that has a generous seat and a back. If you're cutting young children's hair, you should also get a baby beanbag chair. Put the beanbag on the seat and the kid on the beanbag. This setup keeps the child from moving too much, while keeping their ears and other body parts cut-free.

>> **Large mirror:** Cut hair in an area where you have a large mirror to improve the quality of your work. If you can't face a hanging mirror, purchase a full-length wardrobe mirror that you can wheel out any time you cut hair. This type of mirror gives you a great view of your work and allows you to visually balance your cuts as you go.

>> **Floor protection:** Covering the floor around your work area will save you from cleaning up hairy messes. While you can use a number of different materials to do this, I recommend using old-fashioned newspaper printed with soy or water ink, because it does a great job and is biodegradable. Always use enough newspaper to cover a 6-foot (1.9-meter) circumference around your chair. When you're done with your haircut, cleaning up is as easy as wadding up the newspaper and tossing it in the trash or adding it to your compost pile.

TIP

If you will be styling the hair after completing your haircut, make sure to gather up your floor covering and dispose of it *before* blow-drying the hair. If you don't do this, the snippets will scatter like dandelion flowers in the wind. Also, sweep the area and the soles of your shoes to round up any hair escapees. Otherwise, you could be blowing hair snippets all over the room and tracking them to other areas of your home.

>> **Good lighting:** Work with balanced lighting by having a light source overhead and on each side of the person whose hair you're cutting. (If you only have light on one side, you're cutting half of the head in shadow.) Weather permitting, I like cutting hair outdoors in a protected area, such as an enclosed patio, where sunlight allows me to clearly see even the tiniest of details.

If you're feeling really ambitious after getting that annual bonus at work, consider investing in these two gems:

>> **Hydraulic styling chair:** If you plan to cut several people's hair, consider investing in a hydraulic styling chair. I say this because they make your haircuts much easier to do. Many beauty suppliers sell these chairs online, and you can find used equipment for sale on websites such as eBay and on social media pages featuring local sellers.

If you decide to purchase a styling chair, you can skip the stool. (Hang on to the beanbag, though, because it still helps keep fidgety young children in one spot!)

>> **Salon caddy:** A *salon caddy (also called a salon trolley)* — a handy little cabinet on wheels with a flat countertop — can make your haircutting sessions much easier and more convenient. Salon caddies have drawers for storing all your cutting paraphernalia — combs, capes, scissors, clips, and so on — while providing a workspace where you can hang your water bottle and set your comb, scissors, and clips while working. You can purchase one from your local beauty supply store or online seller.

Cutting Up in Your Kitchen

I find cutting family members' hair at home appealing for several reasons. The most important reason, of course, is all the money you can save by cutting their hair, or at least prolonging the time between professional haircuts. The same is true of neighbors or friends who are in need of a haircut but are lacking the funds or time required to have a professional service. (Part 3 focuses on how to maintain professional haircuts, along with a lot of haircutting tips and tricks to use when you're first embarking on your haircutting venture.)

TIP

I also find that haircutting is just plain fun. It allows you to be creative and interact one-on-one for up to an hour with someone you particularly like or love, and it gives you tremendous satisfaction when that person looks in the mirror and says, "I love my hair!"

Mane-taining your own hair

Haircutting not only let you care for other people, but also care for yourself! Making adjustments to your bangs, shortening the hair around your face, or trimming the top of your hair, for example, does wonders to improve the appearance of an overgrown haircut and lift your spirits at the same time. I say the latter because by midmorning of a bad hair day, I almost always feel unattractive and even depressed. To remedy this situation, I have been known to squeeze in a haircut on myself while some good-hearted soul shampoos my next client. (Check out Part 3 to find out more about these self-beautifying trims.)

WARNING

I believe that trimming your own hair under ideal conditions is a good thing. But impulsively cutting your hair in elevators, at stoplights, or seconds before dashing out on a date — as I admittedly have done — is a bad idea. Even minor trims take planning and a sensible work area so you can concentrate on what you're doing!

Chopping your children's hair

Most children's haircuts are simple designs that require mastering less than a handful of skills. From the child's perspective, having a parent cut their hair is often easier than going to a hair salon, especially if you follow the advice given in Chapter 16 and Chapter 22.

REMEMBER

Chapter 16, "Getting Snippy with Children's Styles," gives great advice on cutting children's hair, along with several adorable haircutting tutorials. Chapter 22, "Ten Slices of Advice on Cutting Kids Hair," provides 10 tips (and tricks) on how to avoid common missteps that cause your sweet little angels to squirm, cry, and run away from you the next time you uncase your scissors.

Clipping a companion's hair

Cutting a friend's hair can work well for both of you, especially if you never attempt to tackle a haircut without at least some guidance. To ensure that you always do a good job, follow the easy haircuts in this book. I include step-by-step instructions on:

>> Women's short, medium, and long cuts (Chapters 12, 13, and 14)

>> Men's cuts (Chapter 15)

>> Quick and Dirty basic clipper cuts (Chapter 8, 15, and 16)

REMEMBER

You can cut your kids' hair, your companion's hair, and even your neighbors' hair — for free. But when money changes hands, you're acting as a professional stylist. Being a stylist for hire is forbidden unless you have a cosmetology license. Besides, if you're so good that people want to pay you for a trim, you should become a licensed stylist anyway!

Chapter 2

Strapping On Your Tool Belt

I confess. Before I became a stylist, I'd pick up whatever tool I happened to have handy to comb, brush, or cut my hair. I didn't know the difference between a bad styling tool and a good one and, to be honest, I didn't care. I used brushes until the bristles melted. And, as long as they still cut, I saw no reason why I shouldn't use the same pair of scissors for trimming my bangs, opening the mail, and snipping the packing tape off boxes.

After I began cutting hair for a living, though, I realized that not all tools are alike. Sharp, high-grade scissors allow you to cut through hair like a hot knife through butter, and a smoothly finished comb glides rather than snags through the hair.

Beyond quality, you also have different types of tools and sundries to consider. Some are designed for multipurpose use, while others are strictly specialty items. I explain these tools and the assorted sundries needed for haircutting in Table 2-1, Table 2-2, and Table 2-3 in this chapter.

Running with These Is a No-No

I have to admit that I'm not much of a gizmo girl. In fact, when I see a screwdriver or ratchet, I instinctively walk the other way. Yet the more I know about haircutting scissors (shown in Figure 2-1), the more I realize that scissors are as sexy to a haircutter as prized knives are to a master chef.

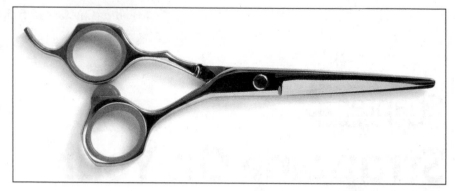

FIGURE 2-1:
Haircutting scissors range from $20 to $1,200 or more, depending on the materials, finishing steps, and brand name.

Manufacturers perform over 100 steps on quality scissors — including hand polishing, sharpening, and balancing — to create a tool that effortlessly cuts the hair. That's why many professional scissors cost hundreds of dollars — a price most beauty pros are willing to pay because their livelihood depends on creating beautiful designs. Still, even the crème de la crème of haircutters must start somewhere, and that place is usually at the lower end of the professional scissors spectrum. I recommend that you start with a $20 model made by a reputable company.

AUTHOR SAYS

My dear friend and haircutter Sean recently moved from Scotland to America to expand his career opportunities. Confusion immediately reigned. "Why are they callin' scissors shears?" he asked. "We use shears for trimmin' bushes and shearin' sheep." Technically, Sean is correct. Scissors are officially defined as having 6-inch or shorter blade lengths. But somewhere along the line, American marketers started calling haircutting scissors "shears." Just for the record, I refer to these haircutting tools as "scissors" in this book, but "shears" is also a commonplace term that you should keep in mind when venturing out into the beauty world on your own.

TIP

Haircutting scissors that cost up to $20 are considered to be disposable because it's cheaper to buy a new pair than pay to have the dull pair sharpened. But don't let this "throwaway" status fool you. A pair of scissors in this price range can adequately care for your family's hair from several months to a couple of years — depending on how frequently you use them and how well you care for them. (See the "Caring for your scissors" section later in this chapter.)

REMEMBER

The quickest way to dull your scissors is to use them for cutting anything but clean, human hair. Cutting mannequins or wigs with synthetic hair dull the blades and may even damage them to the point they must be replaced. Cutting hair coated with styling products will also hasten their need to be sharpened or thrown way.

Selecting scissors

Check the quality of the workmanship when shopping for scissors. First, examine the most expensive pair of scissors in the store and then compare them to lesser-priced brands that fit comfortably within your grooming budget.

>> Run your fingers over the metal to see how smooth and glassy it feels. If it has even one rough spot, pass on the scissors. Unpolished, rough surfaces are open to rusting. Rough spots are also a sign of overall poor workmanship.

>> Close the scissors and examine the tips. Do they meet (good), or is there a gap (bad)?

>> Feel how smooth the *ride* is (the way the scissors feel as you make cutting motions) by opening and closing the blades. Does the ride feel rough (lots of friction) or smooth?

To shop for bells and whistles, consider these important options:

>> **Tension screw:** This feature eliminates the need to use a screwdriver to adjust the tightness of your blades (see Figure 2-1).

>> **Finger tang:** Also called a *finger rest* or *brace,* this option adds a measure of control while cutting the hair. Some stylists can't live without a finger tang while others find it a nuisance. If you are leaning toward using a tang, I suggest that you purchase scissors that have a removable tang so you can have the best of both worlds. (The tang shown in Figure 2-1 can be unscrewed).

>> **Finger and thumb sizing inserts:** Also called *ring sizers,* these rubber-like inserts fit inside the scissors' finger and thumb rings to create a more custom fit (see Figure 2-1). Finger and thumb inserts are especially helpful for people with slender digits as they reduce the interior circumference of the finger ring.

Playing it straight

Straight or *stamped* scissors are the cheapest type of scissors on the market. They're stamped out of metal, cookie cutter-style, have little or no hand finishing, and are sold as $2 paper scissors, $5 kitchen scissors, and $12 (or less) haircutting scissors.

TIP

These ubiquitous tools are referred to as "straight" because the blades are neither beveled nor convex. (The following sections explain these two desirable blade designs.) Straight scissors frequently allow the hair to become bunched or slide down the blades while you're cutting. If you must purchase scissors in this price range, you can partly remedy this problem by cutting a much thinner section of hair at a time.

Making beveled eggs and blades

Beveled scissors are also referred to as *German* or *European* scissors because they originated — and are still produced — in Solingen, Germany. German-style cutlery typically has *beveled blades*, an old-world design with tapered tips. German-style scissors also have *micro-serrated blade edges* (a very fine notching) to help grip and cut the hair. They work well for blunt end cuts, but aren't suitable for more advanced techniques like slide cutting.

The price of German-style scissors typically ranges from $25 to $200. This broad spectrum of costs depends on the number of finishing steps, the quality of the work, the number of deluxe features and, to be honest, the brand name.

TIP

Beveled blades munch the hair like a sharp axe; convex blades slice the hair like a razor.

Caving in to convex blades

Convex, or *Japanese-style*, scissors cut like straight razors. The convex blades are *hollow ground*, meaning that some metal is scooped out of the interior of the cutting blade to create a very sharp edge. Because Japanese-style scissors traditionally offer the smoothest, most effortless cutting experience, they're the tool of choice for most professional stylists.

Due to their keen cutting surface and meticulous finish, Japanese-style scissors are also the most expensive cutting tools. A decent pair starts at about $80 and quickly escalates to $300 and beyond.

Getting a handle on ergonomics

Ergonomics are a godsend for hairstylists who are at high risk for developing carpal tunnel syndrome. Scissors with opposing handles (side-by-side finger and thumb rings) were taken out of the dark ages several years ago when a variety of ergonomic scissor handles were introduced to the professional beauty industry. These handles — offset, crane, or swivel designs — help to eliminate stress on the thumb and wrist joints and, in some cases, the shoulder as well. These features are important to hairstylists who do multiple haircuts every day. (Figure 2-1 and Figure 2-2b show offset handles; Figure 2-2a shows opposing handles. The latter is acceptable for specialty scissors because they are only used briefly or occasionally when cutting hair.)

For the home haircutter who does an occasional haircut, using ergonomic scissors isn't necessary. But if you frequently line up your entire family for back-to-back Saturday morning haircuts, you will experience far less joint and overall hand and shoulder fatigue by using ergonomic scissors.

In terms of handle designs, I prefer using offset handles that keep the thumb in a more natural position. Other people prefer a crane-style handle that places the thumb joint in a stress-free position and the wrist straight and horizontal with the blades.

Swivel handles allow the thumb to move freely, with some designs having both thumb and finger swivel rings. I don't recommend them for home haircutters as they can take you on a wild ride and be downright dangerous in unpracticed hands.

Seeking specialty scissors

Specialty scissor designs are only limited by the tool designer and the stylist's imagination. They are commonly referred to as *chunking, thinning, texturizing, and blending scissors,* depending on the design and the number of teeth, and the whims of the manufacturer. Figure 2-2 shows two types of specialty scissors — texturizing scissors and thinning scissors.

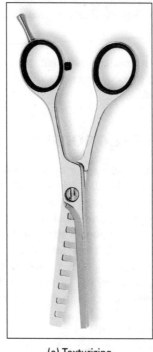
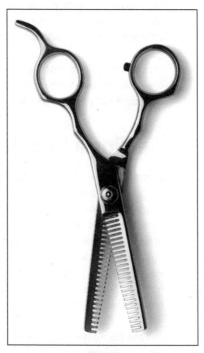

(a) Texturizing   (b) Thinning

© iStockphoto.com/Catalin Plesa (left); Fromm International (right)

FIGURE 2-2:
Nothing blurs *scissor marks* — those pesky lines that show where you've cut the hair — faster than specialty scissors.

Although the names of these tools are decidedly fuzzy, one look at their teeth tells you what they can do: Large, wide-spaced teeth create chunky cuts by removing wider snippets of hair. They are generally used to create interesting patterns in the hair, especially in the bang area. Fine, closely spaced teeth create smooth, diffuse cutting lines by removing finer snippets of hair. (Specialty tools cost anywhere from $20 to $300 or more, depending on the quality, design, and the brand name.)

TIP

The more teeth specialty scissors have, the more diffuse the results, hence scissors with 28 teeth or more are referred to as thinning scissors, and those with 5 to 6 teeth are called chunking (or channeling) scissors.

Although the effects of specialty scissors look impressive, they're actually quick and easy to use as long as you follow three simple rules:

>> Never use specialty scissors near the scalp unless you want bits and pieces of hair to stand on end.

>> Frequently comb through the hair to remove loose snippets that tend to obscure how much hair you've really removed.

>> Use a light touch until you're experienced enough to know what the finished results will be.

Caring for your scissors

Buying the perfect pair of scissors is one thing, but maintaining them is quite another.

If you want to keep your scissors performing like new for months at a stretch, follow these seven easy-care tips:

>> Wipe down your scissors after each use with a soft cotton or microfiber cloth.

>> Put one drop of scissor lubricating oil on the joint of the scissors at the end of each cutting day.

>> Always protect your scissors against nicks or warping by keeping them safely tucked away in a pouch or case when you aren't using them.

>> Avoid cutting hair that's coated with hair spray, styling aids, or other products that can dull your scissors.

>> Never cut synthetic hair with your cutting besties; it will dull the blades.

>> Check your blades periodically to ensure they aren't too loose or too tight. Loose blades cause the hair to bend as opposed to cutting a clean line; overly tightened blades cause bunching and extra wear on the blades.

To make sure that your scissors are properly adjusted, hold them parallel to the floor with the finger ring facing down. Release the finger ring. If your blades open all the way, they are too loose; if they open to within an inch (2.5 centimeters) or so of entirely being open, they are just right.

>> Have your scissors sharpened any time they're not cutting like they did when they were fairly new. Send them to a service center recommended by the manufacturer. If you have an inexpensive pair, it's time to purchase a new tool and use your old pair for practicing your cutting moves on a mannequin head.

Calling All Trimmers

Trimmers are a must for cleaning up hairy necks and shortening and shaping mustaches, beards, and sideburns. Trimmers — the petite cousin of larger, more powerful clippers — are meant to crisply trim the edges along the perimeter of the hair, and shape sideburns, beards, and mustaches. See Figure 2-3 for a comparison of trimmers versus clippers.

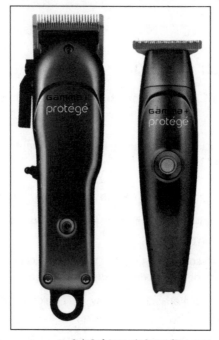

FIGURE 2-3:
Trimmers versus clippers.

WARNING

When people try to use trimmers to do clipper haircuts, chances are excellent that the trimmers will have a mechanical meltdown.

Trimmers work better and last longer when you properly maintain them. The maintenance process includes putting two drops of oil across the top of the blade while it's running (at the end of each cutting day) and keeping debris from building up by frequently removing the blade and brushing away the snippets of hair. (For a more detailed step-by-step on how to maintain your trimmers, check out Chapter 8.)

GETTING CLIPPER HAPPY

Clippers are the grown-up version of trimmers. They are used for classic barber cuts, tight blending, or fading techniques, trendy haircuts, and to shorten the perimeter length of one-length hair.

Clippers are popular power tools with stylists, barbers, and home haircutters. Doing clipper cuts is also a specialty skill that deserves its own chapter. Check out Chapter 8 to get a good grasp on clipper basics and perform easy tutorials, as well as throughout Part 4.

TIP

Nickel-cadmium (ni-cad) batteries power many cordless trimmers. This type of battery has a *memory* — if you only partially charge your trimmers most of the time, the battery will eventually only partially charge before you have to recharge it. To prolong the life of your trimmers, completely discharge the battery at least once a month by unplugging the charging base and turning on the trimmer until the battery is completely dead. Then fully recharge it according to the manufacturer's directions.

You can find these handy machines at nearly all retail stores carrying blow-dryers and curling irons, beauty supply stores, and online. While not all trimmers are created equal — some are more powerful and cut closer to the skin — you can still purchase a fairly decent model for less than $20.

Short List: Tools and Supplies

There's a good reason why styling stations include several drawers. Haircutting requires some tools and supplies that you need, and a few more that you just want to have around. Table 2-1 lists the bare minimum you should have on hand before having your spouse, your little cuties, or your friends sit in your chair.

AUTHOR SAYS

In case you're wondering, some of my extra goodies that aren't on this list: hand sanitizer, nitrile gloves, scissor oil and a microfiber cloth, breath mints, hand lotion, hand mirror, and an emergency protein bar for when lunch has been scratched in favor of accommodating a friend or family member.

TIP

Some of the best haircutting towels are waiting for you at the back of your bathroom cupboard. You know the ones: too good to call rags but too worn to hang out in the open. The profile of a perfect home haircutting towel is one that is older, thinner, and lies flat around the neck and shoulders.

TABLE 2-1	Tools and Supplies You Need for Home Haircutting	
Tool	Where You Can Find It	What It'll Cost You
Haircutting scissors and/or clippers	Retail stores and beauty stores, and online	$15 and up
Trimmers	Retail stores, beauty supply stores, and online	$9 and up
Styling/Cutting combs	Retail stores and beauty supply stores, in person and online	$1 to $15
Wide tooth/Detangling comb	Some retail stores, all beauty supply stores, and online	$1 to $5
Tail comb or pintail comb	Some retail stores, all beauty supply stores, and online	$2 to $15
Cutting capes (adult and child)	Some retail stores, all beauty supply stores, and online	$5 to $15
Assorted hair clips	Some retail stores; best choices sold at beauty supply stores in person and online	$1 to $5 per pack
Spray bottle with mist setting	Most retail stores; best choices are sold at beauty supply stores	$1.25 to $4
Haircutting/Salon towels	Sold at beauty supply stores and online; worn-out hand towels work great!	$1.25 and up each
Floor covering (such as newspaper)	Sold at newsstands, coffee shops, and various stores	$1+

Combing It Over

While there's a dizzying array of combs on the market, most of them are for styling the hair. (Check out Chapter 19 and Chapter 20 for the lowdown on styling tools preferred by stylists, as well as many ways to make the hair bend to your will.) Table 2-2 covers various combs that are useful for prepping and cutting.

TIP

Before purchasing a single comb used for haircuts, collect every comb you have in your house, car, and purse and take them with you when you go on your tool shopping trip. Compare what you have versus what you need. If you're lucky, you may not have to buy any new combs at all.

TABLE 2-2

Combs to Cut By

Type of Comb	What It's Used For
Styling (cutting) comb	Most common type of comb for haircutting; excellent tool for teasing, smoothing, and finishing hairstyles
Barber comb	Has tapered teeth; used for clipper cuts
Tail comb (optional)	Used for sectioning when separating the hair; has a plastic tail (thin handle) that comes to a point
Pintail comb (optional)	Same as a tail comb, except it has a thin, metal tail

REMEMBER

The best quality combs are *carbon composite combs* — also called *carbon fiber combs* — that feel like hard rubber. They're flexible, smooth, heat-resistant, and aren't prone to broken teeth. In comparison, hard plastic combs — the cheapest category of combs — are inflexible, often feel rough, and have brittle teeth. To save your tender-headed family and friends from haircutting angst, only use top-notch carbon composite combs.

WARNING

I don't recommend using a pintail comb when you first start cutting hair, because the metal tail is quite sharp and could damage an eye or an ear if someone fidgets or turns unexpectedly. I also never recommend using a pin tail comb when sectioning young children's hair because they're masters at doing surprise pirouettes, despite never having had a single ballet lesson.

Feeling Secure

Nearly all cuts require hair to be separated and secured in sections. This allows you to keep track of your haircut and to never accidentally (oops!) cut the wrong strands. (Check out Chapter 6 for different sectioning patterns.)

Choosing the right fastener for each section allows you to secure each section while balancing the weight of the clip with the weight of the hair. If you are using a heavy jaw clamp to pin up a section of fine or thin hair, for example, chances are it'll collapse right in the middle of your haircut. Check out Table 2-3 for a list of fastener types and uses.

TABLE 2-3

Clips and Their Jobs

Clip Style	What It Does
Double-prong clippie	Small clips used to secure thin sections of hair and for roller sets
Duckbill clip	Strong, long clips used to secure medium-to-thick sections of hair
Jaw clamp	Also called an alligator clamp; used to hold heavy sections of hair

Practicing with Doll Heads

Many stylists use mannequins to practice haircuts and styles before they give their clients one of their latest and greatest looks. While you may not see manne-quin heads in the area where all the magic happens, they are most likely nearby.

Doll heads are available in different hair lengths and can be made from human hair, animal hair, and synthetic fibers. They're also available in feminine and masculine head shapes and all hair types (covered in Chapter 4). Although you can buy a mannequin head for less than $25, if you can afford to pay more for a higher quality head, I recommend that you upgrade.

To assess the quality of different mannequins, here are some desirable features that you should look for before purchasing your first mannequin head:

>> Hair that's attached in the same directions as it grows on the human head, as opposed to a 90-degree direction (see Chapter 5) or straight back. This factor is particularly important for bobs, lobs, and bangs.

>> Human hair mannequins must be labeled "100% human hair" or it's highly likely they're made with human hair and a mix of animal hair, synthetic fibers, or both. The use of different materials can adversely affect how the "hair" behaves, and you may not be able to use a curling iron to practice hairstyling.

>> Purchase the longest hair you can possibly afford, which will allow you to double or even triple the number of haircuts you can cut on a single manne-quin head.

WARNING

Never use your good haircutting scissors to cut a mannequin head. Synthetic fibers will dull and damage your blades, and even 100-percent human hair can be processed to the point that it will do the same thing. This same advice goes for wigs, hairpieces, and hair extensions.

You can set a mannequin head on your lap, but it's only doable for styling the top of the head. For your purposes, I recommend that you purchase a device that will keep your mannequin head in place while allowing you to swivel the head as you work on different areas of the hair.

» **Table clamps** can be secured on tables or bars and even the back of some chairs. They work best for shorter hair. Table clamps are also handy when you're working on a haircut on and off throughout the day or even week. You can work on your tripod and then use the table clamp to keep it out of the way.

» **Wig or mannequin tripods** work well for short to very long hair. I personally love using mannequin tripods because you can raise and lower the height of the device to ensure you're always comfortable and have the proper view of the hair while perfecting your next masterpiece.

Chapter **3**

Beauty Show and Tell

great haircut is the result of good technical *and* communication skills. You can do the best haircut in the world, but if it's not what the person sitting in your chair wanted, you could have a very unhappy situation on your hands.

Good communication skills involve listening carefully to what the person is saying, thoughtfully repeating their messages in different words, and then reinforcing both of your verbal descriptions with visual cues or images.

In this chapter, I share information about asking the right questions to ensure your visions jibe. I also share how to assess and enhance or minimize certain facial features, provide you with a starter list for finding specific hair images on social media, and guide you on perfecting the art of the "talk."

Chapter 3 is a critical chapter for cutting success, as you will discover in "Getting Acquainted," which includes the legendary case of the severed ponytail.

Getting Acquainted

AUTHOR SAYS

A story about a longhaired male salon customer has been circulating in the beauty industry for many years. A stylist asks the man if he wants to keep his ponytail. When he says, "Yes," the stylist chops it off and hands it to him. In shock, he wanders out of the salon carrying his dearly departed hair. The poor guy then stops at every salon he comes across to ask if anyone there can fix his hair. Although this story probably ranks right up there with the urban legend about alligators living in sewer systems, it does contain a compelling kernel of truth: The number-one reason for haircutting disasters is *failure to communicate!*

"Can we talk?" is the golden question that you should always ask before cutting a single strand of hair. In the case of the severed ponytail, asking the specific question, "Do you want a short haircut?" would have saved this free-spirited victim from the indignity of having a surprise business haircut.

REMEMBER

In real life, good communication eliminates unwelcome haircutting surprises like a shoulder-length style unexpectedly stopping at the jawline, bangs stopping mid-forehead when they were supposed to cover the eyebrows, or graduated ends that weren't supposed to be part of the cut. You can avoid these unhappy events and more by following five simple steps, which are discussed in the following sections.

Being mindful of the past

Although the old saying, "Let bygones be bygones," shows the wisdom of forgiving and forgetting, it doesn't apply to hair. If your bangs have ever been cut so badly that even hot glue wouldn't hold them down, you're always going to be anxious about getting your bangs cut. The same holds true if you once requested a trim and were given the "big chop" instead. Always keep in mind that the people sitting in your chair have probably had similar experiences. It's your job to do all you can to understand where they're coming from and allay their fears.

TIP

To find out what strikes terror in the heart of the person sitting in your styling chair, ask these three questions:

>> Is there anything I should be mindful of while cutting your hair — your bangs, perhaps, or the overall length of your hair?

>> Is there any area of your face, neck, or ears that you want to remain covered, or partly covered, by your hair — the tips of your ears, for instance, or the back of your neck?

>> Do you want to share any other special concerns that you have before we talk about your new style?

Evaluating the present

Comb through every square inch of the hair, or you could be eating your words midway through the service. Do you see any short pieces that preclude certain styles? Is the hair unusually straight, making a curly style too time-consuming to do on a daily basis? Does the neckline shoot up like a waterfall, making it impossible to cut a straight hairline? Is the hair exceptionally smooth and silky, giving it a big thumbs up for a one-length blunt cut?

Discover anything and everything there is to know about someone's hair before the style has been set in stone. Otherwise, you may end up like many stylists I've seen who come rushing into the break room after doing a haircut, crying, "I can't believe it! I was halfway through this haircut when I came across these short pieces. Now there's this big dip in the middle!" This type of disaster will never happen to you as long as you evaluate the hair carefully before you even take your scissors out of their case! (Check out Chapter 4 to find out about the different hair types and their unique styling abilities.)

Getting personal

Everybody has different time constraints, lifestyle habits, and abilities to style their hair that need to be integrated into all haircut suggestions. Imagine having only 45 minutes to shower and style your hair before shooting out the door, only to find that your style takes 45 minutes to blow-dry and curl. Or think about having a haircut that requires the back of the head to be curled when you can barely manage a blow-dryer. Knowing a person's lifestyle and abilities put you in the unique position of creating haircuts that enhance their daily lives.

TIP

Here are four lifestyle questions that you should always pose:

>> How much time do you have (or are willing to spend) in the morning to style your hair?

>> Does your career dictate that you must have a more conservative style?

>> How handy are you with a blow-dryer and curling iron?

>> What type of style — sporty, casual, or elegant, for instance — best suits your lifestyle on a daily basis?

Figuring Out Face Shapes

Human faces come in seven basic shapes. For decades, people treated the oval face as the facial goddess and compared every other face type to its perfect beauty. How dated can you get!

Today, attractiveness is often defined by interesting irregularities like wide-set eyes, a delicate pointed chin, or a square jawline that gives the impression of strength. Still, when facial shapes become too pronounced, people will often request that you de-emphasize something about their face.

Table 3-1 provides info on seven different facial shapes you'll need to consider before suggesting the best styles to enhance your family's and friends' naturally good looks. These guidelines can help you create the illusion of a more pleasing shape by softening or crisping up corners, and minimizing unwanted facial features like a protruding forehead.

TABLE 3-1   **Seven Face Shapes**

Face Shape	Features	Feminine Cutting Tips	Masculine Cutting Tips
Heart Heart	Wide forehead and narrow chin	Cut a side-swept bang, retain enough length to peek around the back of the neck and at the jawline	Keep length on top with less volume; suggest a beard that is slightly fuller and thicker around the chin area
Oval Oval	Symmetrical	Suitable for all haircuts and styles	Suitable for all haircuts and styles
Square Square	Overly strong forehead, jawline, and chin Face is equal length and width	Add see-through bangs and long layers that drape the face (past jawline)	Longer hair that accentuates angles of the face; modern undercuts with tapered sides and angular-shaped beards

TABLE 3-1 *(continued)*

Face Shape	Features	Feminine Cutting Tips	Masculine Cutting Tips
Triangle **Triangle**	Narrow at the forehead and wide at the jawline	Cut a full, wide bang and face frame design	Tapered or faded haircuts with length and volume on top; short, trimmed beards that start just above the jawline
Round (Circle) **Round**	Shaped like a sphere	Cut top layers for lift and/or deep-set bang and long, smooth layers (past jawline)	Longer top with angular perimeter lines; side parts, angular beards
Oblong **Oblong**	Long and narrow	Add fullness to the sides and a smooth top with bangs, or cut a chin-length bob with bangs and movement (waves or curls) around the sides of the face	Cut longer lengths to properly drape the head; or slicked-back styles with a close skin fade paired with a naturally shaped, slightly full beard
Diamond **Diamond**	Wide cheekbones, prominent jawbone, and narrow forehead	Cut a full bang or a *curtain bang*; drape the hair at the edge of the cheeks down to the jawline	Add bangs to high fades; notch or point cut the ends for lift and a deconstructed look; design cuts that hug the jawline

Images © John Wiley & Sons, Inc.; Illustrations by Rashell Smith

SOAPING UP YOUR FACE

Having a hard time figuring out which shape your face is? Try this: Brush your hair straight back to expose your entire face. Next, grab a bar of soap, stand in front of a mirror, close one eye, and trace your face shape onto the mirror. Now open your closed eye. Which face shape do you have?

Playing Show and Tell

Failure to communicate in a precise manner can turn an ordinary haircut into a disaster faster than you can say, "Oops!" One of the best ways to avoid misfires in communication is by using pictures of different haircuts to communicate length, style, and whether or not the tips of the ears should be covered by hair.

To use this strategy effectively, involve the person in your discussion by pointing at pictures and asking things like, "Do you want your hair to stop here or there? "Do you like the way my hair is cut in back, or do you want it more tapered like the model in this picture?" These kinds of questions can save you from making big haircutting mistakes.

AUTHOR SAYS

Here's a true story that happened to a stylist I know rather well. To this day, she still brings it up in conversations and has also confessed to this haircut fail more than once on social media. A regular salon client dropped off her mother for a haircut and then left to go shopping. Normally, this wouldn't have been a big deal, except her mother didn't speak a word of English and the stylist didn't speak the client's native tongue. Instead of communicating through pictures, they solely relied on hand gestures. Bad move. No matter what the stylist asked her, the client kept pointing to her shoulders. So, with all the confidence in the world, the stylist removed 8 inches (20.3 centimeters) of hair to create a beautiful, shoulder-length bob. When the service was complete, the woman paid for her service and left with tears streaming down her face. Uh-oh. When the daughter showed up to collect her mom, the stylist went outside to ask her why her mother was crying. Come to find out, her mother wanted her layers — not her length — to start at her shoulders.

REMEMBER

Talking through pictures — whether there's a language barrier or not — is always the most accurate form of communication.

TIP

Don't feel like you have to narrow everything down the first time you ask the right questions or even use pictures to communicate. People often need some time to feel comfortable enough to openly share what they want done with their hair, and people express themselves differently. By taking your time and verbally rephrasing your questions, the truth will eventually come out.

I WANT MY HAIR TO LOOK LIKE THIS!

Using social media hair pages are the best and quickest way to discover a plethora of styles and haircuts, ranging from short to long and one length to long layers. My go-to social media apps for hair are Instagram and Pinterest. To get you started, here are a few of my favorite pages to visit for inspiration and to visually communicate with my clients:

Topic	Pinterest	Instagram
Kids' Cuts	Childrens haircuts, Kids haircuts, Kids cuts with bangs, Kids curly hair, Buzz cuts, Girls short hair, Girls long hair, Boys haircuts, Kids curly hairstyles boys, Kids clipper cuts, Boys clipper cuts, Boys barber cuts	#childrenshaircuts #kidscuts #kidshaircuts #kidsbarber #kidsfringe #girlshaircuts #boyshaircuts #boyscuts
Women's Short Hair	Women short hairstyles, Women short haircut, Women short haircut black, Women short hair pixie, Pixie haircut, Pixie hairstyles, Short hair ideas	#shorthairstyles #shorthair #naturalshorthair #undercut #undercutgirl #undercutdesign #undercutsforwomen #pixie #pixiecut #pixiehaircuts
Women's Medium-to-Long Hair	Bob haircut, Lob haircut, Shag haircut, Shoulder length hair, Long hairstyles, Long hair with layers, Long layers	#bobhaircut #lobhaircut #shaghaircut #midlengthhair #longhaircut #longlayers #layeredhaircut
Women's Natural Hair	Natural hairstyles, Natural hairstyles for Black women, Natural hair short cuts, Pixie cuts Black women, Fade haircut women natural hair, Fade haircut women, Afro hair	#naturalhairstyles #naturalhair #naturalhairdoescare #naturalhairdaily #naturalhairstylist #afrohair

(continued)

(continued)

Topic	Pinterest	Instagram
Men's Hair	Mens haircut short, Men's hairstyles short, Fade haircut men's, Faded haircut men, Mens haircut long on top, Mens haircut long on top short on sides, Mens hairstyles, Mens hairstyles medium, Mens hairstyles fade	#menshair #menshaircuts #mensgrooming #barber #barbershop #barberlife #barbershopconnect #barbernation #fadehaircut #fades
Men's Natural Hair	Afro men hairstyles, Afro men haircut, Afro men hair, Barber haircuts, Black men haircuts, Black men hairstyles	#mensnaturalhair #naturalhairmen #afrohair #fade #afromenhair #afromen #blackmenhairstyles #barbershopconnect

Chapter 4

Typecasting Different Hair Personalities

Understanding hair type, texture, and density is an important step toward making your little darlings — and your big ones too — look forward to sitting in your chair. Once mastered, evaluating these factors as part of your cutting plan will help you to create cut-above hair designs on even the most opinionated hair.

Carefully evaluating the hair will also help to eliminate so many unwanted surprises like fine hair collapsing on the head, curly hair performing its incredible shrinking act, or thin hair playing peek-a-boo with the scalp.

In this chapter, I walk you through how to determine any hair type, as well as how to spot and handle pesky (but sometimes fun) whorls and cowlicks. You'll learn the meaning of hair density and discover how to determine whether a head of hair is thin, medium, or thick. And because hair texture plays a big role in every cut and style, I'll show you how to determine whether it's fine, medium, or coarse by comparing it to common sewing thread.

Talking about Texture

Hair *texture* defines the diameter of the hair, which ranges from fine to coarse strands. All hair textures behave differently. Fine hair can resemble fine silk, while medium hair is usually spunky without displaying the stubborn characteristics of wiry, coarse hair.

TIP

To help you accurately pinpoint the correct hair texture, use this tried-and-true method: Compare the hair to a length of regular sewing thread. If the hair is the same thickness as the thread, it's medium. If it's smaller than the thread, it's fine. If it's thicker than the thread, it's coarse.

Feeling fine

On the surface, dealing with fine hair seems easy enough. One look at those silky strands lying so neatly next to the scalp and you automatically have the urge to cut a smooth, one-length bob. However, most fine-haired beauties already know that their hair can look fabulous in a one-length bob because they've worn one for most of their lives.

Many people with straight, silken strands hope that you're the haircutter who can change the very nature of their hair by transforming it into a full-bodied mane that naturally lifts away from their head and coils around their fingers. Silly? Perhaps. Do many people with fine hair really hope you can transform their hair with a haircut that isn't a bob? Absolutely.

When discussing fine hair options, firmly guiding people toward more down-to-earth yet interesting hairstyles will allow you to give them something new that works well for their hair texture and their personal style.

Striking a happy medium

Medium hair is the one texture that you can have a field day with, as it's suitable for most cuts and styles. It isn't as flat as fine hair, can still be silky when coaxed, and readily assumes a fuller appearance when styled properly.

Cozying up to coarse hair

Coarse hair is the strongest and most resistant texture. Like a strong-willed child, your best haircutting results come from using its innate characteristics to create well-behaved strands.

Coarse texture has many wonderful qualities that you can incorporate into your hair designs. It has natural lift and frequently has a thicker hair density. Coarse hair excels when cut into a one-length *lob* (long bob) because the length and weight of the hair make it take on a smoother appearance, while still looking full and lush. Stylish layered pixies also receive a big checkmark in the coarse hair category because they can add a thick and chunky finish to the hair. Spiky hair-styles are also the perfect match for coarse hair. And even though it requires a hotter styling iron to literally bend it to your will, coarse hair has great style retention and looks amazing in tousled hairstyles that won't disappear at the stroke of midnight.

What's Your Type?

Hair *type* identifies the shape of the of the hair, which can range from 1A (stick straight) to 4C (coily).

Assessing and learning about your hair type and those sitting in your chair can be an illuminating journey that will not only make you a smarter haircutter, but a wiser one as well. Suddenly things you didn't understand about hair — like why it frizzes or has a Z-shaped coil pattern — suddenly make sense. Hair typing is most important for very curly and coily hair and, to a lesser degree, wavy hair.

TIP

GIVING HAIR AID

The one hair miracle that you call textures comes in the form of a wide array of styling aids. Products like dry shampoos, root lifters, and texture products that bulk up the hair enable those with silky strands to flaunt fuller locks. Coarser hair textures can be calmed and smoothed by using stronger styling aids and nourishing hair oils that help to control the hair, eliminate frizz, and encourage the hair to calm down. (Chapter 18, "Handling the Sticky Stuff," shares the full scoop on styling aids and the best ways to use them.)

The golden rule for creating carefree styles is to never pick a fight with Mother Nature. This means shying away from doing a sleek look on wiry hair, or expecting silky, straight hair to suddenly develop spring-loaded curls. The wisest choice involves maximizing the strengths, while minimizing the drawbacks of all hair types.

Hair types are mentioned throughout this book for both haircuts and styles. To avoid wasting time and needless frustration, I recommend that you dog-ear or bookmark this page.

The following hair typing information in Figure 4-1 and Table 4-1 is inspired by the original system created by Andre Walker, beauty entrepreneur and former personal stylist to Oprah Winfrey. The system I have included in this book is an augmentation of his chart, with more detailed breakdowns of hair types 1A through 4C.

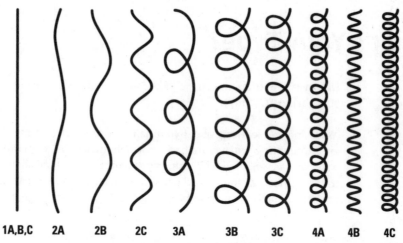

FIGURE 4-1: Hair typing.

1A,B,C   2A   2B   2C   3A   3B   3C   4A   4B   4C

© John Wiley & Sons, Inc.; Illustration by Rashell Smith

TABLE 4-1   **Hair Typing Chart**

Hair Type	Category	Characteristics
1A	Straight	Super straight; lies flat; lacks the body to perform many of your styling commands
1B	Straight	Accepts and holds (less) defined curls; tends to revert back to a straight state within a few hours
1C	Straight	May have faint waves when wet; dries straight; retains defined curl or blow-dry shapes better than 1A or 1B; tends to frizz in humid conditions
2A	Wavy	Loose waves; mostly straight at the roots; S-shaped waves form midway down the hair shaft to ends; excellent for tousled styles; can develop frizz in humid conditions
2B	Wavy	More defined waves; mostly straight at the roots; forms more defined S-shaped waves midway down the hair shaft to ends; tends to frizz in humid conditions; excellent for air-dried and heat-formed styles
2C	Wavy/Curly	Defined waves from roots to ends; prone to frizz throughout the hair; requires tension when heat styling into a smoother shape; moderate shrinkage when dried
3A	Loose Defined Curls	Loose curls from roots to ends; noticeably lifts away from the scalp; responds well to smoothing products; can develop frizz throughout the hair; excels at controlled air-dried and finger styles; moderate shrinkage when dried
3B	Strong Defined Curls	Springy curls varying from ringlets to corkscrews; voluminous whether thick or thin; tends to be dense; tends to dry frizzy; requires special hair care and styling aids; noticeable shrinkage when dried
3C	Corkscrew Curls	Tight corkscrew curls; tends to be voluminous; requires special hair care and styling aids; pronounced shrinkage when dried
4A	Curly/Coily	Densely packed, springy curls and coils; fragile; voluminous; requires special hair care and daily use of styling aids; significant shrinkage when dried
4B	Coily	Densely packed; coils bend at sharp Z-shaped angles; extremely fragile; voluminous; requires special hair care and daily styling aids; extreme shrinkage when dried
4C	Extremely Coily	Densely packed; similar to 4A but with less definition; can be soft or wiry; extremely fragile; requires special hair care and styling aids; most extreme shrinkage when dried

In the Thick of It: Hair Density

Hair density or hair thickness is determined by the number of strands per square inch (2.5 centimeters) on the scalp. Some people confuse texture (circumference of the strand) with density. Common misconceptions include someone with coarse hair (which has the largest circumference) being assessed with having thick hair, or someone with fine hair being assessed as having thin hair.

Here are two ways you can test the thickness of the hair:

>> **Ponytail density test for fine to medium textures:** If the hair is past the shoulders, brush and smooth the hair and then put the hair in a ponytail. If the ponytail diameter at the hair band is the size of dime, the hair is thin. If it's the size of a nickel, it's average. If the pony diameter is the size of a quarter, the hair is definitely thick.

>> **Light density test:** When the sun is directly overhead or the person is standing under a bright light that's a few feet above the head, check the visibility of the scalp. If it's clearly visible, it's thin. If it's slightly visible, it has a moderate density. And if it's not visible, it's thick.

While analyzing whether the hair has a thin, medium, or thick density, use this opportunity to check for thinning areas. Start by brushing the hair straight back from the face. Hair is typically thinner around the temples, but if it's extremely thin or more widespread, you will need to keep that in mind by designing a style that moves forward or down, rather than back. The same holds true for the crown area where many men and some women experience thinning hair. Also check for bald areas anywhere on the head that will need to be covered up with longer layers.

Calming Cowlicks

Cowlicks or *hair whorls* cause the hair to grow in circular patterns. Nearly everyone has at least one small cowlick at the crown area. Many people also have multiple cowlicks, often along the bottom hairline (preventing a straight neckline) and around the front hairline, particularly the fringe area. Figure 4-2 shows an example of a crown with double cowlicks.

Hair growths are also hereditary. If you or your significant other has a cowlick at the nape of the neck, chances are that at least some of your children will have this same growth pattern in their hair.

The swirling direction of a cowlick is less noticeable with longer hair because the length and weight of the strands naturally make it lie down. The minute you begin cutting the hair short, though, cowlicks will start ruling the day by separating the hair and making it look flat or lopsided, or causing it to stick up at odd angles.

NOT-SO-UPLIFTING HAIR

Early in my career, I learned a valuable lesson about the importance of checking for strong growth patterns — cowlicks so outrageous, for instance, that they can stop traffic. An impulsive young hairdresser working next to me was doing a man's business cut. I glanced over and noticed that his hair was lifting up slightly at the crown. I looked over two minutes later and his whole crown was standing on end. I sat there, staring at this scene unfolding with morbid fascination. Soon, his front hairline joined in by becoming so erect that it looked like it had been electrified. The hairdresser didn't say a word, and oddly, he remained stoic even though his hair gradually looked like an angry porcupine. My only guess is that it wasn't the first (or probably the last) time he'd fallen victim to an impetuous hairstylist. Carefully analyzing the growth of the hair before snipping a single end can avoid this type of embarrassing — okay, horrifying — situation.

FIGURE 4-2:
This young person has double cowlicks and double the trouble when trying to alter their natural directions.

© John Wiley & Sons, Inc.; Illustration by Rashell Smith

How to discover growth patterns

When examining the hair, follow these steps to discover hair growth patterns:

1. **Lift up the whole back of the hair without using any tension. Horizontally part and drop the first ½ inch (1.3 centimeters) of the entire neckline. Does it lie flat, partly flat, or is it going every which way in specific areas?**

Continue doing this all the way up to the crown while carefully checking for unusual growth patterns.

If cowlicks or whorls are present at the neckline, a straight-down neck design is nearly impossible. To avoid a cutting fail, design the neckline according to the natural growth patterns.

2. **Do the same thing on the sides of the hair, the top, and the front hairline (see Figure 4-2 to view an image of a cowlick).**

3. **Run your fingers through the hair. Do you feel small areas where hair is growing in swirls, or strongly growing in a forward position? If you do, check how resistant they are to your touch. When you move them in the opposite direction at the scalp, do they stiffly resist, roll over and obey, or do something in between these two extremes?**

After you've found all the whorls and swirls and other strong growth patterns, you can suggest styles that will not force them into a different shape, use them as part of your hair design, or hide them in plain sight using the right haircutting and styling techniques, and styling aids (see Figure 4-3).

FIGURE 4-3: Whenever possible, integrate a strong cowlick into your cutting design.

Photographer: Tom Carson (www.tomcarsonphoto.com); Hair: Ozzy Habibi; L Salon & Color Group, San Mateo, California

Working cowlicks to your advantage

These swirling dervishes can also be used to your advantage when cutting hair. For example:

>> You can use a cowlick to create natural lift at the crown by cutting longer layers to release some weight. This technique gives cowlicks permission to lift up the hair without becoming too obnoxious or separating from the rest of the pack.

>> When cutting short, spiky styles, deliberately cutting a cowlick shorter than you would otherwise dare can add more personality to these haircuts.

>> Using the growth pattern of a particularly large cowlick to dictate the flow of the hair will create a more manageable style.

Some people have the unfortunate distinction of having double cowlicks in their crown area — a royal pain, if you pardon the pun — while others have multiple cowlicks that are commonly found at the crown, the neckline, and front hairline. Strong cowlicks prevent people from having straight bangs, for instance, although the natural lift they create does afford other interesting styling opportunities.

Most haircutters eventually develop their own techniques for dealing with cowlicks, and I'm no exception. Having come from a family with legendary cowlicks — my son has one cowlick that measures a full 3 inches (7.6 centimeters) in diameter — I've learned to take these pesky growths in stride.

REMEMBER

Carefully plan out each haircut — including the best way to handle a person's cowlicks — before taking a single snip of hair. Taking these hair whorls into account allows you to avoid unpleasant surprises while giving you the advantage of shaping these cowlicks to your styling advantage.

2
Mastering Basic Techniques, Stat!

IN THIS PART . . .

Brush up on your geometry skills by getting familiar with lengths, angles, and elevations.

Section hair to make cutting easier.

Deal with the ends: Bevel, diffuse, layer, and more.

Master the basics of using clippers.

Chapter **5**

Understanding Head Shapes, Elevations, Angles, and Guides

To fully participate in this chapter, you need the following tools: scissors, cutting comb, tail comb (optional), clips and clamps, and a mannequin head (optional).

This chapter is filled with technical information. It's the driest chapter in this book and the one you will refer back to the most. This chapter is also the most empowering chapter. Understanding the technical side of haircutting makes the results of every haircut predictable and reproduceable. You'll know how, why, and where you should take each snip. Cool, right?

TIP

If you're missing any of the tools listed, feel free to improvise. If you only have paper-cutting scissors, for instance, separating very thin cutting sections will get you by for this chapter. If you don't have a mannequin head or a willing subject at hand, you can use your own head and hair.

REMEMBER

Once the information and techniques included in this chapter have been mastered, I promise they will be second nature to you when cutting hair. Until then, referring back to this chapter while following cutting tutorials will do the trick!

Getting to Know the Four Pillars of Haircutting

Haircutting is a mechanical process that guides your creativity. If you have a keen sense of balance, for instance, your work will stand apart from other people's haircuts because of the precise symmetry of your cutting style. For someone else, a sharp eye for detail (or even a talent for decorating) may inspire the interesting finishing details you add to your haircuts.

Regardless of your unique cutting style, you should definitely become familiar with the following four pillars of haircutting and use them to guide all your hair designs.

>> **Head mapping:** Pinpointing different shapes and key points found throughout the head

>> **Elevations:** How high or low you hold the hair to create or prevent layering and control bulk

>> **Angles:** Horizontal, vertical, diagonal, or curved cutting lines that control the shape and bulk, and create uniform or graduated layers

>> **Guides (also called guide lines):** Templates that you create to maintain the desired length and shape of each haircutting section

The remaining sections in this chapter focus on each of these four pillars.

REMEMBER

The most important takeaway from this chapter is the need to familiarize yourself with the mechanics of haircutting, which includes very basic geometry.

If you find yourself suddenly regretting that you slept through math class, please relax. While there's a lot of technical information in this chapter, you can easily master the four pillars of haircutting that I share by engaging your mind and using your hands to play along.

TIP

This chapter contains information that you will use as part of every haircut included in the book, as well as all haircuts you will do in the future. In terms of the geometry involved in haircutting, please know that it's tangible math that you create with your hands, as opposed to textbook, two-dimensional drawings. And, if it makes you feel any better, I confess that I have always struggled with math. If I can understand and use the four pillars of haircutting, you can too.

Identifying Head Shapes and Points of Interest (a.k.a. Head Mapping)

As you follow the haircutting tutorials in this book, I keep both of us on the same page by referencing different areas of the head during haircut tutorials, such as addressing the nape of the neck . . . starting at the occipital bone . . . beginning at the parietal ridge . . . or locating the apex of the head. Figure 5-1 visually explains what I am referencing every step of the way.

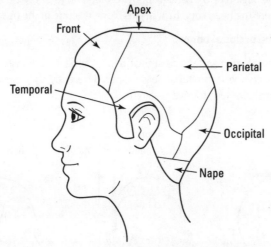

© John Wiley & Sons; Illustration by Rashell Smith

FIGURE 5-1: Key anatomical features of the head.

We've all known more than a few blockheads, but none are based on the actual shape of their head. A human head has flat, rounded, and curved areas that you need to keep track of when cutting hair. (You can help keep yourself on track by frequently referencing Figure 5-2.)

Because most haircutters are visual learners, here's a quick activity to help you become familiar with head mapping. You can identify the following head points on yourself as well as other people. You can also extend your activity by checking out the head shapes of your dog (top ridges) and ducks (very smooth). Every living thing is fair game for this activity. Make sure to have Figure 5-2 close by while doing the following:

1. **Locating the apex.**

   Locate the apex by placing a styling comb on top of the head as shown in Figure 5-2a. The apex, which is the highest point of the head, is where the comb makes contact with the scalp. Finding the apex is key to mapping the top section of the head.

2. **Identifying the parietal ridge.**

   Identify the beginning and ending of the parietal ridge (shown in Figure 5-2b). This is where the head curvature begins along the side of the head.

3. **Finding the occipital bone.**

   Identify the position and shape of the occipital bone as shown in Figure 5-2c. Because everyone's occipital bone is shaped differently, this feature poses unique considerations for every haircut.

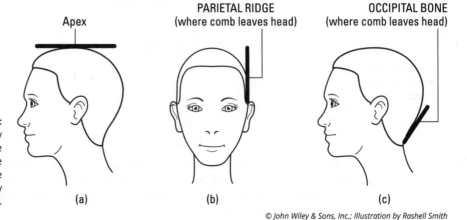

FIGURE 5-2: Locating key points of the head shape should be done before every haircut.

Apex

PARIETAL RIDGE (where comb leaves head)

OCCIPITAL BONE (where comb leaves head)

(a)   (b)   (c)

© John Wiley & Sons, Inc.; Illustration by Rashell Smith

The four corners of the head

Locating the four corners on the top of the head helps to guide how you will cut the hair at top of the head, where the head starts to slope down the sides and back of the head; and how to adjust the hair elevation based on the changing head shape. Practice mapping the four corners on your family members' heads, and while you're at it, map your head too.

How to locate the four corners:

1. **Place a cutting comb on each side of the head, starting at the front of the ear and straight up toward the top of the head.** Repeat this action on the other side of the head. The points where the comb loses contact with the head are the front two corners.

2. **Place the comb at a diagonal, going from one of the front corners to the opposite side of the back of the head.** Repeat this action on the other side. The points where the comb loses contact with the head mark the back corners (see Figure 5-3).

3. **Create a top section by parting out the hair using the corners as your guide.** When done correctly, the section will be in the shape of a rectangle.

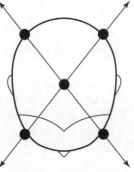

FIGURE 5-3: The four corners of the head help to guide many aspects of individual haircut designs.

© John Wiley & Sons, Inc.; Illustration by Rashell Smith

REMEMBER

Everyone's head shape is unique. If a person has a pronounced occipital bone, for instance, not taking that into consideration could make the hair collapse on the underside of this prominent bone. If a person has a flat occipital bone, building more hair volume in that area will create a far more pleasing shape. A person's head shape and its key points should guide every decision you make during a haircut.

Knowing how to identify key areas of the head is also important in terms of following all haircutting directions, whether they are included in this book or elsewhere.

AUTHOR SAYS

Thinking back to all the great salon haircuts that you've had in your life, you may or may not remember a stylist using a comb to map out key areas of your head. While an experienced stylist doesn't always use a comb to do this, they still use their fingers to surreptitiously check out your head shape while going through your hair. They'll place their hand over the entire occipital bone to get a 360-degree read on its shape; put their hand on the top of your head and lightly contract their fingers to feel where the parietal ridges begin and end; and so forth. When it's necessary to map the four points at the top of the head, most stylists will still use a comb.

TIP

The next time you are having your hair cut by a stylist who doesn't know your head shape, pay attention to what they're doing. This is important because some of the not-so-great salon haircuts that you had in the past could have been caused by the stylist not analyzing your head shape.

REMEMBER

If knowing the key points and shapes, and how to find them, is still a bit fuzzy after finishing this chapter, I promise that by the time you cut your way through this book, you'll be able to recite and identify them in your sleep. It all starts by being a hands-on learner.

Elevating Your Haircuts

Degrees of elevation are based on the hair's direction at the scalp. How high or low you hold the hair determines whether the hair will be cut at a 0-degree elevation for a blunt, one-length bob; a 135-degree elevation for a long-layered haircut; a 90-degree elevation for more structured layers; and so on (see Figure 5-4).

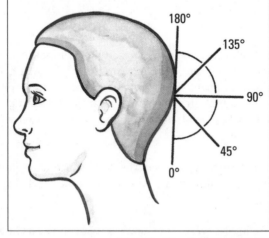

FIGURE 5-4: There may be six degrees of separation, but these are the five main degrees used when cutting hair.

© John Wiley & Sons; Illustration by Lisa Reed

Know your degrees of elevation:

>> 0° = combed straight down

>> 45° = equidistant between 90° and 0°

>> 90° = straight out from the head

>> 135° = equidistant between 90° and 180°

>> 180° = straight up from lower area of the head

REMEMBER

The Golden Rule of Elevation: Anything below a 90-degree elevation adds weight to the hair design; anything above a 90-degree elevation removes weight from the hair design. You'll be referencing this diagram often as you cut your way through this book, so make sure to bookmark or dog ear this page.

TIP

As you're getting familiar with elevations, try this quick activity. Nab a resident human (or yourself). Separate and comb different areas of the hair into various elevations that are detailed in Figure 5-4. Notice how elevations above 90-degrees create a diffuse, light layering, while holding the hair at 90-degrees (straight out from the scalp) creates bulkier, more defined layers.

Getting a Handle on Cutting Lines and Angles

Cutting angles can be straight or curved:

>> **Straight angles** can be horizontal (straight across), vertical (straight up or straight down), or diagonal (at an angle, most common is 45-degrees). Straight cutting lines create strong cutting lines.

>> **Curved angles** are customized to the curvature of the head and what you want to accomplish. For instance, a curved angle can seamlessly connect where the top of the head meets the parietal ridge. Curved cutting lines create softer end shapes.

See Figure 5-5, which visually explains different cutting angles, and Figure 5-2 to view the location of the top and parietal ridge.

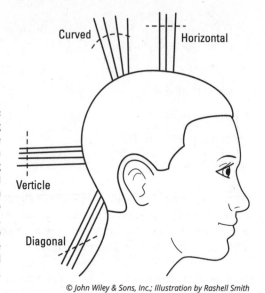

Curved · · · · Horizontal

Verticle

Diagonal

© John Wiley & Sons, Inc.; Illustration by Rashell Smith

FIGURE 5-5: Haircutting angles determine the shape of each haircutting section. Taking all angles used in a haircut into consideration, they determine the overall shape of the finished haircut.

Figures 5-6 and 5-7 show straight cuts and rounded or oval cuts.

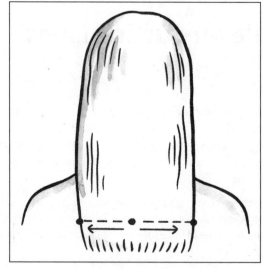

© John Wiley & Sons, Inc.; Illustration by Lisa Reed

FIGURE 5-6: When you are cutting a straight-across perimeter on one-length hair, you are cutting a horizontal line.

Fingers play an important role in cutting hair by holding each cutting section at the desired elevation. Using the second and third fingers of your non-cutting hand, grip the cutting section at the proper elevation with moderate tension and move your fingers to the desired angle. Following your top finger, trim the hair.

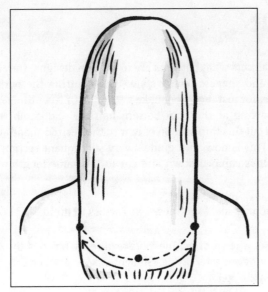

FIGURE 5-7:
When you are
cutting a rounded
or oval perimeter
on one-length
hair, you are
cutting a curved
line.

To practice cutting angles, you can do the following activity. I suggest that you practice all the cutting angles shown in Figure 5-3.

1. Identify the four points at the top of the head (see Figure 5-3).

2. Create the top section by parting the hair and using the four points as the guideposts for your section.

3. Pin away the rest of the hair to avoid cutting confusion. Dampen the top section.

4. Part out a ¼-inch (0.6 centimeter) deep and a 2-inch (5 centimeters) side-to-side *subsection*.

5. Comb the hair straight up (90-degrees) from the scalp (see Figure 5-4).

6. Holding the hair with your second and third fingers of your non-cutting hand, position them so they are horizontal to the scalp and ½-inch (1.3 centimeters) away from the ends. Following your finger angle, trim ¼-inch (0.6 centimeter) off the ends (Figure 5-3).

Repeat these practice steps, cutting the ends at vertical and diagonal angles. Lastly, practice curved angles.

Guiding the Cut

Guides are to haircuts what patterns are to fashion designs; they act as a template for the length and shape of every style. When cutting the perimeter of a one-length hairstyle, for instance, you make a ¼-inch (0.6 centimeter) to ½-inch (1.3 centimeters) parting at the back/bottom hairline and comb this hair straight down. You then cut this thin section of hair to the desired shape and length of your finished style. This is now your guide. Every subsequent section of hair you section out and cut is combed down and cut to the same length and shape of this guide.

REMEMBER

When cutting your guide, keep these two factors in mind:

>> **Hair shrinks when it dries.** The more texture the hair has, the more it will draw up during and after drying. (Straight, wavy, curly, and coily hair types are discussed in Chapter 4.)

>> **Hair is more elastic when it is wet.** This makes it important to never create more than mild tension on straight hair, and no tension on curly hair types when establishing your guides.

REMEMBER

If a person has naturally curly hair, but the hair has been chemically straightened, you should evaluate and cut it as you would straight hair. (See Chapter 4 for more information on hair types.)

WARNING

Be sure to avoid these four pitfalls when following your guide:

>> Cutting the guide along with the rest of the cutting line. This changes the length and sometimes the angle of the hair as you move through the haircut.

>> Failing to keep your guide at the proper elevation from the scalp.

>> Taking thick cutting sections and losing track of your guide.

>> Mistaking other hair as your guide.

The following sections introduce you to the two types of guides: the stable guide and the traveling guide.

Horsing around: Using a stable guide

A *stable guide* — also called a *stationary guide* — is used to create weight, reduce weight, or add graduated layers that seamlessly become longer. As the name implies, a stable guide does not move around during the haircut. Instead, the hair is directed to the guide.

The following are cutting instructions for using a stable guide on a layered haircut (shown in Figure 5-8). This example removes a little weight off the top of the hair for added lift. By only cutting ¼ inch (0.7 centimeter) of length, the cut section will still blend with the rest of haircut. You can do this twice before needing a full haircut.

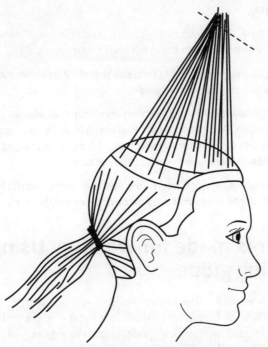

FIGURE 5-8:
A stable or stationary guide.

© John Wiley & Sons, Inc.; Illustration by Rashell Smith

What you'll need: Mannequin, family member with a layered haircut, or your own hair; your new scissors (for human hair) or old scissors (for synthetic hair or processed human hair commonly used for wigs and hair extensions); a cutting comb; and a spray bottle filled with water to wet the hair. (I'm a wuss, so I always use warm water.) If you don't have a spray bottle handy, dip your comb in a bowl of water.

When you're ready, follow these steps:

1. **Make a middle part at the top of the head and comb the hair down on either side of the part to ensure the hair is smooth and tangle-free.**

2. **Separate a ½-inch (1.3 centimeters) section of hair on either side of the middle part. Comb the middle and side partings together (see Figure 5-8).**

   This is now your cutting section. Pin away the remainder of the hair. Dampen and comb the cutting section to ensure even saturation.

3. **Comb and hold your cutting section at a 90-degree elevation (straight up) from the scalp.**

4. **Comb this section once more and hold the hair with your second and third fingers of your non-cutting hand. Slide your fingers up to about ½ inch (1.3 centimeters) away from the ends. Place your fingers at the exact angle as the existing cutting line, which may be a horizontal or a diagonal cutting line.**

   Take your time. If you don't clearly see the cutting line on the ends of the hair, dampen it a little more and comb the ends for better visibility.

5. **Following the existing cutting line, cut ¼ inch (0.6 centimeter) off the ends. This is now your stable guide.**

6. **Separate an identical ½-inch section on either side of your existing cutting section. Dampen the hair and comb it up to your stable guide. Make sure the hair is thoroughly combed from roots to ends. Identify the stable guide and remove ¼-inch length of hair.**

7. **Continue repeating the pattern in steps 2 through 6 until the entire top to just below the recession area on both sides has been cut.**

This hair is made for walking: Using a traveling guide

A *traveling* guide — also called a *moving guide* — travels with each haircutting section. It establishes the perimeter of the haircut and enables you to create uniform or graduated layers. The traveling guide, shown in Figure 5-9, is the most common type of guide used in haircutting, so it's important to show it who's boss at the beginning of your home-cutting adventure.

What you'll need: A willing participant or a mannequin with long hair; scissors, cutting comb, clips or clamps, and a spray bottle filled with warm water (see Chapter 2).

One of the easiest cuts is removing a small amount of length to refresh the ends and keep them looking thick as opposed to straggly. Cutting ¼ inch (0.6 centimeter) of length off every two weeks will keep the hair a consistent length. (Hair grows about ½ inch [1.3 centimeters] per month.)

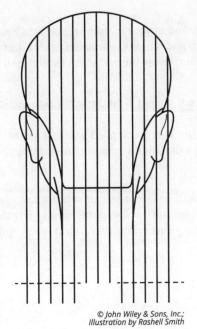

FIGURE 5-9:
A traveling guide moves as the haircut progresses to keep your design on track.

© John Wiley & Sons, Inc.;
Illustration by Rashell Smith

When you're ready, follow these steps:

1. **Brush the hair to ensure it is tangle-free. Lightly spray the hair with water until it is slightly damp. Comb, divide, and secure the hair into six sections — four sections in the back and two sections in the front.**

See Chapter 6 for more information on sectioning.

2. **Part out a horizontal, ¼-inch-thick section closest to the hairline from each of the back sections. Dampen and comb the freed hair straight down.**

Make sure the person or mannequin head you are about to cut is facing directly forward, and the jawline is parallel to the floor.

3. **Visually divide the ends into three sections: middle and two sides. Place the teeth of your comb ½ inch (1.3 centimeters) above the existing ends of the middle section.**

The comb secures the hair and prevents it from drifting while you cut.

4. **Cut ¼ inch (0.6 centimeter) off the ends of the middle section.**

Comb, smooth, and place the hair once again.

5. Incorporate an outside strand of your middle section into your side section. This additional strand is now the traveling guide. Cut the side section from the middle out, based on the length established by your traveling guide.

6. Comb once more and repeat steps 1–5 on the other side section.

REMEMBER

Always check to make sure the hair is combed straight down from the scalp. Double-check the length of the first side section before cutting the second one to ensure it's the proper length.

TIP

If you have an inconsistent length on one side, dampen the hair and comb through the ends. Check your haircut from the middle to the right or left side. Somewhere, while you were traveling, you lost your way. Find your guide and adjust accordingly.

Chapter 6

Parting Ways: Sectioning Hair for Successful Cuts

*T*ools you'll need to fully participate in this chapter: Detangling comb, tail comb, pintail comb (optional), clips and clamps.

When you go to a salon, you can usually tell the experienced haircutters from those who are just starting out in their beauty careers by the way they section the hair for a cut. Beauty schools teach *hair sectioning* (putting the hair in four, five, even seven different sections that are secured with hair clips) as a way to control the hair during the haircutting process. This gives you a much clearer view of what you're doing, while preventing unwanted pieces of hair from falling into your cutting section. Many seasoned salon pros do this by simply combing the hair out of the way, and perhaps casually securing it with a clip or two.

After doing hundreds of haircuts, you may decide to run with the big dogs by skipping these techniques. But, for the present — and for a long time to come — I recommend that you section and pin the hair according to the haircut you're doing. Also, keep in mind that many stylists pin the hair into sections for most haircuts for their entire careers.

TIP

The type of clips that you use to pin a haircutting section depends on the thickness, length, and overall weight of the hair. Chapter 2 details the different hair fasteners that work best on various types of hair. Whichever size and type of clip you use, make sure it's up to the task for gripping and holding each section in place. No sagging allowed!

In this chapter, I have included four-, five-, and two 7-section patterns.

REMEMBER

Depending on the haircut and the hair you are working with, and what makes you most comfortable, your sections may vary. In all cases, make sure that your partings are clean. You can use the edge of a cutting comb, but a tail comb will create a much sharper part. After you have completed your sectioning, look straight down at the head to ensure that the left and right sections match in terms of thickness and shape.

Note: If you decide to skip this section (for now), I recommend that you dog-ear this page, as you will be referencing this chapter quite often as you cut your way through the remainder of this book.

Four-Section Parting

A *four-section parting* is useful when you will not be cutting bangs and the hair is still light enough to be pinned by large clips or jaw clamps (see Figure 6-1). This pattern works well for single-length bobs, blunt cuts, and haircuts with long layers.

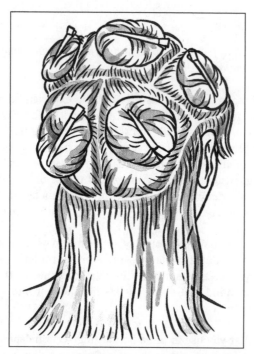

FIGURE 6-1:
Divide the hair
into four sections.

© John Wiley & Sons, Inc.; Illustration by Lisa Reed

To create a standard four-section parting:

1. **Using a cutting comb or tail comb, part the hair from the center front, through the crown, down to the center back hairline** (see Chapter 5 for identifying different areas of the head).

   This divides the hair in half.

2. **Starting at the crown, divide the front/sides of the hair by parting the hair from the crown down to just behind the ear on each side. Twist both side sections, tuck the ends into the twisted hair, and pin each side as you go.**

Four-Section Spherical Parting

Dividing the hair into four spherical-shaped sections is ideal for cutting bobs and long, one-length hair — defined as anything below the shoulders. To create this sectioning pattern, follow these steps:

1. **Part the front section by creating a middle part back to the crown, and then separate the hair into two sections by parting the hair from the crown to behind each ear (shown in Figure 6-2).**

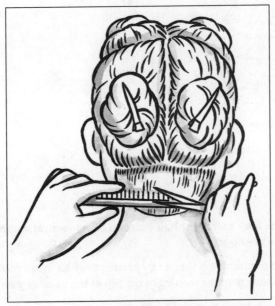

FIGURE 6-2:
Curved sectioning more accurately follows the spherical shape of the head.

© John Wiley & Sons, Inc.; Illustration by Lisa Reed

2. **Create two semi-circular partings at the back of the head. The top/back section starts at the crown. The second back parting starts just above the occipital bone and ends where this bone begins to curve inward toward the neck.**

3. **When you are parting the back of the hair, leave out a thin section all around the lower section.**

   The bottom, unpinned hair is used to establish your traveling guide (refer to Chapter 5 for more creating and working with a traveling guide).

Five-Section Parting

One of the most common sectioning patterns is a *five-section parting* (shown in Figure 6-3). This pattern is used for basic layer cuts, bobs, and many different long-layered hairstyles.

1. **Begin by parting the hair from the crown down to just behind the ear on each side (see Figure 6-3).**

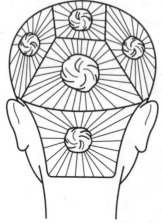

FIGURE 6-3: When creating a five-section parting, make sure that the top section goes all the way back to the crown.

© John Wiley & Sons, Inc.; Illustration by Rashell Smith

2. **Divide the back half of the hair into two equal vertical sections (perpendicular to the floor).**

3. **Separate the front/top section by parting the hair into a rectangular pattern using the four corners at the top of the head as your guide.**

   Mapping these four points is discussed in Chapter 5.

4. **Pin up the two side sections.**

Seven-Section Parting

This basic *seven-section parting* (shown in Figure 6-4) is the first one that beauty school students learn, and the one that you'll probably use the most when cutting your family's hair. It is similar to a five-section (shown in Figure 6-3) except the back of the head is divided into four sections.

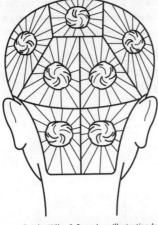

FIGURE 6-4: A seven-section parting is the most common sectioning pattern used by stylists.

© John Wiley & Sons, Inc.; Illustration by Rashell Smith

To create a basic seven section parting, follow these steps:

1. Separate the hair into two halves by parting the hair from the crown down to the back of the ear on each side.

2. Comb the front section toward the face. Separate the back of the head into two halves by parting the hair from the crown down to the middle of the nape. Then separate each half into two horizontal sections (as shown in Figure 6-4). Pin as you go!

3. Separate the top section and two side sections.

Seven-Section Parting with Hairline Sections

An alternative seven-section parting is to create a five-section parting but leave out two small front sections, as shown in Figure 6-5. These sections can be used to cut curtain bangs or for face-framing designs.

Follow these steps to create this alternative seven-section part:

1. Separate a front hairline section that is ½-inch (1.3 centimeters) deep and parallels the hairline. Divide this section in half and secure both subsections as shown in Figure 6-5.

2. Separate the top section, using the four corners of the head (explained in Chapter 5). Secure this section.

3. To part out the side sections, move from the bottom parting of the top section down to just behind the ear on each side. Secure each section as shown in Figure 6-5.

4. Separate the back of the head into two halves by parting the hair vertically right down the middle. Then divide each half in half to create four sections shown in Figure 6-4.

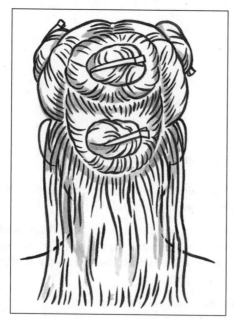

FIGURE 6-5:
This alternative seven-section parting separates the front hairline, which is cut separately.

© John Wiley & Sons, Inc.; Illustration by Lisa Reed

Chapter **7**

Dressing Up the Ends

Tools you'll need to fully participate in this chapter include scissors, blow-dryer, cutting comb, styling brush or round brush, clips and clamps, and a mannequin head (optional).

This chapter is all about graduating the ends, diffusing blunt lines, creating random layering, and perfecting piecey looks. Your best friend for this chapter is a mannequin head because you can cut all the techniques I include in this chapter on a single head of hair. If all you have are live models running around your home, put on your best parent/friend face and sweet talk them into your chair. As long as you both agree on the technique that you want to use, you're both golden.

TIP

If there isn't a head of hair in sight — living or otherwise — you can practice most of the following techniques on your own hair.

REMEMBER

The purpose of the tutorials in this chapter is to teach you how to graduate, notch, point cut, and slide cut the hair as opposed to performing complete haircuts. You can apply these techniques to a wide variety of hair designs.

WARNING

The old hair saying, "curly ends need friends," is true, especially on Type 3 (curly) and Type 4 (coily) hair (see Chapter 4). If you notch, point cut or slice cut curly or coily hair, the hair will expand and have a frizz-for-all party that will last until the affected areas are removed (cut). With the exception of the graduated end cut, the cutting techniques in this chapter should not be done on Type 3 or Type 4 hair.

CHUCKY AND THE DOLL HEADS

When my son was little, I had a favorite mannequin head named "Svetlana" with real blonde hair. I always kept Svetlana on my bedroom dresser, believing she was safe from my son Cody (age 2) and Chucky the dog — also called the Big Hairy Monster. That is, until I walked into the living room one day, and there was Svetlana on the floor with bald patches all over her head and her nose chewed down to a nubbin. Every square inch of her face also was covered with childish scribbles using red, blue, and black markers. I was numb. Svetlana had been transformed from a beautiful hair model to a monster — and it wasn't even lunchtime yet.

After your doll head is as bald as a billiard ball or falls victim to a fatal attack, have a field day. Pin wigs or hair *wefts* on their bare pates to practice hair techniques. Use them for scary indoor or yard décor during the month of October. And, of course, there's always planting season. Did I just say planting season? Some haircutters with a wicked sense of humor love to create creepy garden pots by cutting away the top of the heads, filling them with dirt, and planting herbs or flowers. The main thing to remember is to do everything you possibly can to keep them out of landfills. #repurpose #greenisgood

Graduating with Honors

Like a beveled mirror that gently slopes downward around the perimeter, a graduated perimeter creates a beveling effect by making the top layers longer than the bottom layers. It's done by positioning the head away from you as you cut, whether you're cutting at the back or sides of the hair.

After cutting the hair, you can visually see the graduation you just created by returning the head to an upright, level position. Grasping the tip of a topmost strand with moderate tension and holding it at a 0-degree elevation (see Chapter 5), you'll notice that the strand you're holding is slightly longer than the very bottom ends. Creating graduated ends causes the hair to bevel or cup under (see Figure 7-1).

The graduation or beveling technique is great for straight hair, whether it's natural or regularly styled that way (see Chapter 4). It's also the bomb for the perimeter line of classic bobs and lobs (see Chapter 13).

FIGURE 7-1:
A beveled one-length hairstyle is achieved by cutting graduated ends.

Photographer: Tom Carson (www.tomcarsonphoto.com);
Hair: Katelyn Anderson; Elon Salon, Marietta, Georgia

To cut graduated ends, follow these steps:

1. **Dampen the ends and section the hair into four partings.**

   Refer to Chapter 6 for how to do a four-section parting.

2. **Release a horizontal, ½-inch parting (1.3 centimeters) from both of the back/bottom sections.**

3. **Addressing the head position, make sure the jawline is parallel to the floor and the head is facing straight forward. Then move the head (not the neck or back) straight down with the chin pointing toward the chest (see Figure 7-2).**

   The shoulders should be relaxed as opposed to being hunched. The legs should be uncrossed and facing forward.

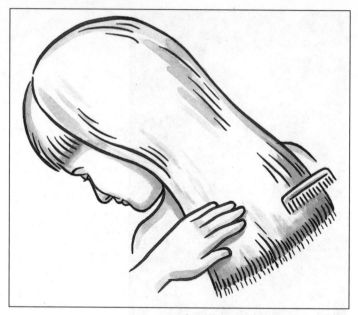

FIGURE 7-2:
How to cut
graduated ends.

4. **Comb the ½-inch (1.3 centimeters) subsection straight down and cut the ends. This is now your guide (see Chapter 5).**

Continue parting out subsections. Following your guide, cut the ends until the entire back of the head as been cut.

Make sure the person's head remains in the correct haircutting position.

If the hair is quite thin, you can drop and cut thicker sections. As long as you can still see your guide peeking through, you're good.

5. **Check your graduated ends by returning the head to an upright and level position. Pointing the nozzle of your blow-dryer straight down, dry the ends using your fingers to keep them in place. Grasp a top strand (outside layer) at the ends with moderate tension and compare the length to the underside of the hair.**

If you've done it correctly, the top layer will be longer.

6. **If everything looks as it should be, dampen the ends of the hair and style them using a styling brush or a round brush.**

Taking It Up a Notch

Notching uses the tips of the scissors to snip the tips of the hair. It can lightly remove weight from the hair, soften and slightly shorten the ends, and help to disguise cutting gaffes. Notching is also used to create piecey end designs around the face and neckline on short hair (see Figure 7-3).

FIGURE 7-3: Notching the ends of the hair creates lightly broken cutting lines.

Photographer: Tom Carson (www.tomcarsonphoto.com); Hair: HBI Design Team, Chattanooga, TN; Color: Ava Gardner; Makeup: Jen Blalock; Planet 21 Salons, Charlotte, North Carolina

Notching can be deeper than ¼ inch (0.6 centimeter). I don't recommend doing this on a family member or friend until you've practiced different cutting depths on a mannequin head.

TIP

If you have someone running around your house with bangs that move up and down every time they blink, you've just found your ideal model. The same is true for longer, single-length hair, or layers of any length. You can also practice notching on your trusty mannequin head. If you still come up dry, head for the bathroom, flip on the light, and get ready to notch your own hair.

Chapter 9 is devoted to different bang and eye-framing styles. It focuses on great hands-on cutting tutorials that are easy to follow and yield amazing results. Many of these tutorials use notching to add interest to the ends.

Technically speaking, notching is a form of point cutting. Stylists normally use the term *notching* for shallow end cuts and point cutting for deeper end cuts.

Follow these steps to practice hair notching:

1. **Choose the area of the hair that you want to notch.**

   Notching is done on the ends only. Possible areas to practice hair notching are the perimeter of all haircuts for a less precise look, the bang area, layered hair that needs lift, and on short, layered haircuts to restore their light, airy appeal.

2. **Thoroughly comb and then lightly dampen the ends of the hair.**

   Notching can be done on dry, damp, or wet hair. I recommend damp hair because you can clearly see the notched pattern.

3. **If the hair is thick, separate horizontal sections (see Chapter 5) and notch the ends. If the hair is thin, you can notch the ends all at once.**

   Here's how it's done: Using the tips of your scissors, notch the hair by cutting the first ¼ inch (0.6 centimeters) of the ends vertically or diagonally (see Figure 7-4).

   Most notching is no deeper than ¼ inch (0.6 centimeters).

   The closer the notches are to each other, the sparser the ends will be.

4. **Using a styling brush, blow-dry the hair straight down. What do you see? If the hair still looks dense on the ends, repeat the process or add point cutting, which is also covered in this chapter.**

To show off notched ends, apply a slight amount of pomade to your palms. Warm the product by rubbing your palms together and then apply a slick of the product to the very ends of the hair. (Chapter 18 covers styling aids.)

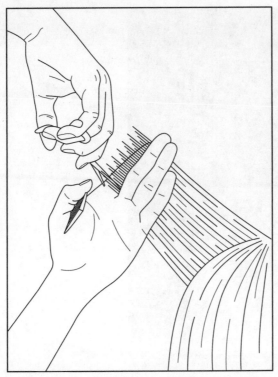

© John Wiley & Sons, Inc.; Illustration by Rashell Smith

FIGURE 7-4: How to notch the ends of the hair.

Point Cutting Remarks

Point cutting is a technique used to remove bulk from the ends, encourage existing layers to more seamlessly blend together, soften blunt lines, and create piecey perimeter lines.

Basic point cutting is done by cutting the ends at a vertical angle (straight up, starting at the tips of the hair). This produces an entirely different result than notching. Point cutting makes bangs lighter and more see-through. When done on the ends of long-layered hair, point cutting creates softer, less structured layers with enhanced movement (see Figure 7-5). On bangs, it removes density to make it a more see-through design (see Chapter 9). Point cutting is usually done after the hair has been cut and dried.

Depending on where you're point cutting the hair, you can remove as little as ½ inch (1.3 centimeters) to as much as 2 inches (5 centimeters) of hair.

FIGURE 7-5:
Point cutting
lightens layers
and opens up the
perimeter of the
hair by giving it a
piecey finish.

Photographer: Tom Carson (www.tomcarsonphoto.com);
Hair: Jillian Woodcock, Douglas Carroll Salon & Spa, Raleigh, NC

TIP

Point cutting is included in several tutorials in Chapter 9 and throughout Part 4.

Ready to try point cutting? Follow these steps and see Figure 7-6:

1. **After you've finished your haircut and dried the hair (smooth as opposed to being curled or waved), pinpoint the area you want to point cut.**

2. **Whether you're point cutting the bangs, layers, or the perimeter, cut straight into the ends of the hair.**

    If you're cutting layers, take 1- to 2-inch sections (2.5 to 5 centimeters) — as opposed to large or random sections of hair — to prevent cutting confusion.

After you've mastered the art of basic point cutting, you may want to try a more advanced technique by cutting the ends at other cutting angles and deeper into the hair strands.

WARNING

Do not point cut at any angle other than vertical until you've mastered this technique and have practiced different angle designs on a mannequin head. (Chapter 5 discusses different cutting lines.)

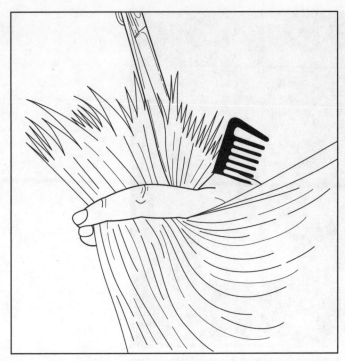

FIGURE 7-6:
How to point cut the ends of the hair.

© John Wiley & Sons, Inc.; Illustration by Rashell Smith

WARNING

Never point cut near or at the root area. Doing so will cause the hair to stick up and do all kinds of obnoxious things. Instead, focus on the ends of the hair and adjust the point cutting depth accordingly.

Any Way You Slide It

A basic slide cut is a dry cutting method that releases weight by creating vertical layers and piecey (as opposed to solid) ends. It's done by pointing your scissors in a downward direction. Your starting point is determined by where you want the vertical layering or separation to begin (see Figure 7-7).

TIP

Chapter 13 includes a gorgeous slide-cutting tutorial!

Sliding is considered a freestyle cutting technique because you tap into your creativity, rather than a guide, to create vertical layers (see Chapter 5 for information about guides). Slide cuts are done to break up dense or saggy areas, remove weight to create more movement, or create random layers. Because of this, slide cutting should be done on dry hair.

FIGURE 7-7:
Slide cutting can transform a haircut from conservative to trendy.

Photographer: Tom Carson (www.tomcarsonphoto.com); Hair: Jesse Soper, Carmen Carmen Salon & Spa, Charlotte, NC

REMEMBER

In order to do the following tutorial, you must use Japanese-style (convex) hair-cutting scissors. This is important because German-style (concave) scissors are not designed for slide cutting (see Chapter 2).

To practice slide cutting, follow these steps:

1. **On dry hair, open the blades and place a strand of hair at the back of the blades (at or near the joint; see Figure 7-8).**

2. **Hold and apply moderate tension on the hair strand with your noncutting hand.**

3. **Move the scissors from where you want the layer to begin toward the ends as you make *slight* cutting movements without closing the blades.**

   This is often described as a fluttering motion. When done correctly, the blade movement is barely noticeable.

WARNING

Slide cutting is a more advanced technique that should be practiced on either a mannequin head or a sewn weft of hair (available at beauty supply stores and websites that sell wigs and extensions). Never slide cut hair worn by a human until you're proficient at this technique.

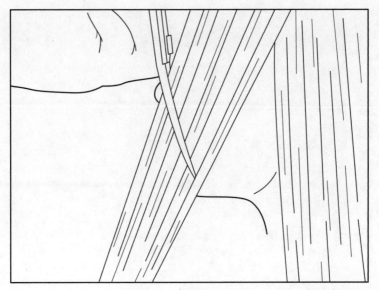

FIGURE 7-8:
How to slide cut
the hair.

Chapter **8**

Cuddling Up to Clippers

Tools you'll need to fully participate in this chapter include clippers, No. 3 and No. 4 clipper guides, scissors, trimmers, blow-dryer (optional), cutting comb, face or neck duster (optional).

Special items you'll need for the balding cut include shave cream or shave gel; shave oil and shave balm, cartridge or safety razor, sunscreen.

Hairdressing pros regard clippers as the automatic transmission of haircutting. They allow you to mow down rows of hair without lifting a finger, square-off corners with a flick of a blade, and do entire haircuts in half the time it takes when using scissors. Most clipper cuts also have a distinctive look, making them the tool of choice for cutting short, crisp styles. You can easily become adept at using these tools by mastering one technique at a time.

In this chapter, you find out how to choose the best clippers for you, as well as how to maintain them. You also get some tips, tricks, and tutorials that will introduce you to the basics of clipper cutting.

REMEMBER

Don't confuse clippers with trimmers. Clippers are larger and more powerful than trimmers; they're meant to clip an entire head of hair. Trimmers, on the other hand, are designed to crisp up perimeter lines, cut hard parts, and trim mustaches, beards, sideburns, and unwanted neck hair. For more information on trimmers, check out Chapter 2.

Getting the Best Clippers for Your Needs

Although you can find many different brands and designs on the market, there are three basic types of clipper motors: magnetic, pivot, and rotary. Which one you choose to use depends on how many clipper cuts you plan on doing and what demands you'll be placing on your machine. Needless to say, the tougher the job, the more powerful the clippers must be.

>> **Magnetic clippers** run at the highest speeds and produce the smoothest cuts. They're ideal for fine hair textures, including fine, curly hair. In general, magnetic clippers are also the lowest-priced clippers and weigh less than their more powerful cousins.

>> **Pivot clippers** run slower than magnetic clippers but make up for it by being twice as powerful. They can sail through thick, heavy hair and sing a song while doing it. The newest tools are also fairly lightweight.

TIP

If you are planning on doing a lot of clipping, I recommend buying pivot clippers.

>> **Rotary clippers** have equal amounts of power and blade speed. They can clip through the hairiest, thickest, and coarsest hair on the planet without skipping a beat. As the true beast of hair clippers, rotary clippers cost the most, weigh the most, have adjustable motor speed settings, and can be used from morning till night without overheating or requiring anything beyond routine clipper maintenance. Rotary clippers are the tools of choice for barbers and some stylists, but they're rarely needed for home haircutting.

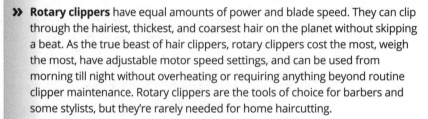

AUTHOR SAYS

THE LITTLE CLIPPERS THAT COULD NOT

When I was a newbie stylist, I knew about clipper brands, but nothing about the different types of motors these companies made. One evening I agreed to take a late appointment when no one else was at the salon except a young boy, his mother, and me. The lad wanted a short clipper cut on his thick, coarse, curly, and overgrown mop. With all the confidence in the world, I whipped out my magnetic clippers and started munching down the hair, beginning at the top/middle of his head. On the first row, my clippers bogged down a bit, but I didn't think much about it. On the second row, my clippers bogged down again, then stopped, and then died — forever. I only had the one clipper tool. The stores were closed. And my little customer had to leave the salon looking like Larry from *The Three Stooges*. Even though I finished his clipper cut the next morning, I believe to this day that the kid and his mother have flashbacks whenever they hear the familiar hum of clippers in action.

Cutting the cord

Corded clippers provide the assurance that your clippers will always be raring to go, and you'll never have to worry about running out of power mid-cut. However, corded clippers limit your mobility in terms of where you must cut the hair and stand while doing it. Because cords also run the risk of accidently being yanked, tugged or tripped over, your clippers risk falling on a hard surface and cracking the casing, chipping the blades, or scrambling the inner workings (been there, done that). Fully charged cordless clippers, on the other hand (see Figure 8-1), can be safely set on the counter and run one to two hours between charges.

FIGURE 8-1: Cordless clippers and charger stand.

StyleCraft (www.stylecraftus.com);
Gamma+ Absolute Alpha

There are also cord/cordless clippers made by several companies, which give you the best of both worlds.

WARNING

Never allow your clippers to remain fully discharged when storing them for even a few days, as this can cause future charging problems. Storing clippers that are partially charged is fine.

The best cordless clippers have a lithium-ion (Li-ion) battery, which allows the clippers to run longer and when stored, remain at least partially charged for up to one year.

Bells and whistles

Beyond corded and cordless models, clippers are available with a variety of features that you should carefully consider before parting with your hard-earned money.

» **Snap-on blade technology:** Removing a blade is easy when you have clippers that use magnetic, snap-on blades. Some professional clippers require a screwdriver to remove the blades. If either of these choices concern you, shop accordingly.

» **Taper lever:** Many clippers include a *taper lever,* a simple armature that allows you to clip slightly longer or shorter lengths of hair in a seamless fashion. Half sizes are accomplished by moving the lever up (half-size shorter) or down (half-size longer). Some deluxe clippers (see Figure 8-2) have multiple settings that eliminate the need for common guide sizes. Check out the next section, "Guiding the cut," to find out about clipper guides and how to use them.

» **Ergonomic features:** These features are important because they make the clippers easier to both hold and control. Ergonomic clipper casings are generally curved (like an arched back) and are balanced from tip to stern to prevent undue stress on the wrist.

» **Anti-fatigue features:** Always shop for clippers that feature reduced vibration and noise levels. Using clippers that nearly buck when you turn them on, or vibrate so bad that they sap your hand, wrist, and arm strength, should be avoided. Noisy clippers can also cause mental and physical fatigue.

FIGURE 8-2:
A taper lever allows you to change the closeness of your cut without changing clipper guides.

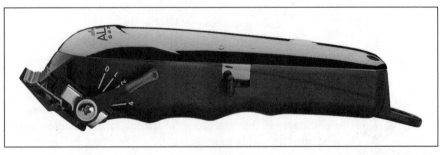

StyleCraft (www.stylecraftus.com); Gamma+ Absolute Alpha

For a long-term relationship to blossom between the two of you, your clippers should comfortably fit in your hand, have minimum vibration, are relatively quiet, and possess the raw power you need to get the job done.

Guiding the cut

Clipper guides (also called *clipper combs or guards*) are must-have tools for all clipper cuts (see Figure 8-3). They are available in a variety of sizes, allowing you to accurately cut specific lengths of hair. Classic clipper guides can evenly cut the hair as short as ⅛ inch (0.3 centimeters) and as long as 1 inch (2.5 centimeters).

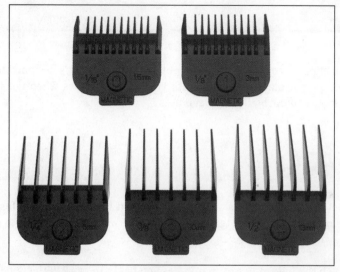

FIGURE 8-3: Clipper guides determine the length you cut the hair.

StyleCraft (www.stylecraftus.com); Gamma+ Alpha

With most clipper brands, when you clip the hair without a guide (sometimes called out as 0), you're cutting the hair approximately ¹⁄₁₆ inch (1.6mm) in length.

If you plan on doing a variety of clipper styles, make sure to have the clipper attachments in Table 8-1 at the ready.

Shop for a clipper kit that includes a set of guides (see Table 8-1). Several companies sell "universal" guides that claim to fit most clippers. In reality, they rarely fit as perfectly as guides designed for the clipper you're using. I recommend always buying clipper guides that are specifically made for the brand and model of your clippers.

TABLE 8-1

Clipper Guide Numbers and Cutting Lengths

Number	Cutting Lengths
1	⅛ inch (3mm)
2	¼ inch (6mm)
3	⅜ inch (10mm)
4	½ inch (13mm)
5	⅝ inch (16mm)
6	¾ inch (19mm)
7	⅞ inch (22mm)
8	1 inch (25mm)

REMEMBER

All clippers come with a blade protector (cover) that's designed to custom fit over the clipper blade. Always sheath your clipper blades when not in use to prevent damage to the blades between uses.

Clipping ABCs

Getting your clipper skills up to speed can happen relatively fast, as long as you allow yourself to master one technique at a time and not try to go full bore with advanced clipper cuts right out of the gate.

Keep the following tips in mind as you begin to work with clippers:

>> Make sure the hair is clean and free of styling aids.

>> Clip the hair damp or dry, but never soaking wet. Towel-dried hair (slightly damp) is ideal for novice clipper cutters.

>> Hold the clipper with your thumb on top and your fingers on the underside of the casing. For most cutting techniques you will be holding the clippers top side up.

>> Clip the hair in short strokes to prevent the clipper motor from getting bogged down and to achieve the cleanest cut possible.

>> Use a comb to remove loose hair after you have clipped a section or any time the loose hair bunches up on the head.

- For most clipper techniques, the hair is clipped against the growth. There are also "with-the-grain" techniques that preserve tight wavy patterns.

- Run the clipper over each section two or three times and in different directions.

- Perfect your *rocking* (also called *arcing*) technique. Rocking entails clipping upward and then arcing the clippers toward you as you reach the point where two different lengths meet. This seamlessly blends these lengths and erases cutting lines. (Check out Figure 8-6 later in the chapter to see how this is done.)

- After the hair has been cut once, re-clip the same hair in different directions (up and then diagonal, for instance) to smooth the cut and make sure that every hair has been clipped to the desired length.

TIP

When trimming the perimeter of the hair, you can keep your clipper in the same position as you did for the rest of the cut or use what is called an *inverted clipper technique* by turning the clipper so that the backside is on top. The latter allows you to see the lines more clearly.

WARNING

If you find yourself feeling impatient, remember that clipper cutting snafus can be ten times worse than those made by scissors.

Maintaining Your Machine

Maintaining your clippers gives them their best chance for a long and useful life; not maintaining these tools will turn them into scrap metal long before they're due to expire. Fortunately, regularly maintaining these lean, mean cutting machines is a quick and easy task.

What you'll need to maintain your clippers:

- Clipper oil

- Clipper brush (or toothbrush)

- Blade cleaner

- Lubricant

- Soft cloth

The following steps walk you through how to maintain your clippers:

1. **Use a soft cloth to remove hair snippets that tend to cling to the casing.**

2. **Use the same cloth to wipe the outside of the blades.**

3. **Use a clipper brush (see Figure 8-4) or stiff toothbrush to remove hair snippets from the sides and top of the blade area and between the blade teeth.**

4. **Follow the directions on the blade cleaner of your choice.**

5. **Apply a clipper oil (see Figure 8-4) per the instructions on the packaging.**

   My usual method is to put one drop of oil on both sides of the blade tips and one drop in the middle of the blade. Once this is done, I run the clippers for a few seconds to distribute the oil, and then turn them off and wipe away any oily residue clinging to the outside of the blades.

FIGURE 8-4:
Clipper oil and a clipper brush.

StyleCraft (www.stylecraftus.com)

TIP

About every six haircuts (or any time you notice buildup), remove the cutting blade and wash it with soap and water. Allow it to completely dry before reattaching it to your clippers. Use this time to examine the blade to ensure that all the teeth are intact and inspect the area where the blade attaches to the machine. Remove any trapped hair snippets with a brush and a soft cloth.

Getting Clipper Happy: Practicing Some Standard Techniques

This section contains two hands-on clipper cuts using basic techniques. These same basic moves also are used as part of all advanced barber cuts. If you have the itch to get clipper happy with your family or friends, you're going to love the tutorials that I have written for you: The Boyish Taper Cut (which includes tapering and clippers-over-comb techniques) and Bald as a Billiard Ball (the art of balding and conditioning the scalp). Of course, these two step-by-steps are just a warm-up for things to come. Part 4 features several partial and full clipper cuts, including step-by-step taper and fade cuts that are to die for.

TIP

Here's a down-and-dirty trick that I suggest you use until you've clipped a few heads of hair: When you are working on existing hair that is considerably longer than your goal length, decide the longest length of the cut you are about to do and then use the appropriate clipper guide to do a rough cut on all areas designated for clipping. You don't have to do a bang-up job but clip it thoroughly enough so that it is fairly even. Doing this makes it much easier to view what you are doing as opposed to clipping through an overgrown head of hair.

The Boyish Taper Cut

Easy

Tools you'll need to complete this tutorial include clippers, No. 3 and No. 4 clipper guides, cutting comb, blow-dryer (optional), face or neck duster (optional).

Whether you're excited to start clipper cutting or are just done with spending too much money and time at the hair shop, the Boyish Taper Cut (Figure 8-5) is a great way to get your buzz on. This tutorial guides you through a complete clipper cut that includes using a tapering technique that seamlessly blends two different lengths of hair and uses the clippers-over-comb technique, which is done for many cuts.

The hair shown in Figure 8-5 is a bit grown out, which is why I list No. 3 and No. 4 clipper guides. To shorten this cut and give it greater longevity, you can use No. 2 and No. 3 guides.

FIGURE 8-5:
The Boyish Taper Cut is a win-win clipper cut: It's easy to do and requires little-to-no styling maintenance.

© saluha/Getty Images

Ready to get started? Follow these steps:

1. **Comb the hair in the direction it grows (straight down in the back, for instance, and forward on top).**

2. **Using a No. 4 guide (refer to Table 8-1), clip the hair from the bottom up. Make sure you are keeping track of the hair growth, and always clipping against the grain.**

    Comb through the cut area frequently to remove loose hair, which can become quite bulky.

3. **If needed, cut cowlicks and whorls in several different directions until the hair blends into the surrounding cut.**

4. **If the hair is thick or coarse on top, use your fingers to comb the hair back for your first pass and then clip the area a second time with the hair lying naturally on the head.**

5. **If you want the bang area to be slightly longer, separate it from the top section and trim it slightly longer using scissors (see Figure 8-5).**

6. **Still using a No. 4 clipper guide, go over the entire haircut in several different directions to ensure that all the hair has been clipped to the new length.**

7. Changing to a No. 3 guide (reference Table 8-1), clip the back of the head from the back hairline and up to the midpoint of the occipital bone (see Chapter 5). Clip the sides of the head up to the same level as the back of the head. Bend the ears and trim around this area of the hairline.

8. Because the sides of the hair typically grow in different directions, clip it in different directions to make sure all the hair has been cut against the grain.

9. Use the *tapering technique* to blend the No. 3 length with the No. 4 length. (See Figure 8-6 to view how to do this technique.) Table 8-1 lists guide lengths.

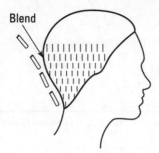

Blend

© John Wiley & Sons, Inc.; Illustration by Rashell Smith

10. Use clippers to design and crisp up the sides and back of the hairline and trim the sideburns. To shorten the interior of the sideburns, use the *clippers-over-comb technique* (see Figure 8-7).

Depending on the size of your clippers, or how close they cut, you may find using trimmers more comfortable to perform step 10. Trimmers-over-comb is done the same way as clippers-over-comb.

11. Using your blow-dryer on a high-velocity setting, remove any loose hair snippets.

12. Using a neck or face brush, remove all loose hair snippets on the face and neck.

TIP

Usually, a No. 3 or No. 4 guide cuts short enough that the cowlick doesn't separate and pop up like a jack-in-the-box (see Table 8-1). If you're dealing with especially gnarly cowlicks, cut them separately by removing the clipper guide and using the clippers-over-comb technique shown in Figure 8-7. Always take small sections and follow the hair growth pattern as you work around the whorl.

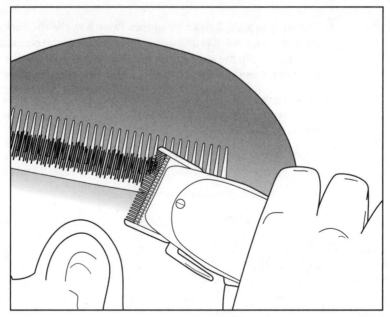

FIGURE 8-7:
The clippers-over-comb technique can be used in lieu of scissors-over-comb to create a crisper finish to the hair.

Bald as a Billiard Ball: Clipper and razor balding cut

Easy

Tools you'll need to fully participate in this tutorial include shave cream or shave gel, shave oil and shave balm, cartridge or safety razor, sunscreen.

In barber speak, *balding* is the act of clipping and then shaving the hair right down to the scalp. It's generally done when pronounced hair thinning or male-pattern baldness is present, although it can make a strong statement in its own right! Balding can be maintained by using a safety or cartridge razor and/or an electric shaver every few days. Specialty balding clippers are also available.

In most cases, balding tools risk cutting the scalp. To minimize the chance of this happening, hold the scalp taut with your fingers when shaving or clipping and move the head away from the area you are balding (for example, move the head forward when cutting the back of the head). Unless you are using electric balding clippers or a shaver, it's also important to prep the skin in the same way you would for face shaving. Make sure to moisturize and apply sunscreen after the cut is complete!

TIP

Cartridge razors have various blade designs to improve your shaving experience. Quality cartridge razors, with up to five blades per cartridge, have a hinge action to allow the blades to follow the curvature of the face or head, and sometimes include serum or lubricating strips. *Safety razors* use single blades that aren't assembled in a cartridge. Enthusiasts love safety razors because they're less irritating to sensitive skin and reduce the amount of waste (single blade vs. cartridge) that ends up in landfills.

WARNING

Always carefully inspect the scalp for odd shapes, bulges, and scars before you start. Uncovering them with a balding cut could be more traumatic for the wearer than hair loss.

Ready to get started? Follow these steps:

1. **Using your clippers without a guide, clip the entire head.**

   Keep the clippers parallel to the head at all times to prevent scraping the skin. Cut the hair against the grain.

2. **Cleanse the scalp with a gentle body wash, liquid shampoo, or shampoo bar.**

3. **Soak a hand towel in very warm water, wring it out until it is no longer dripping, and wrap it around the head. Allow it to remain on the scalp for a few minutes and then gently wipe away the cleanser.**

   Make sure that all product residue and stray hair snippets are removed.

4. **Apply a shave oil to the scalp to protect against razor drag and skin irritation.**

5. **Apply a thin layer of shave cream or shave gel over the oil.**

6. **Starting at the top/back and following the natural growth direction of the hair, shave the hair down to the scalp.**

7. **Soak a towel in warm water, wring it out, and remove the oil and shaving cream.**

8. **For a closer shave, repeat the process going against the grain this time.**

   Exception: Do not repeat this step on sensitive skin or if there are signs of skin irritation.

9. **Soak a towel in cold water, wring it out, and remove all products, and snippets of hair.**

10. **Apply a post-shave balm with calming, antiseptic ingredients. Finish with a light sunscreen to prevent overexposure to UV rays.**

    Products containing zinc to calm the skin are my top picks.

3

Maintaining Hair Moxie

IN THIS PART . . .

Follow step-by-step instructions on how to cut several bang designs.

Work up the courage to trim your own hair.

Do touch-up cuts for your immediate circle of family and friends.

Chapter **9**

Making Bangs and Frames

Tools you'll need to fully participate in this chapter include scissors, cutting comb, tail comb, styling brush, round brush (optional), blow–dryer, clips and clamps, and a mannequin head or hair wefts.

Personally, I've never been a shopaholic or addicted to chocolate cake, but my obsession with bangs runs deep. Creating different bang styles can transform bobs, mid–length, and long–layered looks with just a few snips of your scissors. In this chapter, you discover how to master several popular fringe designs, such as wispy, curtain, curved, and more.

TIP

The term "bangs" or "bang" is used in the United States, while Canada and Western Europe refer to them as a "fringe." When you encounter either of these terms, know that they are one and the same. For the sake of relatability, I use both terms interchangeably in this chapter, which I do in real life as well.

Tips for Creating Bangin' Bangs

Bangs can hide a myriad of flaws and enhance the features you want to show off. Because they can be so transformative, a great deal of thought should be put into choosing a particular fringe design. Here are a few things to take into consideration before designing and cutting bangs:

>> Short foreheads can be visually elongated by making the bang parting slighter deeper than you normally would.

>> High foreheads can look shorter by wearing a long, full fringe.

>> Short bangs open up the face.

>> Creating long side bangs can visually widen or narrow the face, soften the jawline, or make the face appear longer or shorter, depending on how they're cut and styled.

>> Always take the condition of the skin, as well as any deep forehead or frown lines, into consideration before cutting a short bang.

>> Point cutting and notching the bangs will ensure good coverage while allowing light into your design.

>> Fine, straight hair is a natural for straight, tailored bangs.

>> The curlier the hair is, the more bangs must be cared for to maintain a non-frizzy appearance.

>> Versatility is key. Always consider whether the fringe you're cutting will look good with multiple hairstyles.

>> Messier (more imprecise) bangs are ideal for those with stubborn cowlicks or whorls along the front hairline or who love the boho vibe. Precision bangs, on the other hand, are best suited for a whorl-free hairline and urban-chic fashion devotees.

TIP

If you have an oily T-zone, use a light misting of working spray in lieu of products containing oils. Dry shampoo applications also work wonders when natural skin oils seep onto the bangs. Blotting tissues also help control oily buildup throughout the day. (Rice papers work best for my oily T-zone.)

REMEMBER

Fringe remorse is a real thing. People who've never worn bangs are more likely to be unhappy after opting for a fringe cut. When a person (including you) has never worn bangs but wants a full fringe cut, you should recommend that the future bang wearer start out with a minimal fringe that's easily blended into the balance of the hair. Because many bang newbies realize after the fact that they hate how they look, the feeling of hair on their forehead, or having their eyes partially veiled, they'll thank you for your cautious approach to altering their appearance. If they still want a complete bang design in one sitting but end up with fringe remorse, your job is to refrain from saying, "I told you so!"

You can also attach a fringe hairpiece to give them a no-commitment trial run (check out the "Fringe fakery" sidebar later in the chapter). When you purchase the right one, I swear it will blend right in with your hairstyle.

Starting Out with a Bang

Cutting a new bang design or refreshing an existing one can be a piece of cake — as long as you cut the hair methodically and on purpose. Methodical cutting includes cutting the hair in the order of the tutorial steps and not trying to take short cuts. Being methodical also means checking for whorls and cowlicks along the hairline before settling on a final fringe design (see Chapter 4). Cutting on purpose means never losing track of your finished design. Every snip you take should be based on your end goal.

TIP

Cutting less hair than you envision is wise. You can always shorten the hair after the bangs have been allowed to dry and shrink to their heart's content.

The following tutorials give you a range of fringe cuts that will get your creative juices flowing in the safest way possible. All the tutorials presented here take you through every step you need to perform in order to create perfect bangs every time.

Boho bangs

Easy

Tools you'll need to fully participate in this tutorial include scissors, cutting comb, styling brush, round brush (optional), blow-dryer, and clips and clamps.

Boho bangs are free-spirited, loosely groomed bangs that can be worn thick or with point cut or notched ends like the model in Figure 9-1. They can provide full coverage for very high, wide, or protruding foreheads, and they serve as camouflage for scars and deep lines. Equally important, Boho bangs are perfect for fringe lovers who don't like to spend much time on styling their hair into more precise shapes. (See Chapter 7 for different end finishes, including notching and point cutting.)

*Photographer and Hair: Jamie Kindschuh (www.parloureleven.com);
Parlour e.lev.en, Huntington Beach, California*

To cut boho bangs, follow these steps:

1. **Dampen the hair and separate a wide triangular parting, as shown in Figure 9-2.**

2. **Carefully comb the hair to the midpoint or tip of the nose, depending on the desired length (refer to Figure 9-2).**

   Make sure the hair is combed from root to end and held with equal tension throughout the section.

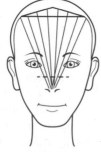

FIGURE 9-2:
How to cut boho
bangs using a
stable guide.

*© John Wiley & Sons, Inc.;
Illustration by Rashell
Smith*

3. **Firmly grip the hair with the index and middle fingers of your non-cutting hand. Release all hair tension by slightly opening and closing your fingers.**

Keep your index finger flush to the skin to avoid noticeable layering on the ends.

WARNING

Make sure that the fringe section is at the center of the nose. If you miss your mark and cut even slightly to one side or the other, your bangs will end up being crooked (see Figure 9-2).

4. **Cut to the desired length.**

Remember that hair shrinks! On straight hair, always cut bangs half an inch (1.3 centimeters) longer than you want them to be when dry. Curly hair will need even more added length. You know your hair and your family's curly hair, but if you're cutting a friend's fringe, ask them about their typical hair shrinkage before cutting.

5. **Release the hair and comb it into place.**

If you're satisfied with the shape of the perimeter line (reference Figure 9-1), you can point cut the hair until the bangs are light and airy. You can also notch the ends for a wispy finish. (Chapter 7 covers how to point cut and notch the ends.)

If you're not satisfied with the shape of the perimeter line, comb the bangs down and then divide and pin them into two horizontal (side-by-side) subsections. Release the bottom subsection, dampen the hair a bit, and examine the perimeter line. Adjust as needed. Repeat this action on the top subsection. When all is well, point cut and/or notch the newly trimmed ends (optional).

Style the bangs using a blow-dryer and a styling brush.

Layered bangs

Easy

Tools you'll need to fully participate in this tutorial include scissors, cutting comb, styling brush, round brush (optional), blow-dryer, and clips and clamps.

Layering a full fringe is one of the best ways to give your bangs renewed lift. It also can be done as a stand-alone cut to create a subtle fluffiness. Layered bangs are also ideal for those who are plagued with an oily T-zone because the layers slightly lift the hair away from the forehead. Figure 9-3 shows a modern layered fringe cut.

THE SKINNY ON "BARELY THERE" BANGS

"Barely there" bangs, like those shown in the following figure, are perfect for people who want to put one toe in the hair pool before executing a swan dive. If you or someone you know is in this mindset, thin, wispy bangs are like a disappearing act. They're easy to cut and wear, and they can be invisibly tucked away into the main body of the hair when you're not in the mood to wear them.

Photographer: Tom Carson (www.tomcarsonphoto.com); Hair: Lisa Kays; Makeup: Jodi Wilcox; Frank Anthony Salon, Chester, New Jersey

Note: When cutting "barely there" bangs, there's one mistake home haircutters make that you should avoid at all costs. When parting out a few wisps of hair, follow the curvature of the hairline as opposed to parting the hair straight across.

Follow these steps to cut layered bangs:

1. **Separate your bang section, as shown in Figure 9-4.**

2. **Dampen the bang section with a light misting of water. Comb through the section to distribute the water and place the hair for cutting.**

3. **Create a middle part dead center of the bang section. Separate a parallel, ¼-inch-subsection (0.6 centimeter) on each side of this center part.**

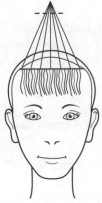

FIGURE 9-4:
How to cut
layered bangs for
a soft lift and
texture.

4. **Combine the two subsections by combing them to the center part and up
    at a 90-degree elevation above the head. Snip the hair to the desired
    length, making it slightly longer as you approach the back of the subsec-
    tion (see Figure 9-4). This is now your stable guide.**

    Chapter 5 discusses elevations and guides.

5. Continue parting and cutting the balance of the fringe section in the same manner.

   For an even fluffier bang, notch the ends of the layers.

6. Comb the bangs into place, and then blow-dry and fluff them with your fingers or a styling brush.

TIP

To create more volume, use a round brush. Place the brush under the bangs, turn the brush a quarter turn to embed the hair into the bristles and create traction. Then move the brush down at a 0-degree (full) or a 45-degree elevation (fuller) to create the desired volume. (Elevations are explained in Chapter 5.) Do not twirl the round brush while doing this, or you'll end up with 1980s-style bangs, and not in a good way.

Sideswept bangs

Easy

Tools you'll need to fully participate in this tutorial include scissors, cutting comb, styling brush, round brush (optional), blow-dryer, and clips and clamps.

Sideswept bangs can be subtle, chic or add a dramatic element to many hairstyles. Sideswept bangs also can be integrated into curly, wavy, and straight styles (see Figure 9-5). Fortunately for all haircutters, they're quick and easy to do.

Follow these steps for sideswept bangs:

1. Create a triangular parting that's 1 inch to 1½ inches deep (2.5 to 3.8 centimeters). See Figure 9-6.

2. Create a center part. Pin up the side of the parting that will be farthest away from your diagonal cutting line.

   If you are moving the hair to the right side of the face, for instance, secure the left subsection and cut it last.

3. Decide on a length, using a facial feature as a landmark.

   If you aren't sure, choose the lips or the bottom of the jawline.

4. Comb the unpinned parting down and diagonally across the face. Secure the subsection with your index and middle fingers. Cut the ends straight across and parallel to the floor (refer to Figure 9-6).

FIGURE 9-5:
Sideswept bangs
can be integrated
into layered hair
to give the front
area lift or worn
straight down
with one-length
hair to create a
smooth beauty
statement.

Tom Carson (www.tomcarsonphoto.com); Hair: Bridgette
Hardy; Makeup: Shelley Beal; Cloud 9 Salon and Spa, Martins
Ferry, Ohio

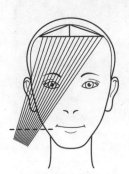

FIGURE 9-6:
How to cut a
sideswept bang.

© John Wiley & Sons, Inc.;
Illustration by Rashell Smith

5. **Repeat step 4 on the second subsection, combing it diagonally across to the same side of the face as the first subsection. Cut the hair, using your first subsection as your guide.**

   When you become proficient at cutting sideswept bangs, you can do this cut in a single section.

Style the hair to your liking. You can blow-dry it flush to the head for a super-smooth sideswept bang, up and over for added volume, or down and back.

FRINGE FAKERY

Faux bangs are a no-commitment way to satisfy the urge to wear bangs. For people who only want to wear bangs some of the time, it's possible to do this with the right haircut. Layered, mid-length hairstyles, for instance, are perfect for sideswept bangs. Just make a deep part on one side of the hair and lift and style the hair to the other side. Boom! You've got luscious, sideswept bangs.

There are also plenty of different bang hairpieces. Either choose a faux bang that matches your hair color or adds an interesting accent color. Installing and removing faux hairpieces is literally a snap. Insert the bangs, push down on the fastener and you're good to go.

Photographer: Tom Carson (www.tomcarsonphoto.com);
Hair and Makeup: Jaime Green; Cloud 9 Salon and Spa, Martins Ferry, Ohio

Curtain bangs

Moderate

Tools you'll need to fully participate in this tutorial include scissors, cutting comb, styling brush, round brush (optional), blow-dryer, and clips and clamps.

Curtain bangs can help accentuate certain facial features while minimizing others. If the face is too wide at the jawline, for instance, curtain bangs can be styled to partially cover this feature to make it appear narrower. For beautiful, high cheek bones, curtain bangs can be lifted out and away to remove shadowing and accentuate these features (see Figure 9-7).

FIGURE 9-7:
Curtain bangs can be dressed up or down and create greater versatility for mid-length and long hairstyles.

Photographer and Hair: Belinda Mills (www.pipsqueekinsaigon.com); Model: Megan Clarke; Salon: Pipsqueek in Saigon, Adelaide, Australia

Modern curtain bangs are fresh, but they're by no means new. They're basically cut like Farrah Fawcett's famous "wings" haircut, which was all the rage in the 1970s. Modern curtain bangs can be styled back, down, or somewhere in-between. They can be curled, waved, or blow-dried into an existing long-layered style.

To cut curtain bangs, follow these steps:

1. **Separate a triangular parting, as shown in Figure 9-8a. Pin away the balance of the hair to avoid cutting confusion.**

2. **Dampen the hair and comb it straight down. Using light tension, hold the hair with the index and middle fingers of your non-cutting hand at a horizontal angle. Cut the hair to the desired length (shown in Figure 9-8a).**

   Make sure to allow for shrinkage. Add ½ inch (1.3 centimeters) for straight hair and, depending on the tightness of the curl, even more length.

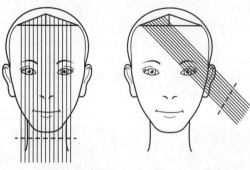

FIGURE 9-8:
How to cut
curtain bangs.

© John Wiley & Sons, Inc.; Illustration by Rashell Smith

3. **Create a middle part to separate the hair into two subsections. Pin away one subsection.**

   To determine the top (shortest strand) of your curtain bangs, use a facial feature as your landmark. A curtain bang can begin at the lips, for instance, or just below the jawline.

4. **Take the unpinned subsection and comb it down and diagonally across the face (see Figure 9-8). Secure the hair with your index and middle fingers of your non-cutting hand. (Figure 9-8b shows the cutting angle and the elevation of the hair.)**

   Comb it thoroughly to ensure that all the hair in this subsection is combed from roots to ends and pointing in the exact same direction.

5. **Cut the ends, as shown in Figure 9-8b.**

6. **Once the entire side has been cut, point cut the ends to soften the perimeter (optional).**

   Refer to Chapter 7 for information on point cutting.

7. **Repeat steps 4–6 on the other subsection, including combing it diagonally across the opposite side of the face (refer to Figure 9-8b).**

   Make sure that both subsections are identical in terms of length and the cutting angle.

Style and play with the curtain bangs using either a styling or round brush. If you want to create a modern version of Farrah Fawcett's wings, finish the hairstyle with a vent brush.

Eye-framing bangs

Medium

Tools you'll need to fully participate in this tutorial include scissors, cutting comb, styling brush, round brush (optional), blow-dryer, and clips and clamps.

An eye-framing fringe is my absolute favorite cut for my own hair. It's easy to do and can be lightly trimmed every few weeks in 10 minutes or less. For those who are fans of longer bangs that frame the forehead and the sides of the eyes, this fringe is for them (see Figure 9-9).

FIGURE 9-9:
Eye-framing bangs give cover to the forehead while drawing attention to the eye area.

Photographer: Tom Carson (www.tomcarsonphoto.com);
Hair: Kim Padgett; Elon Salon; Marietta, Georgia

To cut eye-framing bangs, follow these steps:

1. Create a wide triangular parting starting about 1½ inches (3.8 centimeters) back from the front hairline and tapering down to the temple area on each side (see Figure 9-10).

2. Clip away the rest of the hair to avoid cutting confusion.

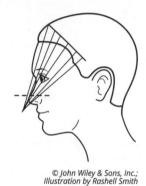

FIGURE 9-10:
How to cut
eye-framing
bangs.

© *John Wiley & Sons, Inc.;*
Illustration by Rashell Smith

3. **Mist the hair until it is damp (not dripping wet).**

4. **Comb the bang parting to the middle of the nose.**

Make sure the section isn't drifting left or right and all strands are thoroughly combed from roots to ends.

5. **Cut the ends to the desired length, as shown in Figure 9-10. Release the hair, comb it into place, and view your handiwork.**

If any shape adjustments are needed, now is the time to do it by repeating steps 4–5.

6. **Point cut the hair at a vertical, straight-up angle until the bangs are light and airy. You can also notch the ends diagonally to give the fringe a more distinctive design.**

Refer to Chapter 7 for more information on point cutting and notching.

7. **Blow-dry the bangs with your fingers. Check how the bangs lie across the forehead and how they frame the eyes. Adjust as needed.**

TIP

If the sides are too long, comb them toward the cutting line while holding them with your index and middle fingers. Cut the hair vertically and then point cut the tips. This will make the side section perimeters separate from the perimeter line along the forehead, which is fine. Being a bit disconnected actually makes the eye-framing bangs look more modern.

If the bangs are too short, you can slightly deepen (thicken) the triangular parting (see step 1) and cut this added hair a little longer than your original cut. It will not completely correct the result, but it will add length and an interesting element to your design. For best results, do not point cut or notch this added hair.

WARNING

Please take "slightly" to heart. If you make the revised bang parting too deep, you will disturb the rest of the haircut and change the overall personality of the fringe cut.

Finish the new look using a blow-dryer and a styling brush or round brush.

Curved bangs

Advanced

Tools you'll need to fully participate in this tutorial include scissors, cutting comb, tail comb, styling brush, blow-dryer, and clips and clamps.

Curved bangs are retro-chic styles that give a nod to classic 1950s bangs. They also have modern appeal by including point-cut ends (see Figure 9-11). The most ideal hair type for this tutorial is type 1 hair, with type 2 being a close second. (See Chapter 4 for information on hair types and Chapter 7 for the basics of point cutting.)

FIGURE 9-11: Curved (inverted U-shaped) bangs can be enhanced with point cutting to change a solid fringe line into a piecey design.

Photographer: Tom Carson (www.tomcarsonphoto.com); Hair: Kim Padgett, Elon Salon; Marietta, Georgia

Follow these steps to cut curved bangs:

1. **Using a tail comb, create a wide, shallow semicircular parting, as shown in Figure 9-12. Clip away the balance of the hair.**

   Make sure there are no cowlicks or whorls along the front of the hairline. If there are, choose another fringe design that doesn't lie flat or require a precise perimeter line. If all looks well, dampen the hair.

2. **Separate a paper-thin, side-to-side, semicircular subsection and pin back the balance of the bang section. Comb the hair straight down and flush to the forehead.**

FIGURE 9-12: Patience and precise measurements are key when cutting curved bangs.

© John Wiley & Sons, Inc.

3. **Determine where you want the sides of the bangs to end. If the bang section you made in step 1 isn't quite wide enough, adjust the entire bang parting now.**

4. **Snip a tiny, identical piece of hair on each side of the parting to mark these two ending points. Also ascertain the very center of the bangs and snip a small piece of hair to the desired length to identify the center of the cut. Re-mist the subsection.**

5. **Trim half of the thin subsection from the middle point to one side, or from one side to the middle (whichever is most comfortable for you), creating a curved perimeter line. Trim the other side to match (see Figure 9-12).**

   This is now your cutting guide (see Chapter 5). If you do not like the shape of the cutting guide, drop a second paper-thin parting and trim it slightly longer than your original cutting line. You can only do this once, so make it count!

   Make sure to comb the hair straight down to where it will lie in the finished style. This is important because if the hair dries in a different position, you'll have an uneven perimeter line.

6. **Separate and drop a slightly thicker subsection and comb it straight down and flush to the forehead.**

   Do you see the guide? If you don't, mist the hair and look again. If you still don't see it, take a thinner subsection of hair.

7. **Continue parting and trimming until the bang has been completely cut. Comb the bangs straight down. Dampen if necessary.**

8. **Point cut the ends at a vertical angle (straight up) and ½ inch (1.3 centimeters) into the bangs. Space out the point cutting as shown in Figure 9-11.**

9. **Brush the bangs straight down and dry the hair by brushing the hair straight down from the scalp to the ends.**

Evaluate the haircut as a whole, and your point cutting in particular. If you need to do additional point cutting, do so at this time.

Lightly mist the hair with a pliable working spray or hairspray of your choice (see Chapter 18 for more information about styling aids). Comb the bangs exactly as you want them to lie. Locating the point cut areas, separate the hair in these areas by using the tail of a tail comb from midpoint to ends. Allow the styling aid to dry and apply a second light coat if needed.

Chapter **10**

Cutting Your Crowning Glory

ools you'll need to fully participate in this chapter include scissors, cutting comb, tail comb (optional), styling brush, blow-dryer with a diffuser attachment, clips and clamps, mirror setup, and small hair elastics.

If you're curious about cutting your own hair — or excited about expanding your DIY haircutting skills — this chapter is for you. The cuts range from easy to moderate. And in case you're worried about having to contort your body to cut the back of your head, most tutorials in Chapter 10 focus on bending and moving the hair rather than your body.

REMEMBER

Chapter 10 focuses on straight and wavy hair, whether it's natural or the hair has been chemically smoothed or straightened. The one exception is the "Dusting cut" tutorial, which can be done on all hair types in their natural state.

TIP

If you want to add a fringe to your new masterpiece, check out Chapter 9 to view several different bangs and frames that you can easily cut to add even more personality to your hairstyle. Chapter 11 shows you how to do perfect touch-up cuts, most of which can be done on your own hair. The same is true for several clipper cuts included in Chapter 8 and throughout Part 4.

Tipping the DIY Haircutter in You

Cutting your hair can be both exciting and clouded by uncertainty. Should I do this? Should I do that? Like most things in life, knowledge is power. The more you know, the less uncertainty you'll have when cutting your own hair.

WARNING

Never reach for your scissors when you're late for an appointment, battling a bad hair day, tired, in a bad mood, double-tasking, or any other situation that could compromise your haircut success and your appearance. Instead, pick a time when you're feeling grounded, focused on the task at hand, and no one is there to bug you about where their socks are, when you're going to call for takeout, or other mundane distractions.

Minding the golden rules of cutting your own hair

REMEMBER

There are right ways and wrong ways to do most things in this world, and haircutting is one of them. Here are a few golden rules to cut by:

>> Trust your knowledge about your own hair, its growth patterns, and how much it shrinks.

>> Keep it simple. Leave the tough stuff to trained stylists.

>> Less is always more. If you want the hair to be a bit shorter, you can always retrim the ends.

>> Until you've got a few DIY cuts under your belt, I suggest that you refresh your existing haircut, rather than creating an entirely new design.

>> Be in the right place, at the right time, and in the right frame of mind when you cut your hair.

>> Never cut your hair while under the influence. You could seriously injure yourself, not to mention create the weirdest haircut that you've ever worn in your life.

Examining the details of your existing cut

Before cutting your hair, always check the cutting lines of your current cut and take photos of your existing style right after returning from your salon appointment. Not doing these things could sabotage your upcoming handiwork.

**AUTHOR
SAYS**

FESSING UP TO YOUR STYLIST WHEN YOU'VE FLUBBED YOUR HAIRCUT

Clients say the darnedest things when they've done something to their hair and need to get it fixed by their stylist. Some truthfully confess that they've given themselves a haircut, while others blame it on a friend or claim they cheated on you with another stylist. One client even told me that she dreamed of cutting her own hair, and when she woke up, there was hair all over the bathroom sink. Really? My advice is to be unapologetic and truthful.

The funniest memory I have about DIY mishaps was the time a good client came into the salon to have her haircut fixed *and* to surrender all her hair tools, including scissors, a towel, a hand mirror, a crochet hook, and a frosting cap. She was so contrite! We both had a good laugh about her gesture and carried on with her appointment.

Remember: If you ever go to a stylist to adjust your cut, you should never feel ashamed or embarrassed. By choosing the right professional, you will be welcomed, feel cared for, and depart the salon loving your new look, even if it's a bit shorter than you'd originally planned.

TIP

Because hair grows a little bit each day, by the third week of your haircutting cycle you may not remember exactly what your original haircut looked like. To help keep track of your style, ask someone to take a snapshot of your crowning glory right after a beauty professional has cut your hair. If you plan on cutting more than your fringe, make sure that you have pictures taken of your profile as well as of the front and back of your hairstyle. These pictures will serve as excellent visual references when doing a refresher trim and also judging the results.

Whether you have straight or wavy hair, following the established haircutting lines of your cut reduces the chance of accidentally cutting your hair at the wrong angle or removing too much hair. Examining your existing haircut also gives you an up-close view of your professional haircut, including many of the nuances that have been put into your style.

TIP

When combing through the hair, make sure to pay close attention to the *haircutting angles* and *elevations*, which can vary from section to section. Chapter 5 explains these important aspects of haircutting; all step-by-step instructions in this book include angle and elevation information that are specific to each haircut.

Analyzing your current haircut

Before refreshing your existing haircut, follow these guidelines:

1. **Detangle and then dampen your hair. Using a cutting comb or a tail comb, make a parting from ear to ear through the crown area.**

   If needed, also spray or apply a leave-in conditioner to detangle and create a smooth glide through the hair. (Combs are covered in Chapter 2. See Chapter 6 for more information about separating the front and back hair sections.)

2. **Firmly secure the back section with clips or clamps.**

3. **Take a ½-inch (1.3 centimeters), side-to-side parting of hair at the crown and comb it straight up from your head.**

   Study the angle of the ends. Are they cut straight across? Are they cut at a diagonal? Are they rounded? (Different cutting angles are discussed in Chapter 5.)

4. **Take an identical parting in front of this subsection and examine the angle of the hair.**

5. **Continue taking side-to-side partings and inspecting them until you've examined the top section.**

   Does your hair become progressively longer as you approach the hairline? Is it longer near the crown? If your hair gradually changes lengths, you need to pay close attention while cutting to ensure that you're preserving this haircutting line.

6. **Repeat steps 3–5, only this time use back-to-front partings.**

7. **After you're familiar with the entire top, check the front/sides of your haircut by taking and examining ½-inch (1.3 centimeters) vertical partings (see Chapter 5), starting at the right or left of your crown section.**

8. **Work your way down the side of the head until you reach the hairline.**

   Does your hair become progressively longer as it approaches the hairline? Is it the same length at the bottom as it is at the top? Does the cutting angle remain constant?

9. **If your style frames your face, check the very front of your cut by taking diagonal and then vertical partings (see Chapter 5 for info on cutting angles).**

   Are they the same length throughout the frame, or do they become progressively shorter or longer? Is the cutting line straight or irregular to soften the lines around the face?

10. **After pinning the front section again, examine the back of the head by starting at the crown and taking vertical partings as you move toward the nape of the neck.**

    Using one of the mirror setups described in the "Mirroring your work" sidebar in this chapter will allow you to easily check the back of your cut.

11. **Comb this hair into the position of your finished style and examine the perimeter ends.**

    Are they blunt? Are they slightly layered on the very tips? Do you see notching or point cutting (see Chapter 7)?

MIRRORING YOUR WORK

Where there's a need, there are gobs of gadgets to make almost any task easier, achieve better results, and do so at an affordable price. Even self-haircutting setups haven't escaped these innovations — and sometimes scams — that promise to make your results better than ever before. By now, I'm sure you know where I'm heading: Shop carefully, read reviews (five stars are the least trustworthy), and investigate the companies' return policies and what guarantees accompany these products.

Here are three types of mirror setups to investigate:

- **Three-way mirror method.** If you're serious about maintaining your hair at home, there are three-way mirror setups that you can purchase for less than $100. These setups are typically hung over a door and have a front mirror and two movable side mirrors to give you a 360-degree view of your hair. When not in use, they can be folded up and stowed.

- **Two-way mirror method.** Another mirror setup is to permanently attach a wall mounted mirror on a hinged, metal arm that allows you to stare straight ahead into your bathroom mirror while viewing the back of your head when the wall mirror is extended. If this appeals to you, shop for a wall unit that's designed for makeup applications with an optional magnified lens.

- **Handheld mirror method.** This is the most difficult setup because you either have to look, then cut, and then look again, or hold the mirror in one hand and trim the hair with the other. As you can tell by how I describe this method, it's definitely my least favorite of the three.

Diving into DIY Haircuts

If you have long- or medium-length hair (whether it's one length or layered) and you want to change-up your style a bit, or even just remove some split ends, you're in the right place.

For this section, I'm assuming that you have straight or wavy hair, you've examined your existing haircut, taken photos, set up your mirrors, and gathered the supplies and tools needed for your planned trim or cut. Phew!

If necessary, cover the floor and work surfaces and wear a haircutting cape to protect your clothing. If you find that the cape interferes with what you're doing, repurpose an old collarless shirt or dress and make it part of your DIY haircutting kit. (See Chapter 1 for more information on floor coverings. Chapter 2 discusses haircutting capes for adults and children.)

Faux cut for straight or wavy hair

Easy

Tools you'll need to fully participate in this tutorial include scissors, styling brush, cutting comb, tail or pintail comb (optional), blow-dryer, and small elastic hair bands.

This haircut is most effective on one-length hair that's at least 3 inches (7.6 centimeters) past the shoulders.

Freshening up the tips of the hair can noticeably improve the appearance of mid-length and long hair. This haircut is so slight that it only removes approximately ⅛ inch (0.3 centimeters) of length. (For perimeter trims of up to several inches, check out "Getting Edgy cut" later in this chapter.) You can repeat the Faux Cut as often as every week to help keep your ends in tip-top shape (see Figure 10-1).

To complete the Faux cut, follow these steps:

1. **On damp hair, use a cutting or tail comb to part the hair in half by moving from the middle of the forehead, over the top of the head, and down to the back neckline (see Chapter 6).**

Use your mirror setup to check your parting. It must be exactly center of the head, and the parting line straight down to the center/back hairline. If you've missed your mark, or your lines look more like squiggles, repeat step 1.

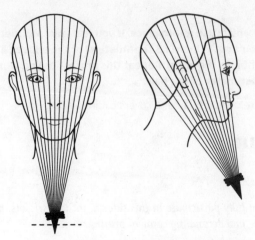

FIGURE 10-1:
How to do a faux
haircut.

© John Wiley & Sons, Inc.; Illustration by Rashell Smith

2. **Brush each half forward past the shoulders and down until both sides are precisely at the center of the chest or neck, depending on the length of your hair. Secure the two sections together with a small elastic band. Slide the band down to within an inch (2.5 centimeters) of where you are going to cut the hair (see Figure 10-1).**

I recommend using small elastic bands that are tough and have minimal elasticity. Traditional hair bands are too stretchy and tend to move while you're cutting the hair.

Make sure to use equal tension on both halves of the hair.

If your hair is quite long, use two bands — one mid-shaft and the other within an inch (2.5 centimeters) of where you're going to trim the ends. To ensure that the hair stays in the proper position, first apply the two bands close together and then slide the bottom band down to 1 inch (2.5 centimeters) above where you're going to cut the hair.

3. **Check all areas of your hair. If either section has drifted or has unequal tension, remove the bands and repeat step 2.**

Use your mirror setup to examine your hair from all different angles.

4. **Once you're sure the hair is perfectly secured, lightly pick up the ends without disturbing the bands and horizontally trim ⅛ inch (0.3 centimeters) off the length using the tips of your scissors (see Figure 10-1).**

   Alternative technique: **Spread the ends like a fan just below the bottom elastic band by applying pressure with your thumb and forefinger and then notching the ends.**

   If you need a refresher, Chapter 7 discusses how to notch the hair.

5. **Free the hair and brush it into place. If you feel your perimeter ends are too dense, point cut ½ inch (1.3 centimeters) of the ends at a vertical angle (straight into the ends). Repeat this process as you work your way around the perimeter of the hair.**

   If you need a refresher, Chapter 5 covers cutting angles.

Dusting cut

Easy

Tools you'll need to fully participate in this tutorial include scissors, blow-dryer with a diffuser attachment, and detangling comb or brush.

Removing split ends — those little forked devils that make your hair look rough and dull — from all hair types can really transform your hair from having a rough texture to a sleeker, smoother finish. This technique is commonly referred to as a *dusting cut* because so little hair is removed. I recommend that if your hair tends to develop split ends, do a dusting cut once a month. (Refer to Chapter 4 to learn more about hair types.)

Dusting cuts can be done on all hair types in their natural or smoothed state.

TIP

Doing a dusting cut can be a bit mind numbing, especially after you've been at it for 10 minutes or so. Make sure that you stay focused at all times to avoid cutting mishaps, including accidentally snipping off pieces of healthy hair.

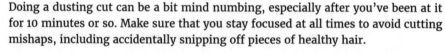

WARNING

If you or someone in your family is plagued by split ends, it's important to find out what's causing the hair to degrade. Common culprits: not using a heat shield product, using overly hot styling tools, improperly curling the hair, using high-velocity wind when drying the hair, brushing the hair too aggressively, not using a proper hair care regimen (shampoo, conditioner, deep treatment, and so on), or infrequent hair trims.

Follow these steps for dusting the ends of your hair:

1. **Shampoo but do not condition the hair on Type 1 and Type 2 hair. Lightly condition Type 3 and Type 4 hair (see Chapter 4 to learn more about hair types).**

2. **Blow-dry the hair.**

   If the hair is natural Type 3 or Type 4 hair, use a blow-dryer with a diffuser attachment until it is 80 percent dry.

3. After twisting a ½-inch-thick (1.3 centimeters) vertical section of hair, trim off the split ends that pop out from the strand. (See Figure 10-2 to view how this is done.)

4. Reverse the direction of the twist and remove all split ends in the same manner.

5. Repeat this process throughout the hair.

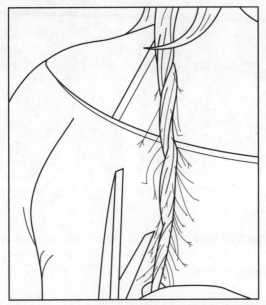

FIGURE 10-2: How to twist and trim split ends.

Condensed Bob Chop

Moderate

Tools you'll need for this tutorial include scissors, cutting comb, styling brush, blow-dryer, and small, thin hair bands.

The Condensed Bob Chop for straight and slightly wavy hair (including straightened or smoothed textures) is shorter at the back and lengthens as it moves toward the face (see Figure 10-3). The ends are notched and point cut to create an irregular perimeter line. Like all bobs, it can be worn with or without bangs.

Photographer: Tom Carson Photography (tomcarsonphoto.com); Hair: Amanda LaPenta; Makeup: Marissa Osborne; Frank Anthony Salon; Chester, New Jersey

FIGURE 10-3: A light, imprecise bob trim releases weight to allow the hair to return to its original fullness and movement.

If you are working with Type 3 or Type 4 hair, do not notch or point cut the ends. Instead, blunt cut the ends to remove ¼ inch (0.6 centimeter) of length off of the existing bob haircut.

TIP

For the Condensed Bob Chop, I recommend that you first have your bob professionally cut by a beauty professional (see Figure 10-3) to establish the proper cutting lines and angles. From there, you can continue cutting your bob at home until it needs a beauty professional to realign the cut.

Note: The following cutting instructions include a condensed refresher trim, which is achieved by combing all the hair to one point and removing a small amount of length. (Check out Figure 10-4 for placement.) If your existing bob has shorter layers, Chapter 11 shows you how to restore their perky personality as well. To add or trim bangs, Chapter 9 provides multiple tutorials on creating everything from plain to framed fringes.

WARNING

The Condensed Bob Chop tutorial is not suitable for classic bobs with precise perimeter lines.

FIGURE 10-4:
A condensed bob trim is done by combing or brushing all the hair into a low centered ponytail and cutting the ends.

Hair band

© John Wiley & Sons, Inc.; Illustration by Rashell Smith

Follow these steps to compete the Condensed Bob Chop:

1. Wash, condition, and towel-dry the hair with an absorbent cotton or microfiber towel.

2. Use a styling brush and then a cutting comb to put your hair into a low ponytail that begins *below* the back hairline and is precisely center of the head (see Figure 10-4). Secure the low ponytail with a small, elastic hair band that has very little elasticity.

Examine the ponytail. Make sure that the lower layers of the hair do not move up to the ponytail band. All the hair should be straight down at a 0-degree elevation (see Chapter 5). This is why it's important to secure the ponytail below the bottom hairline.

The thin, small bands described in step 2 are tough with only a slight stretchiness to keep the hair precisely in place. They are available at stores that sell hair sundries. I don't recommend using thicker, more elastic bands, as they tend to slip while you're cutting the hair.

3. Determine your cutting line.

For touch-ups, I recommend cutting no more than ¼ inch (0.6 centimeters) off the length (see Figure 10-4).

4. After adjusting your mirrors to view the back of your head, hold the low ponytail straight down in one hand and snip it straight across using the tips of your scissors.

This often takes multiple snips. While the hair is still secured in the low ponytail, view your end trim from different angles to make sure it is cut straight across, smooth, and completely level from side to side.

5. Release, dampen, and then comb your hair into place. If you always wear a side part, then part the hair accordingly. If you vary your part, use a middle part.

6. **Loosely dry the hair into place with your fingers (as opposed to forcing it into a style) and examine your perimeter area. Is it the same length on both sides? If it isn't, lightly correct the shape at this time.**

7. **Dampen and re-pin the back section into two horizontal (side-to-side) subsections — one section on the lower 2 inches of the head and the top section firmly secured with clamps to prevent it from interfering with the cut.**

8. **Using a mirror setup, separate a ½-inch-thick (1.3 centimeters), horizontal (side-to-side) section from the lowest section. Comb the hair straight down and examine the perimeter.**

   It should be a uniform line. If there are irregularities, re-trim and notch the perimeter line at this time. (See Chapter 7 for more information about notching.)

9. **Drop the balance of the bottom section and lightly point cut the ends ½-inch-deep (1.3 centimeters) or less and notch cut (if desired) the last ¼ inch (0.6 centimeters) of the ends.**

10. **Release the rest of the back hair and fluff it at the scalp to encourage a more natural placement. If desired, notch cut the perimeter.**

11. **Release the side sections and comb them straight down. Separate a thin strand from the back section that's right next to each side section. If there is a step (non-blended cutting line), lightly trim the ends to create a continuous line.**

12. **Double-check the haircut, especially the hair nearest the bottom hairline. Shorten or point cut any length irregularities that do not blend with the rest of the cut.**

Getting Edgy cut

Moderate

Tools you'll need to fully participate in this tutorial include scissors, cutting comb, styling brush, small elastic bands, and a flat iron.

This innovative cut is for long Type 1 and Type 2 hair. It allows you to remove an inch or more of length without creating a V-shaped perimeter. If you're looking for a slightly diffused perimeter — as opposed to one that's crisp and blunt — this haircut could be perfect for your hair (see Figure 10-5).

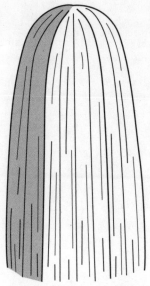

FIGURE 10-5:
By carefully following the Getting Edgy tutorial, you can create a perimeter that encircles the back and shoulders with a diffused line.

© John Wiley & Sons, Inc.; Illustration by Rashell Smith

WARNING

I do not recommend the Getting Edgy cut for Type 3 or Type 4 hair because point cutting — which is taboo for these textures — is key to this cut (see Chapter 7 for point-cutting tips).

To get this edgy cut, follow these steps:

1. **Wash and condition the hair. Apply a heat shield (protectant) product that protects the hair up to 400° Fahrenheit.**

2. **Blow-dry and then use a flat iron to smooth the hair (see Figure 10-6).**

    Reference Chapter 19 for information on flat irons, including safety tips and temperature recommendations. And check out Chapter 20 for the lowdown on the best way to flat-iron the hair.

3. **Separate your hair into four sections, starting at the center/front hairline and moving back and down to the bottom hairline. Then separate the front sections by moving from the apex to just behind the ear on each side of the head. Secure each section with clips or a clamp.**

    See Chapter 5 for information about how to find the apex. See Chapter 6 for more information on four-section partings.

4. **If you wear a center part or frequently vary your part, your front sections are ready to be cut. If you wear a side part, release your two front sections, separate the hair according to your side part, and re-pin.**

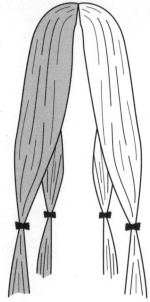

FIGURE 10-6:
The key to success with the Getting Edgy cut is precisely sectioning the hair and positioning the bands level with each other.

© John Wiley & Sons, Inc.; Illustration by Rashell Smith

5. **Comb your first side section straight down at a 0-degree elevation (see Chapter 5). Then hold it with your fingers while applying tension to the entire section. Comb it a few more times to make sure it's perfectly straight. Then secure the section with a thin, small elastic band (see Figure 10-6).**

   Examine the section and band carefully. Make sure that the hair is still straight down and that the band is at the center of the section.

6. **Repeat this action on the remaining three sections. Make sure that all four bands are at the same level and center of each section.**

TIP

   For the back two sections, use a hands-free mirror that allows you to view the back of your head. Thoroughly brush each back section straight down. Grasp one of the back sections just below the nape and secure it with a hair elastic without moving the hair from its brushed position. Make sure the band is positioned at the center of the section to ensure even tension and cutting results. Then move the band directly down until it's level with the bands on the front sections. Repeat step 6 on the other back section.

7. **Addressing a front section, hold the section straight down and with tension while sliding the band down to ½ inch (1.3 centimeters) above where you want to cut the hair. Adjust the bands on the remaining three sections in the same way.**

   Check and double-check to ensure that the bands are all at the same height and still center of each section. Check your sections to ensure the hair within each section is still 100 percent smooth and pointing straight down.

8. **Without using any tension, lightly lift one front section with your fingertips and move it toward your line of vision where you can see the ends of the hair.**

   When moving this section toward your field of vision, do not tug or disturb the banded hair.

9. **Point cut the ends. Continue point cutting the ends until they are no longer bulky and are at the desired length.**

10. **Repeat steps 7–9 on the other front section.**

    Before cutting the other front section, compare the bands to ensure they're exactly level with each other.

11. **Repeat steps 7–9 on the back sections.**

    Before cutting the back sections, compare the bands to ensure they're exactly level with each other and center of each section.

12. **Remove the elastic bands and comb or brush the hair straight down. Examine your handiwork.**

    If you have slightly irregular lengths along the front sections, point cut the ends until the lengths are level. Repeat this action on the back area of the hair.

Layers and Lift cut

Moderate

Adding long layers to one-length straight, straightened, or smoothed hair can transform your hairstyle stat! The following Layers and Lift tutorial shows how you can cut layers without having to be a contortionist, even at the back of your head. The model shown in Figure 10-7 has preexisting, long curtain bangs that give the front of her hair a nice lift. (Check out Chapter 9 to learn how to cut curtain bangs.)

WARNING

I do not recommend the Layers and Lift cut for natural Type 3 or Type 4 hair, because point cutting — which is taboo for these textures — is key to this cut.

Follow these steps for the Layers and Lift cut:

1. **Wash and condition the hair. Apply a heat shield product that protects the hair up to 400° Fahrenheit (204° Celsius).**

2. **Blow-dry the hair and then flat-iron it until it's smooth.**

FIGURE 10-7: Adding long layers to Type 1 and Type 2, medium-to-long, one-length hair removes weight and creates movement throughout the interior of the hair.

Photographer: Tom Carson Photography; Makeup Artist: Jess Ross; Skin & Nail Salon, Glen Mills, PA

3. **Separate your hair into four sections, starting at the center/front hairline and moving back and down to the bottom hairline. Then separate the front sections moving from the apex to just behind the ear on each side of the head.**

    Check out Chapter 5 for information on how to find the apex of the head.

4. **After the hair has been separated into four sections, clamp each one to ensure they do not mingle.**

5. **If you wear a center part or frequently vary your part, your front sections are ready to be cut. If you wear a side part at least 80 percent of the time, release your two front sections, separate the hair according to your side part, and re-pin.**

6. **Unpin one front section and use your cutting or pintail comb to divide this section in half using a horizontal parting. This will give you a top half and a bottom half. Brush the top subsection straight up and secure it center of the section (not leaning in any direction) with a thin elastic band about 2 inches (5 centimeters) from the ends. Repeat on the other side.**

    Take your time when brushing the hair straight up above the head. Getting this exactly right is crucial to the success of the Layers and Lift cut.

After doing this step, the subsections will be a bit floppy. While it may look wrong, this is exactly how you want them to look.

7. **Repeat the same process on the two back sections.**

   Make sure that all sections are brushed straight up and not leaning to one side or the other. When applying the bands, concentrate on keeping the hair stationary.

8. **Starting with a front section, pick up one of the top subsections and move it toward your field of vision without disturbing the banded hair and point cut straight into the ends. (Figure 10-8 illustrates how to position the ends.) Point cut up to 1 inch (2.5 centimeters) of length.**

9. **Repeat this same process on the other three sections.**

   I recommend point cutting no more than 1 inch of hair. If you remove more than an inch, you risk creating a noticeable separation between the top layers and the perimeter.

FIGURE 10-8: After banding the top subsections, point cut directly into the ends to create light, airy layers.

© John Wiley & Sons, Inc.;
Illustration by Rashell Smith

Chapter 11

Perfecting Touch-Up Cuts

Tools needed to fully participate in this chapter include scissors, blow-dryer, trimmers, clippers (optional), cutting comb, detangling comb, pick (pic) comb, tail or pintail comb (optional), mannequin head (optional).

Say goodbye to shaggy edges, droopy tops, and ragged ends. Mastering the art of refreshing a variety of haircuts will keep those closest to you looking their absolute best. Equally appealing? Most refresher trims are quick and fairly easy to do.

In this chapter, I share how to release weight on the top, sides, and all over the hair, as well as clean up business cuts by trimming off just ¼ inch (0.6 centimeter) of hair. Beyond these step-by-steps, though, you can also refresh several fringe and eye-framing designs that are detailed in Chapter 9. Any of the cuts that are covered in Chapter 10 also can be used to refresh various haircuts between having the whole shebang done at the salon, barber shop, or in your cutting space.

A Little Goes a Long Way

While reading through this chapter, you may be asking yourself, "Why only trim a measly ¼ inch (0.6 centimeter) off the ends?" I totally understand where this question is coming from because at first read, it does seem like much ado about nothing. But here's the scoop: Hair grows about ½ inch per month (1.3 centimeters). By cutting the hair a quarter inch every two weeks, you can make the hair look and behave better between full haircuts.

WARNING

Avoid cutting off too much hair at all costs. Any time you cut areas of the hair noticeably shorter, chances are excellent that these areas will no longer blend into one seamless hair design. Too, by focusing on a single area of the hair (front and sides, for instance) and doing a refresher trim too many times between complete haircuts, you'll end up with two separate styles — one where you refreshed the hair and one where you didn't. This is why I never recommend doing a refresher cut more than twice on medium and long hair, and only once on short hair, before receiving or giving a full haircut.

TIP

Any time you wait three weeks to refresh a medium or long haircut, you can cheat a bit by removing ⅓ inch (0.9 centimeter) without going a snip too far. The same is *not* true for short styles like business and pixie cuts.

Cutting Back: Refresher Trims

Everyone can benefit from a refresher haircut, including all members of your family. To hone your skills, I suggest that you scan through the following refresher trims and then decide who would be perfect for each of them. No living candidates within your current grasp? Bring out your sweet-natured mannequin head and get to cutting (see Chapter 2 for info on mannequin heads). If you don't have a mannequin head, keep this chapter close at hand. Everyone's hair grows about ½ inch (1.3 centimeters) a month. Sooner rather than later, they will be in need of your refresher haircutting skills.

Getting Down to Business cut

Moderate

Tools you'll need to fully participate in this tutorial include scissors, cutting comb, trimmers, styling brush, blow-dryer.

For business haircuts to look sharp, they need a full haircut approximately every three weeks. You can stretch out this time by doing a simple touch-up trim at the two-week point. The first business cut in this section is for Type 1 to Type 3b (straight, wavy, and curly) hair (see Figure 11-1). Tips on how to refresh Type 4 (very curly/coily) immediately follow this tutorial. (Check out Chapter 4 to learn more about hair types.)

Follow these steps and check out Figure 11-2 to give someone with Type 1 to Type 3B hair the Getting Down to Business cut:

PICK-UP TIPS

The following suggestions are for Type 1 and Type 2 (straight to slightly wavy) hair. (If you haven't done so already, check out Chapter 4 to learn about different types and textures of hair.)

- **Bangs:** Change the ends of a fringe design by slide cutting the last ½ inch (1.3 centimeters) of hair. You can also point cut the last ½ inch of the hair, notch cut the last ¼ inch (0.6 centimeter), or both. (Chapter 7 shares how to do these techniques.)

  Note: I strongly suggest that you practice your slide cutting moves on a mannequin head until you have them down pat.

- **Sides and back hairlines:** On very short hair, cut out design pieces of hair along the sides of the face and the back of the hairline for added interest. This design technique, which creates instant attention, is covered in Chapter 12.

- **Interior layers:** If the hair is short, coarse, and straight or slightly wavy, remove ¼ inch of length by diagonally notching the tips of the top section and then randomly isolating a few thin pieces that are no more than ⅓-inch-wide (0.9 centimeter). Horizontally blunt cut ⅛ inch (0.3 centimeter) off the ends to create a chunkier look when combed forward and more dimension (or patterned effect) when you lightly apply a working spray and use your fingertips (down to the scalp) to move the hair in the direction of the finished style.

1. **Begin by cleaning up the haircut at the back of the head. Using trimmers, crisp up and shorten the bottom hairline ¼ inch (0.6 centimeter) (see Figure 11-2).**

2. **Addressing the hair along the right side of the back hairline, comb it to the right and past the hairline (see Figure 11-2). Using trimmers, cut ¼ inch of length. Repeat this same action on the left side.**

   Once completed, make sure that the sides seamlessly connect with the bottom hairline. If they do not, adjust the cutting line you just did on the back/sides of the head.

3. **Addressing the front hairline, comb the hair forward along the sides up to the recession area. Trim ¼ inch off the length (see Figure 11-2).**

   If the person has a receding hairline and the hair along the recession areas is longer, separate these longer areas and trim the ends ¼-inch.

   This is important because cutting the recession areas the same length as the rest of the hair will expose the retreating hairline.

WEIGHTLIFTING: SHORT LAYERED CUTS

Short-layered haircuts like pixies and crops quickly lose many of the details that make their personalities so attractive in the first place. Just a couple of weeks after getting snipped, the hair starts sticking out over the ears, and the layers begin hugging the head or poofing out in all directions, depending on whether the hair is straight or curly. You can easily refresh a short-layered haircut by point cutting the ends on the top section, trimming the hair directly above the ears so that it lies flat, and cleaning up the hairline. A refresher trim on short-layered haircuts also gives you the opportunity to change up the design a bit by using the scissors-over-comb technique (see Chapter 15) to taper the back area of the head, notching the back/bottom hairline, and more aggressively point cutting or slide cutting the fringe. (Notching, point cutting and slide cutting are covered in Chapter 7.)

Photographer: Tom Carson (www.tomcarsonphoto.com);
Hair: Ben White; Makeup: Nikki Courtney Davis;
Bob Steele Salon, Atlanta, GA

FIGURE 11-1:
Refreshing a business cut every two weeks creates a consistently well-groomed appearance.

Photographer: Tom Carson (www.tomcarsonphoto.com); Hair: Jessica Ingenito; Makeup: Brenna Burke; Frank Anthony Salon; Chester, New Jersey

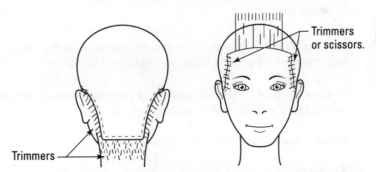

FIGURE 11-2:
How to refresh a classic business cut on straight to curly hair.

© John Wiley & Sons, Inc.; Illustration by Rashell Smith

4. **Comb the hair straight down around the front/bottom hairline to behind the ear. Bend the tip of the ear toward you to prevent it from being accidently cut or obstructing your view. Using trimmers or scissors, trim ¼ inch off the hairline from the front of the ear to the back of the ear.**

When done correctly, this should connect the side and back hairlines. If they do not connect, retrim the area so that the line is continuous from the back/side to in front of the ear.

5. **Identify the four corners of the top of the head and separate the hair within these points into a top section (refer to Chapter 5). Starting at the back of this section, separate a ½ inch (1.3 centimeters) side-to-side parting (see Figure 11-2).**

6. **Notch the ends of Type 1 and Type 2 hair that is 2 inches (5 centimeters) or less in length; point cut ½- inch deep on hair that is more than 2 inches in length. For Type 3 hair, blunt cut ¼ inch of length.**

   Continue taking side-to-side sections as you move toward the front hairline. Stop ¼ inch away from the hairline.

7. **Using trimmers, shorten the sideburns to the desired length and then thin them using the scissors-over-comb technique. (See Chapter 15 to see how a scissors-over-comb technique is done.)**

8. **After you trim the sideburns, cut any fine hairs between the sideburns and the perimeter lines you cut at the front of the ears.**

   Unless the cut is quite angular, cut a curved line from the sideburns to the front of the ear.

Getting Down to Business cut for Type 4 hair

Moderate

Tools you'll need to fully participate in this tutorial include scissors, cutting comb, pick (pic), trimmers, clippers (optional), styling brush, blow–dryer.

To shape up Type 4 hair, crisping up the perimeter lines every two weeks will keep the cut sharp and the wearer looking well–groomed (see Figure 11–3).

Follow these steps for the Getting Down to Business cut for Type 4 hair:

1. **Use trimmers to sharpen the back hairline, starting at the bottom and then trimming the back sides up to right behind the ears. Then trim the hairline around the ears (see Figure 11-4).**

   Do not comb or disturb the hair in any way.

2. **If the original haircut included a crisp clipped line around the front hairline, use trimmers to clean up and sharpen this line (see Figure 11-3).**

3. **If a hard part is present, use trimmers to clean up and sharpen the part line (see Figure 11-3 and Figure 11-4).**

FIGURE 11-3: Business cut with hard part on Type 4 hair.

© fizkes/Adobe Stock

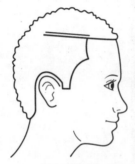

FIGURE 11-4: How to refresh a Type 4 hair business cut.

© John Wiley & Sons, Inc.;
Illustration by Rashell Smith

4. **Using a pick (also spelled pic) comb, gently lift the hair at the scalp only (see Chapter 2 for info on combs.) Study the overall shape of the cut. Normally, at the two-week point, the hair still has an excellent shape, but if you see any areas that are too high or too full, lightly reshape these areas by lightly snipping or clipping the hair and using your eye to guide the trim.**

Do not comb through the ends of the hair as this distorts the end shape of the haircut and can cause the hair to frizz.

5. **Soften the skin in the nape area with a warm, moist towel. Apply a shaving gel and then shave the neck area using a safety or cartridge razor (with a new blade) and following the direction of the hair growth. Remove the shave gel with a wet (not dripping wet), cool towel and then apply a soothing shave balm.**

A Little off the Top and Sides trim

Moderate

Tools you'll need for this tutorial include scissors, cutting comb, tail or pintail comb (optional), detangling comb, small hair band (hair elastic) with minimal stretch, clips and clamps.

No one with mid-length hair should have to go around with a style that looks like a deflated balloon. By strategically trimming the front area of the head (back of the ears forward), you can bring new life to a layered hairstyle for up to three weeks (see Figure 11-5). The trick is to never take off too much of the length, as this will cause a separation from the rest of the hair. The angle you cut the ends is also critical to achieving exactly what you envisioned, whether you're cutting your own hair or someone else's tresses.

FIGURE 11-5: Removing a little off the top and sides restores some fullness at the top and enhances style manageability.

Tom Carson (www.tomcarsonphoto.com); Stylist: Anna Raudabaugh; Elon Salon, Marietta, Georgia

A Little off the Top and Sides removes the tips of the hair. This eliminates just the right amount of length to restore the hairstyle closer to its original shape. ***Note:*** When cutting mid-length hair, you can refresh the layers twice before needing a full haircut.

Follow these steps for the A Little off the Top and Sides cut:

1. Dampen the hair with a spray bottle and then comb through the hair to evenly distribute the water.

2. Separate the hair from the top of the crown to behind each ear (see Chapter 6 to see how this is done).

3. Identify the four corners of the top of the head and separate the top section based on their locations. Use clips to secure the sides of the hair.

Chapter 5 shows how to map the four corners, as well as how to locate the apex of the head.

If bangs are present, separate and secure the existing bang parting. This section will be cut separately.

If there are receding areas along the front hairline, part out the hair around these recessions and keep them separate from the balance of the hair.

4. Take a top/center, back-to-front parting. Following the previous cutting line, trim ¼ inch (0.6 centimeter) off the ends (see Figure 11-6).

This is now your stable guide (see Chapter 5) for the top section.

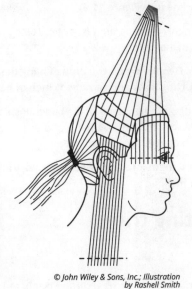

FIGURE 11-6:
Trimming just ¼ inch (0.6 centimeter) off the ends gives new life to sagging tops and sides.

© John Wiley & Sons, Inc.; Illustration by Rashell Smith

5. **Carefully comb the rest of the top section up to your cutting point and remove ¼ inch of hair (see Figure 11-6).**

   Addressing the recession areas, if the hair is longer than the original haircut, only trim the ends ¼ inch. If the existing hair around these receding areas is the same length as the surrounding area, don't cut them. Instead, assess these areas after you have cut and dried the hair. Do they need to be shortened a tiny bit to blend in with the rest of the haircut, or left as is to provide adequate cover for the receding areas?

6. **Notch or lightly point cut the ends.**

   This helps to blend the ends into the existing hairstyle.

7. **Release one of the side sections. Separate a horizontal parting nearest the top section. Comb it up and to the stable guide or cutting line and cut the ends ¼ inch (see Figure 11-6).**

   The sides of the hair are often slightly longer than the top when combed up to a stable guide. This is done to keep the sides fuller and to ensure that they blend with the rest of a layered cut. When you comb the sides of the hair up to your stable guide, cut ¼ inch off the ends, no matter how much longer they are than your top. This will keep your original haircut intact.

8. **Continue cutting the sides until you are 1 inch (2.5 centimeters) away from the side/bottom hairline (see Figure 11-6).**

   The last inch of hair is commonly cut separately (see step 10) to preserve weight along the perimeter of the hair.

9. **Release the fringe section. Depending on the type of bang design you're dealing with, follow the cutting lines and remove ¼ inch of hair.**

   Never use tension when cutting the perimeter of the bangs. Instead, allow them to hang naturally to avoid surprise movements and shrinkage after they've been left to their own devices for a few minutes.

10. **Release the sides and comb them into their final style position. Trim the bottom perimeter ends ¼ inch.**

Tipping and Dusting trim

Moderate

Tools you'll need to do this tutorial include scissors, cutting comb, tail comb (optional), detangling comb or wet/dry brush, clips and clamps.

Refreshing medium-to-long layers improves the appearance of the ends and the behavior of the overall style (see Figure 11-7). When you add a dusting cut to the refresher trim (great for all hair types), the improvement to the quality of the overall style is quite noticeable.

FIGURE 11-7:
This end refresher on longer hair can be followed by a dusting cut for smoother, healthier looking strands.

Photographer: Tom Carson (www.tomcarsonphoto.com); Stylist: Laura Torpin; Makeup: Alexis Degroat; Frank Anthony Salon, Chester, New Jersey

TIP

A *dusting cut* is an easy specialty technique that removes split ends — those forked little devils that can appear throughout the hair. Refer to Chapter 10 for instructions on how to perform a dusting cut.

Follow these steps for a Tipping and Dusting trim:

1. **Dampen the hair and remove any tangles using a detangling comb or wet/dry brush.**

   Make sure to keep the hair damp throughout this cut.

2. **Separate the front/top of the hair by locating the four corners. Secure the section with a clip or clamp, depending on the weight and length of the hair. (Chapter 5 explains and illustrates how this is done.)**

3. Moving parallel to the hairline, separate and secure a ½-inch-deep (1.3 centimeters) subsection on each side of the top section to the back of each ear (shown in Figure 11-8).

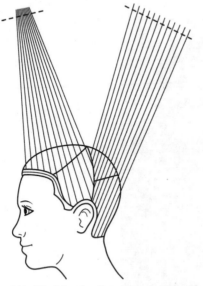

FIGURE 11-8: Separating the cut into sections makes this refresher trim easier to handle and yields more seamless results.

4. Separate and secure the side sections by parting the hair from the back of the top section down to behind the ear.

5. Addressing the back of the head, make a horizontal parting to divide the hair from the back of the top section down to the top of the occipital bone (see Chapter 5). Secure this section.

6. Secure the back/bottom section.

7. Unpin the top section. Using a styling comb, comb the hair up and forward. Holding the hair at a 45-degree elevation, trim ¼ inch (0.6 centimeter) off the ends. Re-pin the newly cut section.

8. Unpin and comb the back/top section to a 45-degree elevation away from the face. If the hair is too unwieldly, vertically divide the section in half and cut these newly created subsections one at a time. Holding the hair with your non-cutting hand, trim the ends ¼ inch (0.6 centimeter).

9. **Release one side section and comb or brush the hair back to the ends of the back section. Using this previously cut section and angle as your guide, cut ¼ inch off the length. Repeat on the other side.**

If the hair on the sides is too short to reach the back section, comb the hair straight up to the top stable guide. If it's longer than the top guide, still only trim ¼ inch of the length.

10. **Using a detangling or styling comb, release the front hairline subsection and comb it straight down. Then comb the uncut back/bottom hair straight down. Remove ¼ inch off the perimeter of the hair.**

11. **Dust the ends (optional).**

Reference Chapter 10 for how to do a dusting cut.

4 Getting Snippy

Chapter 12

Getting Snippy and Clippy with Women's Short Styles

Tools you'll need to fully participate in this chapter include scissors, clippers and No. 2 guide, trimmers, blow-dryer with air concentrator nozzle attachment, cutting comb, pick (pic) comb, large and small round brushes, styling brush, and clips and clamps.

Many people love wearing short, up-to-the-minute styles that dry quickly and look great with a minimal amount of fuss. These snippy styles can be expressive by allowing wearers to make a crisp, businesslike statement, emphasize their athletic lifestyle, or use their petite halo of hair to show off their stylish personalities. People who are partial to short haircuts also make great haircutting devotees because they must have their hair trimmed every four weeks to keep it in tip-top shape.

Checking In Before You Begin

Here are five things you should examine before settling on a specific short haircut:

>> Look for cowlicks, whorls, swirls and other irregular growth patterns. In most cases, you will need to integrate these growth patterns into your haircut. (Chapter 4 covers information about irregular hair growths.)

>> Look for thin and receding areas throughout the head. You will need to camouflage these areas by cutting longer layers or styling the hair in such a way that fuller, thicker hair can help provide cover.

>> Look for scars that would be exposed by a short haircut.

>> Check the ears. If they are overly large or noticeably protrude, you will need to at least partially cover them with hair.

>> Study the face shape. If the face is round or oblong, for instance, a pixie cut will bring attention to these shapes. (Chapter 3 contains a wealth of information about face shapes and matching a person's personal style with their hairstyle.)

Life on the Short Side of the Street

People who are devoted to short hairstyles live in what I call a centimeter world. If a tiny amount of hair touches their ears, or the bang area is a centimeter past their eyebrows, they start checking out their hair in every window or mirror they pass. They also tell those close to them (proximity or relationship) that their hair is driving them crazy. Their saving grace? Short-haired lovers book their appointments in advance, knowing that going one day past their haircut due date could be a style catastrophe.

REMEMBER

Short hair types also check out every fresh haircut with a trained eye and a fine-tooth comb. To compound this behavior, short haircuts often fail to disguise even the most minor cutting mistakes. For these reasons alone, it's important to always think before you cut, keep the four basic pillars of haircutting in mind (refer to Chapter 5), and cut the hair conservatively. (You can always go back and shorten or sharpen the haircut by doing a second pass.)

Short haircuts can be freeing to the wearer. The hair dries much faster than mid-length or long hair and can be styled in minutes. They also offer creative opportunities, such as adding design elements around the front and back hairlines. The following section includes tutorials that give you step-by-step instructions on how to cut a popular, super-short pixie cut, a conservative cut, and a scissor-and-clipper cut with plenty of sass.

Being Pixie Perfect cut

Advanced

The tools needed for this short, sassy cut include scissors, trimmers (optional), a tail or pintail comb (optional), a cutting comb, and clips or clamps.

TIP

You can really make this haircut shine if you concentrate on emphasizing the person's best facial features. The model in Figure 12-1, for instance, has beautiful eyes. Placing a design detail in line with her eyes draws attention to this exceptional feature. Her cheekbones are also quite remarkable.

FIGURE 12-1:
Ultra-short, carefree pixie styles can be customized to each person's face and personal preferences.

Photographer: Tom Carson (www.tomcarsonphoto.com); Stylist: Maria Dickson; Makeup: Jodi Wilcox; Frank Anthony Salon, Chester, New Jersey

The Being Pixie Perfect cut in Figure 12-1 is best suited for Type 1 and Type 2 hair and smoothed Type 3 hair. (Check out Chapter 4 for information on hair typing and hair types.)

When you're ready to cut this short and sweet style, follow these steps:

1. **Working on damp hair, comb the back of the hair down to the back hairline. Trim the bottom hairline until it is ¼ inch (0.6 centimeters) in length (see Figure 12-2).**

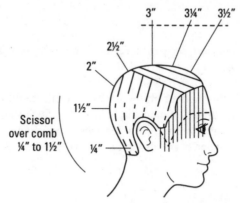

FIGURE 12-2:
How to do a basic pixie cut.

2. **Over-direct the hair growing right along the side/back perimeter onto the neck. Trim the hair to ¼ inch in length, moving from the corner of the neckline up to the back of the ear. (Chapter 10 illustrates how this step is done.)**

This is where the natural hair growth comes into play. If the neckline grows straight, thank your lucky stars. If it grows sideways or up in places, the neckline should be cut to incorporate these anomalies. (The neckline on the model in Figure 12-1 is combed to the side.)

If you're feeling frisky and want to add some design elements along the back hairline, leave this area alone until you reach step 20. You can then add details to the front and back hairlines at the same time.

3. **Using scissors or trimmers, remove unwanted hair at the back of the neck.**

This step can also be done last.

4. **Moving to the front of the face, separate a ¼-inch-deep section that parallels the front hairline and begins and ends at the front of each ear. Comb the hair onto the face and trim the hair to 2 inches (5 centimeters) in length (see Figure 12-2).**

You will return to this section at the end of the haircut to add finishing details and give the front hairline its final shape.

5. **Separate a top section using the four points of the head to determine the perimeter lines and create a top section. (Refer to Chapter 5 to see how to locate these four points.) Comb this section forward (see Figure 12-2).**

   Pin down the balance of the hair that is adjacent to your new top section to avoid cutting confusion.

6. **Starting at the top/back perimeter line, separate a back-to-front subsection that's ¼ inch wide and 2 inches long. Comb this subsection to a 90-degree elevation (see Chapter 5) and hold this subsection with the second and third fingers of your non-cutting hand. Move your fingers into a diagonal position to allow the hair to lengthen to 3 inches (7.6 centimeters) in length. Cut the hair using a diagonal cutting line.**

7. **Separate the next subsection directly in front of your original subsection.**

   It should be the exact width and length as the first subsection.

8. **Incorporating a strand from your first back-to-front subsection to use as your traveling guide, cut the second parting to 3 inches in length.**

   Make sure you are following the curvature of the head as shown in Figure 12-2. (Check out Chapter 5 for information on head shapes, traveling guides, cutting angles, cutting lines, and elevations.)

9. **Repeat this cutting pattern until the entire top section has been cut.**

   Do not cut or disturb the front section you created in step 4.

10. **Separate a vertical subsection that's ¼ inch wide by 2 inches long, starting at the top/back perimeter line of the section you created in step 5 and moving down the back of the head.**

11. **Borrow a thin strand of hair from the top/back perimeter line and incorporate it into the subsection you parted out in step 10.**

    This is now your traveling guide that moves down the back of the head.

12. **Hold the subsection at a 90-degree elevation out from the scalp. Using a horizontal cutting angle, cut the hair to 3 inches in length.**

13. **Use the end of this subsection as your traveling guide for your next subsection. Comb this subsection to a 90-degree elevation and trim the hair to 2½ inches (6.4 centimeters) using a curved cutting line.**

    For this haircut, curved cutting lines allow you to taper the length as you progress down the head. They are discussed and illustrated in Chapter 5.

14. Gradually reduce the length of the hair from 2½ inches to 1 inch (2.5 centimeters) as you reach the bottom of the occipital bone. Repeat this pattern until the entire back of the head down to the bottom of the occipital bone has been cut.

The occipital bone is discussed in Chapter 5.

15. Starting at the bottom hairline and moving upward, taper the hair from ¼ inch at the neckline to 1 inch at the base of the occipital bone using the scissors-over-comb technique.

The scissors-over-comb technique is explained and illustrated in Chapter 15.

16. Addressing the sides of the head, separate a vertical subsection that starts at the perimeter line of the top/back section and moves down the side of the head. Borrow a thin strand from the top/side perimeter to act as your traveling guide (see Figure 12-2).

17. Comb the subsection at a 90-degree elevation from the head. Cut the hair with a curved angle to gradually taper the hair from 2½ inches down to ½ inch (1.3 centimeters) in length. Repeat this cutting pattern until both sides are cut.

Remember not to cut the front section that you created in step 3.

18. Trim the hairline around the ears to ¼ inch in length. Then use the scissors-over-comb technique (see Chapter 15) to blend this area with the ½-inch-long hair above it.

When trimming around the ears, make sure to connect the back/side perimeter line with the perimeter line you're cutting around the ears.

19. Shape and add details to the forehead section.

The hair you cut around the forehead is 2 inches long. The hair right behind it is 3 inches long (7.6 centimeters). You can do one or more of the following steps to shape the front hairline along the forehead.

- Leave as is.

- Comb the 3-inch top section forward. Cut the hair that reaches the ends of the front section to 2 inches.

- Slice cut or point cut the 3-inch section that's just behind the front section and style it over the shorter perimeter (see Chapter 7 for tips on slicing and point cutting the hair).

- Create design details that are discussed in step 22 (see Figure 12-3).

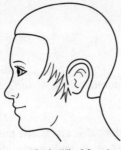

20. **Shape and add details to the hairline along the sides of the face and the back hairline (optional).**

The hair you cut around the front/side sections is 2 inches long. To finish the style, you can do one of the following suggestions.

- Trim the hair to ½ inch to make it blend with the sides of the hair.

- Create design elements.

   Decide where you want to place the design details along the sides of the hairline (see Figure 12-1 and 12-3).

   Dampen and comb the hair as shown in Figure 12-3.

   Cut the hair between your designated design elements to ½ inch to create negative space.

21. **Taking side-to-side partings on the top section of hair, point cut the ends at a vertical angle and ½ inch deep for lift and movement (see Chapter 7).**

22. **If needed, use the scissors-over-comb technique to taper and blend the hair that you cut to ½ inch in step 20 with the sides.**

The Being Pixie Perfect in Figure 12-1 can be styled with a large round brush around the crown area to lift the hair and take advantage of the natural cowlick. The sides and back (below the crown) are smoothed and directed using a styling brush.

Using a flexible pomade on the tips of the hair can bring out the piecey ends, and using the tail of a tail comb to separate the design pieces polishes the look.

Keeping It Simple cut

Moderate

Tools you'll need to fully participate in this tutorial include scissors, cutting comb, tail or pintail comb (optional), clips and clamps.

Although haircutters love the fanfare of fashionable styles, the meat-and-potatoes, conservative haircut shown in Figure 12-4 is an enduring style that dates back decades. Typically worn by those in their golden years, this cut can also be seen in a variety of variations on mature people who prefer simple over fashionable any day of the week. The only change from days gone by are less structured curls and little-to-no teasing.

FIGURE 12-4:
This short-layered haircut is popular among those who want to wear a classic hairstyle that's styled away from the face.

Photographer: Tom Carson (www.tomcarsonphoto.com);
Hair: Ozzy Habibi, L Salon & Color Group, San Mateo, CA

Keeping It Simple is ideal for Type 1and Type 2 hair and smoothed Type 3 hair. (Hair types are discussed in Chapter 4. If it's been a while since you skimmed through that chapter, I recommend that you go through it again with your more experienced eye.)

When you're ready to Keep It Simple, follow these steps:

1. **After dampening the hair, comb it straight down at the nape and cut the hair to ½ inch (1.3 centimeters) below the hairline (see Figure 12-4).**

   If the hairline has strong cowlicks or growth directions, cut it to 1 inch (2.5 centimeters) and then revisit the length once the hair has dried. At that point, you can be a better judge of whether it can be shortened without allowing the irregular growth patterns to run wild.

2. **Locate the four points at the top of the head (refer to Chapter 5). Using these points as the four corners of the section, part out the top section. Pin the hair around the perimeter of this section to avoid cutting confusion (see Figure 12-5).**

   If you separate this section correctly, it will have a rectangular shape.

FIGURE 12-5:
Tapering the layers allows you to softly parallel the shape of the head.

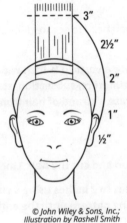

© John Wiley & Sons, Inc.;
Illustration by Rashell Smith

3. **Part out a ¼-inch-wide (0.6 centimeters), back-to-front subsection, starting at the back of the top section.**

4. **Comb the hair to a 90-degree elevation. Using a horizontal angle, cut the hair to 3 inches (7.6 centimeters) in length.**

   This subsection is now your first traveling guide (see Chapter 5).

REMEMBER

5. **Separate a side-by-side subsection right in front of the previous subsection you cut in step 4.**

6. **Borrowing a strand of hair from your first subsection to act as your traveling guide, comb this subsection to a 90-degree elevation. Holding your gripping fingers at a horizontal angle, cut the hair to 3 inches in length.**

   Make sure to keep track of the head shape. As you can see in Figure 12-5, the head slopes as you approach the hairline. All elevations are based on the position of the hair to the scalp.

7. **Continue taking vertical partings until the entire top section has been cut.**

   If there are pronounced recessions along the hairline, separate and cut these areas separately. For slight recessions, cut these areas ¼ inch longer. For more pronounced recessions, cut them up to 1 inch longer.

8. **Separate the sides from the back by parting the hair from the top/back perimeter line down to the back of each ear. Pin away the back section to avoid cutting confusion.**

   Chapter 2 covers the clips and clamps you need to secure different areas and lengths of hair.

9. **Addressing the side of the head, create a vertical ¼-inch-wide by 2-inch-long (0.6 centimeters by 5 centimeters) subsection, starting at the top/back point. Borrow and incorporate a strand of hair from the original subsection.**

   This strand is your new traveling guide.

10. **Comb the hair to a 90-degree elevation and cut the hair 3 inches long.**

11. **Gradually taper the length on the sides to 2 inches using a curved cutting line (see Chapter 5). Repeat this cutting pattern until the entire side has been cut.**

    Repeat this pattern on the other side.

12. **Moving to the back of the head, take a ¼-inch vertical subsection (moving downward), starting at the top/back perimeter line.**

    Borrow a thin strand of the original subsection to act as your guide.

13. **Following your traveling guide, cut the hair to 3 inches in length while holding it at a 90-degree elevation.**

14. **Part out an identical vertical subsection directly below the previous subsection. Comb it to a 90-degree elevation and cut it at a curved angle.**

    A curved cutting angle will gradually shorten the hair to 1 inch at the bottom of the occipital bone and ½ inch at the neckline.

15. Repeat this haircutting pattern until the entire back of the head has been cut.

16. Check the length of the neckline. If it can be shortened to ½ inch without disturbing the hair growth, do so now.

17. Use trimmers or scissors to remove unwanted neck hair.

When using trimmers, cut the hair against the grain (opposite the natural hair growth).

To style the Keeping it Simple cut, apply a light gel and use a 1-inch round brush to style the back area below the crown and down the head from there.

Use a larger round brush for the front and top, as well as the back to just below the crown area. The size of this round brush will depend on how fluffy or curly you want the hair to be. Blow-dry the sides right above the ear either out and back (more fullness), or straight back (less fullness).

Pulling the Plug cut

Moderate

The tools needed for this disconnected style include scissors, clippers with a No. 2 guard, trimmers, blow-dryer with air concentrator nozzle attachment, clips or clamps, tail or pintail comb, pick (pic) comb, and cutting comb.

Although traditional haircuts usually flow smoothly from beginning to end, many trendy styles combine two or more separate haircuts in a single design. These *disconnected shapes* can be conservative, defiant, or somewhere between. They're often popular with teens and the 20-something set, but never judge a book by its cover — or in this case, people's tastes in hairstyles according to their age. Disconnected shapes can be fun and flippy or add a touch of elegance to an otherwise conservative style (see Figure 12-6). Depending on how you style it, Pulling the Plug falls into two categories: sassy and stylish chic.

Get ready for some fun and follow these steps to compete the Pulling the Plug cut:

1. Locate the four corners of the top section. Separate a top section by parting the hair from point to point to form a rectangular parting. (Chapter 5 provides guidance on how to do this.) Secure this section with clips or clamps, depending on the length and bulk of the hair. (Chapter 2 gives you the scoop on hair fasteners.)

FIGURE 12-6:
Disconnected cut
on natural curly
hair.

*Photographer: Tom Carson (www.tomcarsonphoto.com);
Stylist: Katie Kacere; Makeup: Kristian Bailey; Sheer
Professionals Salon, Wooster, Ohio*

2. **Create an entire upper section (see Figure 12-7b) by continuing the part from the side perimeters of the top section down to just before or at the midpoint of the occipital bone (see Chapter 5). As you part the back of this section, gradually narrow the two side partings until they end at 1 inch to 1½ inches (2.5 centimeters to 3.8 centimeters) apart. (Figure 12-7a and 12-7b provide excellent views of these lines.)**

   In addition to the top section you created in step 1, you now have an entire upper section (to be cut with scissors) and lower section (to be cut with clippers).

TIP

   Use a tail or pintail comb to create the perimeter lines of the upper section. This will enable you to create a much cleaner parting. When complete, pin the balance of the upper section away from the perimeter lines to give you a better view of the partings and to avoid cutting confusion.

3. **Checking the partings from above the upper section, facing the front and back of the head, and from side-to-side, examine the lines for balance, sharpness, and accuracy. If necessary, re-part one or both lines at this time.**

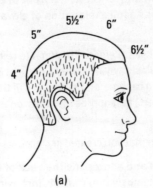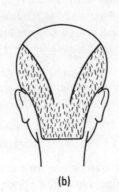

FIGURE 12-7:
How to cut the
Pulling the Plug
disconnected
style.

5" 5½" 6"
4" 6½"

(a)   (b)   (c)

7" 6½"

© John Wiley & Sons, Inc.; Illustration by Rashell Smith

TIP

4. **Using a clipper with a No. 2 guard, clipper cut the entire lower section (see Figures 12-7a and 12-7b).**

Start at the neckline and work your way up toward the upper section by clipping up to, but not past, the perimeter partings. Clip the hair against the growth direction. Use short strokes and cut this same section of hair in three different stages and directions (up, diagonally, and side-to-side). This process creates a very smooth finish to the hair. (Chapter 8 shares detailed information about clippers and guides, as well as two hands-on clipper tutorials.)

5. **Addressing the bottom neckline, use trimmers to shorten and shape this area. You can either cut a square, masculine hairline as shown in Figure 12-7b, or create a feminine, rounded hairline. Trim any unwanted hair on the back of the neck.**

6. **Use a blow-dryer to dislodge any snippets that are clinging to the hair each time you change directions. Do not disturb the curls.**

Restrict the blow-dryer to the clipped area only. This can be done by using an air concentrator nozzle on your blow-dryer.

Review the entire clipped area. Is the hair uniformly one length, or do you need to shorten stray hairs that escaped your clippers?

7. **Unpin the top section that you separated in step 1. Separate a side-to-side subsection at the hairline that is ½ inch deep (1.3 centimeters) and the complete width of the top section (see Figure 12-7c). Secure this subsection to avoid cutting confusion.**

This section will be cut later.

8. **Your top section will be cut at a diagonal angle to make the hair length shorter at the back of the section and longer at the front of the section (see Figure 12-7a). (Chapter 5 gives a full explanation of elevations, guides, and cutting angles.)**

Check the hair type and existing length. (Refer to Chapter 4 to refresh your memory about hair typing.) The hair shown in Figure 12-6 (curly) is Type 3C. It is approximately 5½ inches long (14 centimeters) at the back of the top section and 6½ inches long (16.5 centimeters) as it approaches the front subsection that you separated in step 7.

Do not disturb the front subsection that you created in step 7.

9. **After dampening the top section and addressing the back of the top section, separate a back-to-front subsection that's ¼ inch wide (0.6 centimeters) and 2 inches long (5 centimeters). Comb this subsection to a 45-degree elevation from the scalp and toward the hairline. Moving your fingers to a diagonal cutting position, trim the hair starting at 5½ inches long and gradually lengthening to 6 inches (15.3 centimeters). See Figure 12-7a.**

This subsection is now your first traveling guide.

10. **Separate a same-size parting right in front of your first subsection. Add a traveling guide (a strand of hair from your first subsection that's right behind your new subsection). Comb this second subsection to a 45-degree elevation and, following your traveling guide, cut the hair so that it lengthens from 6 inches to 6½ inches in length (see Figure 12-7a).**

Continue doing this cutting pattern until the entire top section has been cut. Refer to Figure 12-7a to view the gradual lengthening of the hair.

11. **Release the front hairline section. Comb the hair to the side and up to a 45-degree elevation. Trim this section starting at 6½ inches and lengthening it to 7 inches (17.8 centimeters), as shown in Figure 12-7c.**

If you intend for the hair to be worn smooth and curly, the hair must reach below the bottom of the earlobe.

12. **After completing step 11, comb this section to a 0-degree elevation from the scalp and down the side of the face to the final styling position. Trim the very bottom ends at a diagonal (longer in back to shorter in front) near the earlobe and to the desired length. This establishes your bottom perimeter.**

The diagonal angle will give the ends a slight taper.

13. Moving to the top/back section, separate a ¼-inch-wide by 2-inch-long vertical subsection moving down the back of the head. Borrowing a strand of hair from the back of your top section to use as your traveling guide, comb the hair at a 90-degree elevation (see Chapter 5) and trim the hair to 5½ inches in length (see Figure 12-7a).

REMEMBER

Anything below the four points at the top of the head is a curved surface. This means that all subsections at the back of the head, must be elevated based on the curvature of the head (see Chapter 5).

14. Continue cutting the hair in vertical sections by following the curvature of the back of the head. As you progress down the back of the head, gradually shorten the hair to 4 inches (10.2 centimeters) at the end of the upper section (see Figure 12-7a).

Depending on the amount of curl, adjust the tapered cutting line of the upper section. For super-curly hair, for instance, the hair will need to be left longer.

To taper the length, cut each subsequent subsection gradually shorter by using a slightly rounded cutting line (see Chapter 5).

Style the hair by dampening the hair and then applying a light curl cream. Shape curls by twisting each one. Place the hair into the desired style position by using a pick comb (also spelled pic). Insert the pick comb at the scalp and lift and move the hair without breaking through the curls. Diffuse the hair. Do not touch the hair until it is completely dry.

Chapter 13

Getting Snippy with Women's Mid-Length Styles

Tools you'll need to fully participate in this chapter include convex (Japanese-style) scissors, blow-dryer, styling brush, vent brush (optional), large-sized round brush, cutting comb, clips and clamps, hair bands (elastics), and mannequin head or hair wefts (optional, but highly recommended).

I was 8 years old when I did my first mid-length haircut. My cousin Emily and I locked ourselves in the bathroom with a pair of rusty barber shears and a great idea: "Let's give Emily a haircut!" It was my first masterpiece. Even though her mother (and mine) seemed to think that I had created a disaster, I was instantly smitten with shoulder-length hair. While the mothers were fussing and fuming, I remember standing in the corner and thinking, "Why would Emily want all those waist-length curls anyway?"

I'm happy to report that I'm not alone. Of all the different lengths of hair, mid-length cuts remain eternally popular styles. As sure as the sun will rise tomorrow, you can count on cutting a lot of these beauties.

Checking in Before You Begin

Here are four basic checkpoints you should examine before settling on a specific mid-length haircut:

>> Check for *strong* cowlicks, whorls, swirls, and other irregular growth patterns. If the hair splits flat just at or below the crown area, for instance, having longer layers in that area will help lift the hair away from the scalp (see Chapter 4).

>> Look for thinning areas on the sides and at the crown area of the head. If either is present, you'll need to build density in these areas (see Chapter 24).

>> Check for overall thickness. Hair that's thin throughout the head, for instance, is ideal for one-length blunt cuts and long-layered cuts (see Chapter 24).

>> Study the facial features and the neck. Make plans to accentuate or minimize specific facial features and, if needed, to visually minimize the appearance of a short, thick, or aging neck (see Chapter 3).

Being in the Middle: Mid-Length Cuts

Mid-length hair is neither short nor long; it's a medium length that offers many people the best of both short and long hair. It's a length that's also perceived by the eye of the beholder. Someone with hair down to their waist, for instance, may think that a long bob is a short haircut. Someone who's sporting a pixie may think a shoulder-length style is long.

Because there are different perceptions of what is short, medium, or long hair, I've made my own judgment call for this chapter: Any hairstyle that goes from below the jawline to 3 inches (7.6 centimeters) past the shoulder is mid-length hair.

REMEMBER

The following are some benefits of mid-length hairstyles:

>> The hair is long enough to be cut into several different styles.

>> It can be stylish or simple, depending on how it's styled.

>> The hair is still short enough to be relatively healthy.

>> The hair has natural lift and can nicely contour the head shape.

>> It can be cut in a variety of ways to enhance the face shape and facial features.

>> Mid-length hair can camouflage a host of imperfections far better than short or long hair.

Chapter 13 starts out with a face-framing cut, the most advanced cut in this chapter and the most popular mid-length cut to date. If you have mid-length hair, chances are almost 100 percent that you've had, do have, or will have a face-framing cut at some point in your hair future. To ensure you're successful with your first face-framing cut, I've included detailed instructions to walk you through every snip needed to create this cut. Also included in this chapter are a graduated bob, an asymmetrical lob, and a shoulder-length haircut with slide cut strands that's gaining popularity among those who want lift without traditional layering or a less structured style.

It's a Frame-Up cut

Advanced

The tools needed for this tutorial include scissors, blow-dryer, clips or clamps, ponytail band (hair elastic) (optional), tail or pintail comb (optional), cutting comb, and manne-quin head (optional but highly recommended).

Face-framing haircuts create a picture-perfect effect along the sides of the face and neck. They're cut at a vertical (straight up) angle. The It's a Frame-Up cut has a continuous line from the shoulders up to the jawline or wherever you want your face frame to begin and end.

The face frame style shown in Figure 13-1 was cut vertically and then slide cut on the ends to create a piecey finish. (Note how the whole perimeter has also been slide cut.) The sideswept bangs are actually faux bangs. They were styled by borrowing the top portion of the face frame on one side and sweeping it over to the other side.

REMEMBER

This tutorial requires that both sides of the hair are long enough to be combed down at a diagonal to the opposite side of the face. It should also be either one length or have existing long layers that start no higher than the base of the occipital bone (see Chapter 5 to review the anatomy of the head).

The It's a Frame-Up tutorial is designed for Type 1 and Type 2 hair and smoothed Type 3 and Type 4 hair. If you're working on Type 3 or Type 4 hair, I recommend that you create a piecey perimeter (see Figure 13-1) by using a soft gel or styling paste to separate the ends rather than slide cutting them, as this could cause frizzing and failure to obey your hair commands.

FIGURE 13-1:
Add a little variety to your look with this face-framing cut.

Photographer: Tom Carson (www.tomcarsonphoto.com); Hair: Terry; Color: Liza; Style: Antonia; Makeup: Solimar; Barbaria Salon, Foster City, California

REMEMBER

When cutting a face frame, it's important that the person sitting in your chair keeps their head straight forward and their jawline parallel to the floor. For best results, I strongly suggest that you first cut a face-framing design on a mannequin head.

When you're ready to try the It's a Frame-Up cut, follow these steps:

1. **Use a cutting comb to locate the apex, the highest point of the head.**

   Chapter 2 shares information on combs. Chapter 5 explains and illustrates how to locate the apex of the head.

2. **Create a front section by separating the hair from the apex down to behind each ear (see Figure 13-2c). Dampen the entire front section. Secure the back section with clamps or put the hair in a ponytail to avoid cutting confusion (see Figure 13-2c).**

   Cutting a face frame when it's damp makes it easier to handle and to follow your guide. Make sure to keep all areas of the hair you're cutting damp throughout the cut because cutting some areas dry and others damp could cause a cutting failure.

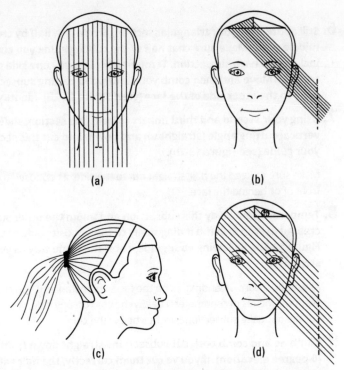

(a)

(b)

(c)

(d)

FIGURE 13-2:
How to cut a
face-framing
design.

© John Wiley & Sons, Inc.; Illustration by Rashell Smith

3. **Part out a triangular subsection, starting 1½ inches (3.8 centimeters) back from the hairline and to the recession area on each side of the forehead (see Figure 13-2a). Secure the rest of the front section with clips or clamps (see Chapter 2 for more information on hair fasteners).**

4. **Comb this triangular section straight down the face. Grasp this section with the second and third fingers of your non-cutting hand and then move your fingers down to where you want your framing to begin (refer to Figure 13-2a).**

   I suggest starting below the jawline.

5. **Slightly open and close your fingers once to release tension on the hair and then locate the center of this subsection. Cut the center strands in this subsection horizontally and to the desired length (see Figure 13-2a).**

   This is now your first traveling guide and the shortest hair of your face-framing cut.

TIP

I suggest that you cut this guide a little longer than you envision the first few times you cut a face frame, as it will give you the leeway to re-trim if necessary.

6. Still addressing your triangular section, divide it in half by creating a middle part. (Make sure that half of the cutting guide you cut in step 5 is included in each subsection. Temporarily pin away one side of the triangle. Move and then comb your unclipped cutting subsection diagonally to the other side of the face (view Figure 13-2b). Identify your guide.

7. Using your second and third fingers to hold this section, slide them into a vertical cutting angle (straight up and down) and cut this section up to your guide (see Figure 13-2b).

Make sure to keep the hair straight out to the side, as opposed to holding it in front of or behind the face.

8. Temporarily pin away this subsection and unpin the other subsection you created in step 6. Comb it diagonally to the opposite side of the face (see Figure 13-2b). Following your guide, cut it the same way as you did in steps 6–7.

REMEMBER

Always be aware of landmarks on the face. For instance, if you cut one section 2 inches (5 centimeters) below the chin on one side, you also need to cut the opposite subsection 2 inches below the chin.

9. Combine and comb both cut subsections straight down from the scalp (0-degree elevation). If you've cut them correctly, the hair will form a triangle (inverted V).

If your cutting results are uneven, there are four common reasons for unevenness:

- You lost your guide.

- You combed and held the subsections at different angles.

- You didn't cut the hair at a vertical (straight up) angle in places.

- Your triangular parting is either off center or the sides of the triangle are two different lengths or angles.

REMEMBER

If you've cut the hair a little unevenly or at the wrong angle, it's not the end of the world. Starting at the beginning of this tutorial, go through each step, identify the error, and correct the mistake. If you have cut a small section of hair too short, leave it alone. As you add more hair to the face frame, chances are good that it will be covered. My philosophy: Check. Correct or ignore. Move on.

10. Identify the side subsection that you made in step 2. Release one side of this section and comb it down to where it will naturally fall in the style.

11. On the unpinned subsection, part out one or two diagonal subsections as shown in Figure 13-2c.

12. **Move and then comb the subsection nearest to the face down and to the opposite side of the face. Find your guide, then position and cut the hair as shown in Figure 13-2d.**

Do not cut the hair until you are absolutely sure that you see your guide. If you cannot see your guide, part out a thinner diagonal subsection. Make sure the hair is evenly damp.

If some of the hair does not reach your cutting line at any time during this cut, ignore it and stay true to your guide. By checking the hair length prior to cutting, this problem can be largely avoided.

13. **Drop the second diagonal parting shown in Figure 13-2c. Move and comb it diagonally across the face as shown in Figure 13-2d. Use the subsection that you cut in step 12 as your guide.**

After cutting each diagonal subsection, comb the hair into place and check your cutting line to make sure it is vertical.

Repeat this process until both sides have been cut.

14. **While the hair is still damp, check and compare the sides to make sure they're both cut at the same angle and length. Correct if needed (see step 9).**

15. **Dry the hair with a styling brush. Re-check the cut to make sure that both sides match.**

Make any minor adjustments needed, such as a few stray bits of hair that are not in line with the cut.

16. **If you want to slide cut the last 2 to 3 inches (5 to 7.6 centimeters) of hair (see Figure 13-1) on Type 1 or Type 2, medium-to-thick hair, do it now.**

Slide cutting basics are discussed and illustrated in Chapter 7.

To style the hair, place the hair at a 0-degree elevation, and use a blow-dryer and round brush to dry and style the hair from the occipital bone down to the nape. Dry the back area above the occipital bone at a 45-degree elevation for lift and fullness. Use a blow-dryer and styling brush to dry the sides of the hair forward and flush to the face. Lift the top by blow-drying the hair at a 90-degree elevation. Separate the perimeter ends and use a light gel or pliable pomade to accentuate the piecey end finish.

Do not slide cut Type 3 and Type 4 hair. (See Chapter 4 for more information on hair types.)

Her Name Is Bob cut

Moderate

Tools needed for this bob cut include scissors, blow-dryer, clips or clamps, tail or pintail comb (optional), cutting comb, and a round brush.

The classic bob is the poster cut for mid-length hair. Because the popularity of this cut is eternal, bobs have morphed from being little more than a bowl cut to a classic style that can be cut in so many different ways that I could write an entire book on them. In this book, I have included a graduated bob, straight bob, and an asymmetrical lob haircut.

TIP

Bob haircuts are the all-stars of the beauty world because they're suitable for fine, medium, and coarse hair. The bob shown in Figure 13-3 is meant for Type 1 and 2 hair, and Type 3 and Type 4 hair that is consistently worn in a smooth style. (Refer to Chapter 4 to familiarize yourself with hair types.) Most bobs can also make thin hair look thicker and more luxurious, while convincing flyaway strands to be on their best behavior by maintaining weight at the ends of the hair.

FIGURE 13-3:
A graduated (beveled) bob is the most popular type of bob cut on the planet.

Photographer: Tom Carson (www.tomcarsonphoto.com); Stylist: Acacia Cronic; Elon Salon, Marietta, Georgia

TIP

Before diving scissors-first into the graduated bob shown in Figure 13-3, I recommend that you take a moment to study the design details. Notice how the hair *bevels* (cups inward). The length is also considered to be ideal because it's long enough to shimmer and sway without having the perimeter line broken up by brushing across the shoulders.

When you're ready to try the Her Name Is Bob cut, follow these steps:

1. **Dampen the hair and use a styling or detangling comb to evenly distribute the water throughout the hair.**

2. **Using a tail or pintail comb, part the hair into six sections: four back and two front sections.**

   Chapter 2 covers all combs needed to detangle and cut the hair. See Chapter 6 for sectioning patterns.

TIP

   Alligator or duckbill clips work well for larger sections because they firmly secure thicker sections of hair, preventing it from sagging and getting in the way of cutting the rest of the hair. (Check out the scoop on clips and clamps in Chapter 2.)

3. **Addressing the back of the hair, use a tail or cutting comb to part out a ¼-inch-deep (0.6 centimeters) horizontal parting from both bottom sections (see Figure 13-4a). Comb the parting straight down.**

TIP

   If the person you're cutting has a fading hairline — one that's so sparse it seems to disappear — release a slightly thicker parting of hair.

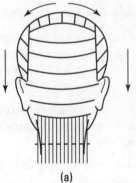

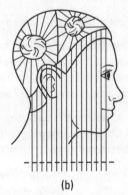

FIGURE 13-4:
How to cut a
graduated bob.

(a)   (b)

© John Wiley & Sons, Inc.; Illustration by Rashell Smith

4. **Ask the person you're cutting to look straight ahead and then, keeping the neck in its original position, bend their head down toward their chest to create a graduated (beveled) end cut. Comb the hair straight down.**

   Graduated ends are discussed in Chapter 7.

5. **Place your index finger of your non-cutting hand about 1 inch (2.5 centimeters) above where you plan to cut the hair to keep it from drifting. Trim the hair ½ inch to 1 inch (1.3 to 2.5 centimeters) below the hairline, depending on the end length you want for the finished style. Cut the hair straight across (horizontally), as shown in Figure 13-4a.**

This is now your first traveling guide. (Refer to Chapter 5 for a refresher on guides.)

The position of the head in step 4 creates *graduated* (finely layered) ends. Graduation (also called beveling) is fully explained and illustrated in Chapter 7.

If cowlicks or whorls are present along the hairline, comb and cut the hair without tension.

6. **Ask the person in your chair to lift their head until they're facing forward and their jawline is level (parallel) to the floor. Comb the hair down without applying tension and check the length and evenness of the traveling guide. If needed, adjust the shape of the guide line before proceeding with the next steps.**

   If you're uncertain about the length, blow-dry the cut area using only your fingers or a vent brush, and then recheck where the hair falls on the neck. Make sure to wet the hair before resuming the haircut.

7. **Reposition the person you're cutting according to step 4. Separate a horizontal ½-inch-deep parting right above your guide and comb the hair to a 0-degree elevation. Following the guide, cut the hair.**

   Can you see your guide? If you can't, you need to take a thinner parting of hair.

   Repeat this cutting pattern until both of the back/bottom sections are cut.

8. **Reposition the person in your chair according to step 6. Addressing the back/bottom sections you just cut, comb the hair straight down.** Check the length and shape of the perimeter line to ensure it's even and each side is identical in length and shape.

9. **Addressing the back/top sections, reposition the head according to step 4. Continue dropping ½-inch, horizontal partings, using the bottom perimeter as your guide (see Figure 13-4).**

   Check your haircut midway through cutting the back/top section to make sure you are on track. When all back sections have been cut, comb the hair into the style position and examine the hair for evenness.

10. **Unpin your front sections and establish your top part. (The one shown in Figure 13-3 is a middle part.) The part should be the one that is used at least 80 percent of the time. If the parting frequently varies, choose a middle part. Re-pin one front section.**

WARNING

Be careful not to spray water into the ear. I know this sounds ridiculous, but it's easy to do. I protect the ear by covering it with the back of my hand when I spray the hair in this area.

11. **Addressing one side of the head, separate a ½-inch horizontal subsection at the front/bottom of the section. Borrow a thin strand of hair from the back section that's adjacent to your front/bottom parting to act as your guide. Ask the person in your chair to face straight ahead with their jaw parallel to the floor, and then tilt their head (not their neck) away from you. Comb the hair straight down without using any tension. Following your guide, trim the hair at a horizontal angle to the desired length.**

Continue separating and cutting the front section until it's complete. Unlike the front/bottom subsection, use slight tension while cutting the balance of this section.

Move to the other front section. Repeat steps 10–11.

12. **Check both front sections. Have the person return their head to an upright position. Make sure the head is facing straight ahead and the jawline is parallel to the floor. Compare the length of each side of the head to ensure that they're identical. Check the rest of the haircut in the same manner.**

When cut correctly, you should have a continuous line that goes all the way around the perimeter of the hair.

If possible, both of you should face a mirror that's about 3 feet (1 meter) away from your chair. Check the front hair sections for evenness:

- Grasp these sections with your fingers and move down the two sides starting at the same point and remaining level with each other.

- If you're still unsure that both sides are even, measure the length of both sides using the handy ruler on the back of your cutting comb. Not there? Use a regular ruler.

- Have the person sit sideways so you can view one whole side of the head. Is the entire perimeter line the same level and shape? Repeat this action on the other side.

- Shake the hair by placing your hand fairly firmly on the head and using your fingertips to move the hair back and forth. Comb the hair into the final style position. Do the ends still look even?

If you need to correct any area of your perimeter line, do so now.

13. **Dry the hair using a styling brush and, if desired, bend the ends with a 2-inch (5 centimeters) round brush.**

If you're excited to cut the beautiful bang design shown in Figure 13-3, head over to Chapter 9.

Bobs can be styled in many ways. For the graduated bob shown in Figure 13-3, separate the hair into 1-inch-thick horizontal partings. Starting at the back of the head, blow-dry the hair one parting at a time. For a very full bob, apply a working spray on each parting and dry the hair at a 45-degree elevation.

TIP

A *straight bob* like the one shown in Figure 13-5 is cut the same way as a graduated bob, except the head remains facing forward with the jawline parallel to the floor for the entire haircut. Notched ends give a straight bob modern curb appeal (refer to Chapter 7). Blow-dry a straight bob with a styling brush held at a 0-degree angle. For a super straight look, finish the style by flat-ironing the hair (see Chapter 19 and Chapter 20).

FIGURE 13-5:
A straight bob.

Photographer: Tom Carson (www.tomcarsonphoto.com); Hair: Brandon David; Makeup: Betty Mekonnen for Douglas Carroll Salon & Spa, Raleigh, NC

The Tilted Lob Bob cut

Moderate

Tools needed for this lob cut include scissors, blow-dryer, clips or clamps, tail or pintail comb, cutting comb, and a round brush.

Lob haircuts are long bobs with a few design twists of their own. And like bobs, the classic lob continues to introduce new variations. The model in Figure 13-6a and 13-6b is wearing an asymmetrical lob, which begins to slant downward at the mid-shoulder and continues at this same trajectory to the end of the front perimeter line (see Figures 13-6a and 13-6b).

FIGURE 13-6:
The lob (short for "long bob") is a haircut alternative that gives wearers the benefit of having both shorter and longer hair in one cut.

(a) (b)

Photographer: Tom Carson (www.tomcarsonphoto.com); Hair: Brianna Rademacher; Makeup: Brenna Burke; Frank Anthony Salon, Chester, New Jersey

Lob variations can make a dramatic slant along the perimeter line after they pass the midpoint of the shoulders (see Figure 13-6) to ensure a clean, continuous perimeter line. Depending on the length, a classic lob can be elevated (cut just below the occipital bone in back) or longer (cut at the back hairline). The asymmetrical lob in Figure 13-6 starts low and has a moderate length on one side (Figure 13-6a) and a shorter length on the other side (Figure 13-6b).

TIP

A short or mid-length asymmetrical haircut means that one side of the hair is longer than the other. An asymmetrical cut can start at the back of the head or at any point along the perimeter of the cut.

What I find so interesting about lobs — with the exception of the general design — is that once beauty lovers rock lob haircuts, they rarely want to give them up. It's a hair clique of sorts that I call the "Lob Mob."

When you're feeling ready to cut the Lob Bob, follow these steps:

1. **Dampen the hair and use a styling comb to evenly distribute the water throughout the hair.**

2. **Using a tail or pintail comb, part the hair into six sections: four back and two front sections.**

   Chapter 2 covers all combs needed for this chapter. Chapter 6 explains and illustrates different sectioning patterns.

3. **Addressing the back of the hair, use a tail or cutting comb to part out a ¼-inch-deep (0.6 centimeters) parting from both bottom sections. Ask the person in your chair to look straight ahead and then bend their head (not their neck or back) down toward their chest.**

   The position of the head in this step creates *graduated* (finely layered) ends. (Graduation is fully explained in Chapter 7.) Frequently check the head to ensure it is still in the correct position.

4. **Using a cutting comb, comb the hair straight down. Place the teeth of the comb or your index finger of your non-cutting hand to about 1 inch (2.5 centimeters) above where you plan to cut the hair to keep it from drifting. Cut the hair at a horizontal (straight across) angle.**

   This is now your cutting guide (see Figure 13-7). If you need a refresher on guides, refer to Chapter 5.

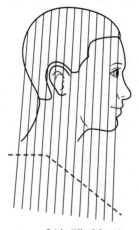

FIGURE 13-7:
How to cut an asymmetrical lob.

© *John Wiley & Sons, Inc.;*
Illustration by Rashell Smith

If you're cutting someone with a fading hairline — one that's so sparse it seems to disappear — release a slightly thicker subsection of hair for your guide.

5. **Drop a ½-inch (1.3 centimeters) horizontal parting right above your guide and use the fine-tooth side of a cutting comb to position the hair at a 0-degree elevation.**

Reposition the head as instructed in step 3.

Can you see your guide? If you can't, you need to take a finer parting of hair. If you can see the guide, cut this subsection.

Repeat this cutting pattern until both of the back/bottom sections are cut.

6. **Release a ½-inch-deep horizontal parting from a top/back section and comb it down to a 0-degree elevation. Using the ends of the last subsection as your guide, cut the hair. Continue this process until both back/top sections are cut (see Figure 13-7).**

After you've completed the back of the head, comb the hair straight down and check the cut. Is it the same length on each side? If cutting adjustments are needed, do them now.

7. **Unpin your designated longer front section and take a ½-inch-thick horizontal bottom parting. Separate a strand of hair from the back section that is directly next to the front parting and incorporate it into your front/bottom subsection.**

Re-pin the balance of the front section. If needed, dampen the hair you're about to cut.

8. **Do a practice run without cutting the hair. Addressing the front/bottom perimeter of the longest side of your lob, comb the section straight down at a 0-degree elevation and without tension. Using your second and third fingers to grasp the hair, and starting at the back of this section, angle your fingers down so that the hair gradually lengthens. Does it end at the desired length?**

Repeat step 8 using a cutting comb in lieu of your fingers. Continue doing this until you have the perfect cutting angle for your lob.

9. **Make sure the person you're cutting is sitting straight, and the head is facing straight ahead. Then tilt the head (not the neck) away from the side that you're cutting. Cut your front/bottom subsection, as shown in Figure 13-7. This is now your guide. Drop the balance of the same front section in ½-inch partings. Following your guide, cut the front/side of the hair.**

10. **Repeat steps 6–9 on the shorter side of the lob.**

Cutting the shorter side is a bit like Goldilocks and the Three Bears. If you cut the hair too short, the hair won't move past the shoulder properly. If you leave the shorter side too long, the difference between the two front/side lengths may be too little and look like a haircutting mistake. But when you find a happy medium, the shorter side will be long enough to hang properly and short enough to make the overall look have a definitive style.

Repeat step 8 on the shorter side before actually cutting the hair.

11. **If you want to add a light bang, do it now.**

If bangs are on the menu, I recommend the wispy bangs found in Chapter 9.

To style this graduated lob, separate the hair into horizontal 1-inch partings, starting at the nape of the neck. Apply a light-hold styling aid and dry the hair using a round brush. Completely dry each horizontal parting before moving onto the subsection above it.

Let It Slide cut

Moderate

Tools needed for this cut include convex (Japanese-style) scissors, blow-dryer, clips or clamps, tail or pintail comb, cutting comb, and a styling or vent brush. For practice only, you'll need a mannequin head or hair wefts.

I was torn on rating this haircut *Easy* or *Moderate.* It's actually an easy cut that uses one advanced technique. Make sense? (I can see your brows knitting as I write this.)

The moderately difficult technique used in this haircut is called *slide cutting.* In a nutshell, slide cutting is a method that releases weight by creating planned but unstructured vertical layers. It's done by pointing your scissor blades at a downward angle and toward the ends of the hair. Your starting point is determined by where you want the vertical layering to begin. The slide cut technique used in this haircut is fairly deep to create lift in the interior and exterior areas of the hair. Slide cutting is explained and illustrated in Chapter 7.

The Let It Slide cut, shown in Figure 13-8, is designed for Type 1 and Type 2 hair. (Hair types are discussed in Chapter 4.) This cut falls just below the shoulders. For ideal results, make sure that the hair you're about cut is one length or has very long layers.

REMEMBER

The slide cutting technique used in this tutorial requires *convex (Japanese-style)* scissors (see Chapter 2 for more information on scissors). Convex scissors have smooth, razor-like blade edges that glide through the hair. *Concave (German-style)* scissors, which are not designed for slicing, have micro-serrated teeth that will shred the hair as you glide down the strands.

FIGURE 13-8:
Slide cutting can transform a simple, one-length haircut. When combined with a thin curtain bang, it adds planned messiness and youthful appeal.

(a) (b)

Photo and Hair: Belinda Mills (Instagram @bel_pipsqueekinsaigon); Model: Georgia Bess; Salon: Pipsqueek in Saigon, Adelaide, Australia

TIP

To get the knack of slide cutting, you should practice this technique on a mannequin head. If you don't have one available, you can use 4-inch-wide (10.2 centimeters) or wider human hair wefts (hair extensions). Hair extensions of all types are sold online and at brick-and-mortar beauty supply stores.

When you've had a bit of practice and feel ready to try this cut, follow these steps, which are grouped into multiple parts.

Part A: Basic haircut

The basic haircut in Part A is cut the same as the Her Name is Bob cut earlier in this chapter with two key differences:

>> The Let It Slide haircut is longer.

>> The ends are blunt cut (not graduated).

While cutting Part A of the Let It Slide cut, refer to Figures 13-4a and 13-4b to visually understand the instructions that follow. Just remember that you're now cutting longer hair that's just below the shoulders, and you're not graduating the ends of the hair.

1. Dampen the hair. Section the hair into a six-section pattern (two front sections and four back sections), as shown in Chapter 6.

TIP

Using a tail comb or pintail comb makes sectioning more precise and much easier to accomplish.

2. **Drop a horizontal ½-inch parting (1.3 centimeters) from one of the back/bottom sections. Using a cutting comb, comb the hair straight down to just past the shoulders at a 0-degree elevation (see Figure 13-4).**

   Chapter 5 shares the highs and lows of haircutting elevations.

   Make sure the person sitting in your chair is looking straight ahead with their jawline positioned parallel to the floor. The torso should be erect, as opposed to leaning forward or side-to-side.

3. **Grasp the hair by your second and third fingers of your non-cutting hand. Rest your finger lightly against the skin and cut the hair at a horizontal cutting angle. This is now your first haircutting guide.**

   Placing the third finger next to the skin creates a slight layering (and lift) on the ends.

4. **Continue dropping subsections, using your previous cut as your guide, until the one back/bottom section has been completely cut.**

5. **Comb and examine this section to ensure that your cutting line is straight and true.**

6. **Cut the other back/bottom section. Part out your first horizontal ½-inch subsection and comb it straight down. Borrowing a strand of hair from your first cutting section to act as your guide, cut the hair exactly as you did in steps 3–4.**

   Check the perimeter of the back haircut by comparing the two back sections to make sure they've been cut at the same length and angle.

7. **Cut the two back/top sections the same way you did in steps 2–6.**

   Make sure that you're combing the hair straight down and at a 0-degree elevation. This will ensure that you're following the curvature of the head within each section.

   Frequently check the position of the person's head to ensure it is still in the correct position.

8. **Comb the entire back of the hair into the finished style position. Check the length to ensure that the perimeter line is even and cut correctly.**

   Re-pin the back four sections.

9. **Unpin one front section. Part out a ½-inch horizontal bottom subsection. Release an adjacent back/bottom strand to use as your guide. Comb the guide and your first front subsection straight down. Do not apply any tension. Following your guide, cut the ends at a horizontal angle (see Chapter 5 to learn more about cutting angles).**

For reference only, view Figure 13-2. The positioning of the hair is the same, but the length you're now cutting is much longer than the bob shown in this figure.

10. **Repeat step 9, using a slight amount of tension until the entire section has been cut. Check your perimeter line to ensure that it seamlessly connects from front to back.**

Part B: Slide cutting

When you've completed Part A, you're now ready for the hair sliding portion of the cut:

11. **Re-pin the front hair sections to avoid haircutting confusion.**

Never slide cut the hair close to the scalp.

12. **Horizontally (side-to-side) divide one of the back/bottom sections into two equal top-and-bottom subsections. Pin away the top subsection.**

13. **Select and part out a thin 1-inch-wide (1.3 centimeters) subsection. Hold this hair with tension at a 45-degree elevation with your second and third fingers of your non-cutting hand.**

14. **Point your blades toward the ends. Open the blades and insert them about 3 inches (7.6 centimeters) down the strand. Move the contact point of the strand to the back of the scissors (next to the joint).**

15. **Move down the strand to the ends while almost imperceptibly moving your cutting thumb ⅓ inch (0.9 centimeters) in a cutting motion to remove the top surface of the strand.**

This movement is often referred as *fluttering*.

16. **Continue slide cutting the hair until you complete both of the back/bottom sections.**

If the hair is on the thick side, space your slide cuts 1 inch (2.5 centimeters) apart. If the hair is on the thin side or it's naturally fluffy, just slide cut a few pieces in each of the back sections.

Never completely close the blades when slide cutting as this will create short strands where they aren't supposed to be.

17. **Comb through the hair. Observe the amount of hair that you removed and how the intact hair looks. Do you like the slide cut strands? The entire result? If you feel you should have cut more hair, wait until the end of the haircut to add more layered pieces.**

18. **Unpin one of the back/top sections and repeat steps 12–16. For the top sections, start your slide cutting 3 inches up from the ends.**

Repeat these cutting actions until both back/top sections have been cut.

19. **Moving to the front sections, comb both sections straight down. Check to make sure that your center part is straight and dead center of the hairline.**

20. **Addressing one of the front/side sections, horizontally divide this section into two equal subsections (top and bottom subsections).**

21. **Pin away the top subsection you're not cutting to avoid confusion.**

22. **Pick up a ⅛-inch-wide (0.3 centimeters) strand in the middle of the front/ bottom subsection and hold it at a 0-degree elevation. Starting 2 inches (5 centimeters) away from the ends, slide cut the hair at a 0-degree elevation. Repeat this action, but this time pick up a strand of hair toward the back of this subsection.**

Avoid slide cutting the hair on the front area of the front section, as this will change the haircut by removing too much weight from the hair.

Ignore the front/top subsections for now. You can decide whether to slide cut them after you've cut the light curtain bang.

Part C: Curtain bangs

If you want to add curtain bangs, now is the time:

23. **Cut a shallow (thin) curtain bang, following the directions in Chapter 9.**

Part D: Haircut check

24. **Brush the hair into place and check your haircut:**

- Is it cut at a consistent length throughout?

- Are there any stragglers along the perimeter line that you need to trim?

- Do you have areas that look dense or saggy that could benefit from a couple more layers?

- Compare the ends of your cut with the model's hair in Figure 13-8. If your hairline is still too dense, point cut any problematic areas at a 0-degree angle.

- Do the front/top subsections need to be slide cut?

TIP

For this haircut and style, a root lift product was applied at the base, and a flexible hairspray was lightly applied on the midshafts and ends to lift, define, and affix the hair. Chapter 18 shares information on different styling aids. Chapter 20 delivers great styling tips.

Chapter **14**

Getting Snippy with Women's Long Styles

Tools you'll need for this chapter include scissors, blow-dryer, clippers, tail comb, detangling comb, cutting comb, styling brush, round brush (optional), and clips and clamps.

Although beauty trends tend to favor shorter styles, plenty of women enjoy their ongoing love affair with long hair. Their ample tresses — defined in this book as hair that cascades at least 4 inches (10.2 centimeters) past the shoulders — often need only a light trim on the ends to look fabulous for weeks. And when long-haired aficionadas become bored with their single-length hair, you can easily create a lively new look by adding long layers, a sexy fringe, or a frame cut around the eyes, neck, or jawline.

Preparing Thyself for Long Locks

Generally speaking, the longer someone's hair is, the more challenging it is to control. The difficulty of twisting wet sections of hair and firmly pinning them with jaw clips, or dealing with tangles that magically reappear, is compounded by every inch (2.5 centimeters) of added length. If the person's hair is curly or thick to boot, every inch of hair can add up to a handful of extra bulk.

TIP

To ensure that the long hair you work with behaves, follow these simple rules:

>> **Always treat long hair as though it's frail and fragile because it's probably both of these things (see Chapter 17).** Long locks are the senior citizens of the hair world. They've been around long enough to experience thousands of sunny days (UV ray damage), be subjected to hundreds or even thousands of high-heat stylings (heat damage), and have suffered right along with the wearer when time-crunched schedules lead to overly rough treatment (mechanical damage).

>> **Never ask a girl to do a woman's job, and never expect a flimsy clip to hold long, heavy hair.** If you do, your sections will collapse in a heap. Implements like alligator jaw clamps should be your fasteners of choice for pinning long hair. (Chapter 2 shares information about hair clamps.)

>> **At the start of every long haircut, always use a wide tooth or detangling comb to remove all tangles.** If the hair is relatively free of tangles, a wide tooth comb works well. When more tangling is present, do yourself (and the person sitting in your chair) a favor by using a *detangling comb*. This comb loves to go on snarl patrol and can easily remove even gnarly tangles.

>> **Anytime you decide to take a shortcut by not thoroughly conditioning long hair, you're in for a tough haircutting or styling session.** If you don't want to wash the hair prior to cutting it, dampen the hair with a spray bottle filled with a mixture of water and one capful of regular rinse-out conditioner and comb through the hair. The comb should effortlessly glide down the hair shaft. If it's still bumping along, you need to apply an undiluted leave-in conditioner or detangling spray. (Chapter 17 gives great information on several different types of leave-in hair conditioners.)

>> **Anytime you wash long hair prior to a haircut, take the extra time to thoroughly towel-dry the hair until it's damp rather than dripping wet.** If you don't do this, you're bound to find yourself standing in a puddle of water with your shoes looking more like you've been singing in the rain than cutting hair. Use a soft cotton or microfiber towel, as these will cause the least amount of friction on the hair. A cotton or microfiber T-shirt can also be used to soak up excess water.

Never rub the hair with a towel. Instead, gently squeeze the hair and then wrap it up with a towel or T-shirt until the hair is damp.

Shape-Shifting Styles for Long Hair

Long, single-length hair can be the ultimate hair status for many hair-hugging lovelies. But no matter how much they love their crowning glory, there comes a time when straight, one-length hair no longer complements their overall appearance, it becomes incongruous with their career or lifestyle, or they simply yearn for a new look.

AUTHOR SAYS

When working behind the chair, I had one client who always held her finger and thumb ½ inch (1.3 centimeters) apart in front of my assistant, so she could bear witness to the requested end trim. One time she even strutted around the salon to make everyone aware of her end goal. (She was joking, not joking.) As obnoxious as her behavior was, I understood why she was worried about losing too much length.

The source of this fear usually comes from a previous experience when they entered a salon expecting a light trim and departed missing 6 inches (15.3 centimeters) of hair. I've never done that to anyone, but I do know why it sometimes happens: Some stylists cannot control their urge to do what's best for the hair rather than simply what the client requests.

TIP

Whenever you run across this situation (for instance, they want a ½-inch cut but need 6 inches or more removed), trim the ends as requested and offer to do a dusting cut, which removes split ends and broken hair without affecting the length (see Chapter 10). Doing this won't completely correct the situation, but it will remove some damage and make the hair look much healthier.

Changing up a one-length cut

Long, single-length hair is definitely one of the easiest styles to care for, making it an excellent choice for children, active teens, and anyone who wants beautiful hair with a minimal amount of fuss. But even the most passionate long-hair devotees can become bored with the sameness of having single-length hair. When they do, you can change-up their style while only removing a minimal amount of hair. Here are some options to consider:

>> Point cut the ends to add a piecey look (Chapter 7).

>> Cut graduated (beveled) ends (Chapter 7).

>> Add a curtain bang (Chapter 9).

>> Design an eye-framing cut (Chapter 9).

>> Add a light face-framing cut (Chapter 13).

>> Slide cut the mid-lengths and ends to create a more unstructured style (Chapter 13).

>> Cut a different perimeter shape (see Table 14-1).

The simple variations presented in Table 14-1 allow you to say goodbye to ho-hum long hair.

TABLE 14-1 **Perimeter End Shapes**

Shape	About	Ideal Hair Types
Square	Emphasizes weight and thickness	Hair Types 1–3
Oval/round	Soft and girlish	Hair Types 1–2
Fan	Very feminine	Hair Types 1–3
Diamond	Goth, old-time punk rock	Hair Type 1

Being Single-Length and Loving It

Easy

One-length haircuts come in a variety of perimeter designs, such as square (straight-across) and oval shapes, as well as blunt and graduated ends. The model's hair in Figure 14-1 has a square perimeter that's been cut at a *0-degree elevation* (Chapter 5 gives you the scoop on elevations). However, the instructions in the following Being Single-Length and Loving It tutorial can be applied to all perimeter shapes.

Tools you'll need for this tutorial include scissors, blow-dryer, clamps, tail comb (optional), detangling comb, and cutting comb.

TIP

A one-length cut works well for a variety of lengths, but it truly excels when the hair is long enough to cascade several inches past the shoulders to accentuate the perimeter design (see Figure 14-1). It also looks best on hair that lacks visible damage, such as roughness, breakage, and split ends — conditions that cause the hair fiber to fray and snap like a dry twig. (Chapter 17 provides information about different hair conditions. Chapter 7 shares details on different end designs.)

FIGURE 14-1:
A square-cut perimeter on long hair expresses simplicity and an affinity for natural beauty.

Photographer: Tom Carson (www.tomcarsonphoto.com);
Hair: Vanis Salon & Spa, Schererville, Indiana

Follow these steps for the Single–Length and Loving It cut:

1. **Dampen the hair and part it into six sections (refer to Chapter 6).**

TIP

   If your model always wears a side part like the model in Figure 14-1, use this side parting as the dividing line between the two front sections. If the hair is thick, heavy, or cumbersome, divide the back sections into smaller, more manageable subsections.

   For bulky hair, use a tail comb (shown in Chapter 2) to divide the hair into sections.

2. **Place the person's head in a level position.**

   Make sure they're looking straight forward, and the chin and jawline are parallel to the floor.

   If you're cutting graduated ends, bend the head (not the neck or torso) forward until the chin is touching the chest and then cut the hair. (See Chapter 7 for more in-depth directions.)

3. **Drop a ¼-inch to ½-inch (0.6 centimeters to 1.3 centimeters) horizontal parting from the back/bottom sections (just above the bottom hairline).**

4. **Comb the hair straight down to a 0-degree elevation. After making sure the person is in the correct position (reference step 2), cut the ends to the desired length and shape.**

If the hair is longer than mid-back, have the person stand while cutting their hair. Make sure they're standing straight, their head is facing forward, and their jawline is parallel to the floor. Comb the hair straight down in the direction that it naturally falls.

If you're cutting a curved perimeter line (see Table 14-1), cut the hair from the center to each side. If you want to correct the shape, either re-cut the parting or drop another thin parting and cut it to the desire shape. **Note:** You can only do this once, so make sure you give it your best effort.

This hair parting is now your *cutting guide* — the template that dictates the length and shape of your haircut design (see Chapter 5).

REMEMBER

Before you continue with the cut, check your guide for length and accuracy. Are the sides of the hair the same length? Is the perimeter line cut at the proper angle?

5. **Make a ½-inch horizontal parting in each of the back/bottom sections that are directly above your bottom guide. Comb the hair straight down. Following your guide, cut the hair.**

If you're cutting graduated ends, make sure to position the head forward with the chin touching the chest (see step 2).

Continue repeating this haircutting pattern until all of your back sections have been cut.

6. **Addressing one front section at a time and starting at the parting, brush and then comb each section back to the bottom perimeter line.**

When you comb each of the front sections back to the perimeter line, make sure you're combing them into the finished style position.

Brush and then comb all the hair together to seamlessly blend the front and back sections.

7. **Following your cut perimeter line as your guide, cut the sides of the hair.**

For graduated ends, follow the directions in step 2.

Making a Clean Break

Moderate

Tools you'll need to fully participate in this tutorial include clippers, styling brush or detangling comb, and cutting comb.

Here's a fun, super-blunt clipper cut that you can do, stat! If you can get your hands on anyone with one-length hair that's 4 inches (10.2 centimeters) or longer past the shoulders, you're in for a treat (see Figure 14-2).

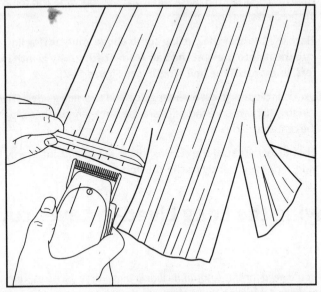

FIGURE 14-2: Using clippers to cut the perimeter of one-length hair creates a crisp, distinctive line.

The Making a Clean Break perimeter trim is ideal for Type 1 and Type 2 hair, whether it's natural or smoothed, and Type 3 and Type 4 hair that's been chemically smoothed or straightened. Unless the hair is unusually thick, this design can be cut in one section. (See Chapter 4 for detailed information on hair types.)

When you're ready to try it, follow these steps:

1. **Brush or use a detangling comb to unsnarl the hair. Separate the front of the hair by first creating a part that's worn at least 80 percent of the time. (If the person frequently changes their part, make a middle part.) Lightly dampen the hair and comb through it until the water is evenly distributed and the hair is perfectly smooth.**

   Make sure the person in your chair is facing straight ahead, the torso is erect, and the jawline is parallel to the floor.

   Decide on the finished length and shape of the perimeter. A square perimeter is the preferred design for a novice clipper cutter.

   If you want the hair to remain back as the person goes through their day, leave the hair at least 4 inches (10.2 centimeters) below the shoulders.

2. **Comb the back of the hair into the finished style position.**

Comb the hair back and straight down the back at a 0-degree elevation (see Chapter 5).

This is a crucial step so make sure you take your time and comb every hair into the finished style position.

3. **Place the teeth of the cutting comb above your cutting line and straight into the hair to prevent the hair from drifting. Clip ½ inch (1.3 centimeters) or more off the hair length (see Figure 14-2).**

Use your clippers to cut a center guide and two side guides. Check them carefully to make sure the sides are the same length. Then clip the hair from the center to each side.

4. **Check to make sure the cutting line is sharp and cut evenly from side to side. If needed, lightly re-clip the line.**

Slaying the Long Lived-In Layer cut

Advanced

Tools you'll need for this tutorial include a blow-dryer, scissors, cutting comb, tail comb, wide tooth or detangling comb, clips and clamps, styling brush, and a large round brush (optional).

Long layers can transform all long hairstyles from plain to stylish, whether the hair is one length, has graduated ends, or includes a taper cut from the shoulders up to the jawline. The results can be flirty, sexy, stylish, or all of the above.

While Chapter 10 shares what I call a quick-and-dirty tutorial on how to layer longer hair with a single snip, it's best suited for haircut touch-ups between professional haircuts. This Long Lived-In Layer cut tutorial is a professional method for first-time layered cuts and refresher trims.

TIP

The Long Lived-In Layer cut, shown in Figure 14-3, pairs well with eye-framing or curtain bangs (Chapter 9), as well as a face-framing cut (Chapter 13).

It's ideal for Type 1, Type 2, and Type 3A hair that measures 10 to 14 inches (25.4 to 35.6 centimeters) in length on smooth hair, and 12 to 16 inches (30.5 to 40.6 centimeters) in length on curly hair. (See Chapter 4 for information on hair types.)

The Long Lived-In Layer cut is an advanced cut and, therefore, has several components. I've broken down this tutorial into six different parts to help simplify the process.

Photo and hair: Belinda Mills; Model: Georgia Bess; Pipsqueek in Saigon salon (www.pipsqueekinsaigon.com); Adelaide, South Australia

FIGURE 14-3: This long-layered haircut looks completely different on straight and curly hair.

Part A: Cutting the perimeter of the hair

To cut the perimeter of the hair, follow these steps:

1. **Dampen and smooth the hair using a detangling comb and then a cutting comb.**

2. **Separate the front, sides, and back of the head:**

- Create the front/top part according to how the person normally wears their part at least 80 percent of the time. If there isn't a consistent part, create a middle part.

- Create and secure a ½-inch-wide (1.3 centimeters) section that follows the front hairline from ear to ear (see Figure 14-4a). This section will be addressed near the end of the tutorial.

- Separate the front and back areas by parting the hair from the back of the top part down to the front of each ear.

- Separate the hair in the back of the head into four sections (see Chapter 6).

3. **Part out a side-to-side bottom parting from both back/bottom sections. Comb the hair straight down and cut the hair to the desired length. This is now your first perimeter guide.**

Continue parting out side-to-side subsections and cutting the hair. Release the top sections and repeat steps 2–3.

4. **Release one side section. Comb the hair into its finished style position. Borrowing a strand from the back section that's nearest the side section to use as your guide, trim the perimeter of the hair.**

Repeat step 4 on the other side of the hair.

Part B: Cutting the top and sides of the hair

To cut the top and sides of the hair, follow these steps:

5. **Create a layering and top guide by taking a strand of hair right behind the top part. Grasping it with your fingers, move it down the back of the head at a 0-degree elevation (see Chapter 5 for more on cutting elevations). After deciding how long the top layer will be, snip this strand to the desired length (see Figure 14-4a).**

Lived-in long layers generally begin about 3 inches (7.6 centimeters) above the perimeter line.

When deciding on the length of the layers, always take into account that hair shrinks and visibly loses length when volume or curl is added to the hair.

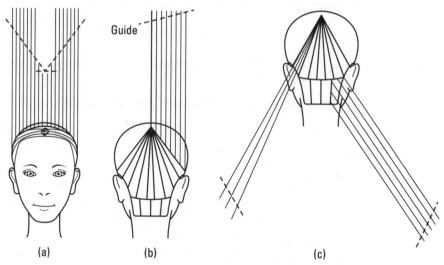

FIGURE 14-4: How to cut long, lived-in layers on long hair.

(a)   (b)   (c)

© John Wiley & Sons, Inc.; Illustration by Rashell Smith

6. **Addressing the top of the head, separate a ¼-inch (0.6 centimeters) back-to-front subsection on each side of the part that you established in step 2. Comb both subsections together and straight up from the head at a 90-degree elevation. Following the guide you snipped in step 5, cut the**

hair at a horizontal (straight across) angle. (Figure 14-4a shows the top subsection and cutting line.)

Comb the hair back into place, including your original part line.

7. **Addressing the top/side of the head, separate a ½-inch-wide by 2-inch-long (1.3 by 5 centimeters) vertical subsection starting at the center part line and bordering the front subsection you separated in step 2. Comb this subsection straight up from the head. Using the hair from the part line as your guide, cut the hair at a diagonal angle (short-to-long) as shown in Figure 14-4a.**

8. **Separate a ½-inch-wide by 2-inch-long vertical subsection right below the subsection you cut in step 7. Borrow a thin parting from this previous subsection to act as your guide. Thoroughly comb the new vertical subsection and your guide straight up from the scalp. Following your guide, cut the hair at a diagonal angle (see Figure 14-4a).**

9. **Continue repeating the cutting instructions in step 8 until you're 1 inch (2.5 centimeters) away from the front/bottom hairline.**

10. **Moving back to the middle parting, continue separating vertical subsections as you did in steps 7–8 until you reach the back of the side section.**

Repeat steps 7–8 on the other side of the head.

Compare the length and angle of the hair on both sides of the head to ensure that you have stayed true to your traveling guides.

11. **Secure both front/side sections by parting the hair from the back of the part to the front of each ear and securing the hair.**

Part C: Cutting the hair at the back of the head

To cut the hair at the back of the head, follow these steps:

12. **Secure the back of the head into four sections. In this case, instead of being four equal sections, the bottom two sections are parted out at the lower occipital bone area (making them smaller than the top sections). Chapter 5 provides information about this area of the head.**

Secure the bottom sections. They will be cut later in the tutorial.

13. **Continue the vertical cutting pattern that you did on both sides of the head for the top back sections by moving from the outside perimeter to the middle on each side (see Figure 14-4b).**

It's easy to lose your way when cutting the back of the head, so be extra vigilant. This is usually caused by losing track of your guide, cutting your guide, or varying the elevation or direction. The solutions are simple: Take your time and never lose focus on what you're doing. If you're ever uncertain, return to

WARNING

the previous subsections and comb through the hair. You can also take thinner partings or cut each subsection in two or three parts, as opposed to trying to handle and cut the full parting at one time.

Re-pin the back/top section before proceeding to the next back/top section.

14. **Unpin one back/bottom section. Release a 1-inch-thick (2.5 centimeters) parting from the bottom of the top section that is the same width as the bottom section.**

This is now the traveling guide for all the vertical subsections in the back/bottom section (see Figure 14-4c).

Re-pin the balance of the back/top section.

15. **Comb the unpinned hair straight down. Separate a 1-inch-wide vertical subsection closest to the ear and comb it to a 45-degree elevation (see Figure 14-4c).**

16. **After making sure that the hair is carefully combed to a 45-degree elevation, use the second and third fingers of your non-cutting hand to grip the section at a diagonal angle. Diagonally trim the tips of the hair (see Figure 14-4c).**

Unlike the rest of the haircut, the goal when cutting the back/bottom sections is to lightly blend the ends with the rest of the hair without layering it. Doing so will preserve the weight along the perimeter and maintain fullness where the bottom of the occipital bone recesses.

17. **Repeat steps 14 and 15 until the entire section has been cut.**

Repeat these same steps on the other back/bottom section, starting at the ear and working your way toward the center of the head.

Part D: Cutting the front section

Follow these steps for cutting the front section:

18. **Unpin the front section that you parted out in step 2. Separate it into three subsections: center and both sides. Part out an identical subsection directly behind the center subsection to act as your guide. Using your cutting comb, comb the hair down to a 45-degree angle and without tension. Cut the hair following the shape of the guide.**

If the front section is shorter than your guide, leave it as is. Repeat this same cutting pattern on the side subsections.

Part E: Notching and point cutting the ends

Follow these steps to notch and point cut the ends:

19. **Pin the hair into seven sections — four back sections, two side sections, and one top section (shown in Chapter 6).**

20. **Unpin the sections in step 19 one at a time.**

- On medium-to-thick hair, separate the hair in 1-inch (2.5 centimeters) horizontal subsections and point cut the ends 1 to 1½ inches (2.5 to 3.8 centimeters) deep, depending on the length of the hair and how piecey you want the hair to look.

- On thin hair, lightly notch the tips of the hair.

Remember that the thickness of the hair will vary throughout the head. The sides, for instance, are always much thinner than the back/bottom of the hair.

Part F: Checking the haircut

This final part of the tutorial involves checking the haircut and making any necessary final tweaks. Here's how:

21. **Moving to the top/back of the hair, create a side-to-side parting that's 3 inches wide by 1 inch deep (7.6 centimeters by 2.5 centimeters). Comb this parting straight up from the scalp and study the shape of the ends. If you've cut the hair correctly, the ends will form a soft "V" shape (see Figure 14-4a).**

Repeat step 21 until you reach the front hair section you created in step 2.

If the hair doesn't form a soft V, comb through the hair to make sure the cut didn't go astray. If it is incorrect, lightly trim the hair to bring it into the proper shape. Phew, you made it!

When it comes to styling long hair with laid-back layers, you have a lot of options. You can blow-dry it with a vent brush, a styling brush, or a large round brush. You can use a flat iron to smooth the hair or wrap the hair around the flat iron and glide through the hair to add curl. To give the hair ultimate oomph, use a curling iron with a 1-inch or 1½-inch diameter barrel (2.5 to 3.8 centimeters). You can also alternate between forward and back rolling directions throughout the hair. Chapter 19 contains information about styling tools, and Chapter 20 shares cool styling tips and tricks.

Chapter **15**

Getting Snippy with Men's Styles

*T*ools you'll need for this chapter include scissors, clippers, Nos. 1–4 clipper guides, trimmers, cutting comb, blow–dryer, styling brush, vent brush, and barber pencil (a.k.a. barber chalk) (optional).

Novice haircutters are drawn to basic men's haircuts because most of them are easier to master than their female counterparts. The biggest challenge with these basic designs is the demand for no-fuss grooming. You can easily meet this challenge by mastering some basic male haircutting techniques — scissors-over-comb, trimmers-over comb, and clippers-over-comb, as well as hard partings and angular design lines.

**AUTHOR
SAYS**

To get into the groove of masculine haircuts, I suggest that you grab someone who's unwittingly wandering around your home with an overgrown mop and let your clippers or scissors fly. If you find that this approach isn't your style, consider a more conservative one by first maintaining your family's barber cuts between professional appointments. This tactic will help stretch your household grooming budget while giving you invaluable practice. (Chapter 11 shares tips and a tutorial on how to extend the time between men's basic haircuts.)

Cutting Corners and Other Barbering Techniques

Short, masculine haircuts typically have distinctive angular lines that include sharp, straight-across or pointed sideburns, a square-shaped neckline, and sharp angles going from the square corner of the neckline up to the back of the ears.

TIP

Square necklines are commonly associated with masculine cuts, while oval or round necklines are considered more feminine cuts. Some men, though, look better with more rounded lines — especially around the nape area — when they have an unusually thick neck or a wide, square-shaped head.

Using the "over-comb" cutting technique

The *scissors-over-comb technique* (see Figure 15-1) involves using your comb to lift and hold the hair in position while cutting short hair, creating a seamless blend and erasing isolated cutting lines. You should also use this technique whenever the hair's too short to hold with your fingers or you want to create a softer finish than you would with clippers. When doing this technique, always cut against the growth direction of the hair.

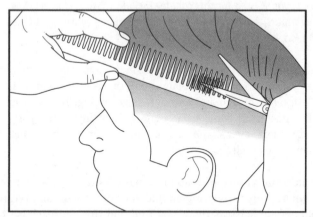

FIGURE 15-1:
Use the scissors-over-comb technique to taper cut short hair.

© John Wiley & Sons, Inc.; Illustration by Rashell Smith

TIP

Straight, fine hair is the worst for showing cutting lines. The scissors-over-comb technique can be used to erase them. You can also use texturizing or thinning scissors (see Chapter 2) to achieve similar results.

Here's how to do the scissors-over-comb tapering technique:

1. **Beginning just below the neckline, place your cutting comb flat to the skin with the teeth side up. Move your comb up until you see the hair poking through the teeth. (Chapter 2 covers comb information.)**

2. **While continuing to move the comb upward, and keeping the scissors parallel to the teeth, trim the exposed hair.**

   Always move the comb against the natural growth direction.

TIP

Both clippers and trimmers can be used in lieu of scissors in the over-comb cutting technique to create crisper layering and tapering. Both of these tools are placed perpendicular (as opposed to parallel) to the comb and then moved across the teeth (see Chapter 8).

Absolute power tools

Clippers, guides, and clipping tips are covered in Chapter 8, along with two tutorials: a taper cut involving two blended lengths and a balding cut that includes how to condition the scalp and avoid skin irritation.

Besides cleaning up necklines, trimmers and clippers can give your entire haircut a distinctive edge by creating clean perimeter lines and sharp corners that simply aren't possible to do with your scissors. They're also used to create design lines in short areas of men's haircuts.

Parting the hard way

The *hard part* has many different names, such as a *shaved part, razor line,* and *side part line.* Hard parts are shaved or clipped down to the scalp. The shaved line is highly versatile as it perfectly complements many masculine and feminine barber styles. When cutting a hard part, make sure to move and secure the surrounding hair to avoid clipping mishaps.

The tools used to create a hard part are clippers, trimmers, or a haircutting razor. For novice cutters, I recommend using trimmers because they cut sharp lines and are small and easy to handle.

TIP

A hard part requires a steady and practiced hand. Before creating a hard part on a family member, cut several hard parts on a mannequin head until you feel confident of your results.

Follow these steps to create a hard part using trimmers:

1. **Create a clean side part where the hair is commonly separated (a pintail comb works great for this task).**

2. **Pin away the area around the part so you can clearly see and follow the part line.**

3. **Invert the trimmers so the back side is on top and point the blades toward the scalp. Starting at the front of the part, clip the hair to the scalp.**

Move slowly and be as precise as possible. You can cut the hard part several times until the line is absolutely clean. Do not widen the part while doing this unless that was your plan all along.

Note: If you prefer to use clippers instead of trimmers, cut the hard part without a clipper guide.

Finding Your Masculine Mojo

Besides having more angular necklines than their feminine counterparts, masculine haircuts have sharper cutting lines where the hair transitions from the top to the sides of the head. And unlike most feminine styles that require more involved styling (which hides a myriad of mistakes, by the way), most men want a brush-and-go style.

TIP

Despite having a few unique challenges, the design possibilities of men's cuts will always keep your mind and creativity engaged. As you go through the tutorials in this chapter, focus on creating super-smooth tapers, awesome fades, sharp angles, and crisp design lines. I promise that you can master these skills surprisingly fast in terms of time and practice.

REMEMBER

Creating flawless haircuts hinges on your passion to perfect your skills!

Tips for longer masculine styles

In terms of longer masculine styles, you cut them *almost* the same as you would longer feminine styles. In fact, nearly all haircuts included in *Haircutting For Dummies* can be adapted for masculine designs.

Tips on converting feminine styles into more masculine designs:

>> Choose haircut designs that do not need to be styled with an iron or round brush. The best style choices are air-dried and blow-dried styles using the fingers or a vent brush (see Chapters 2 and 19).

>> In most cases, skip the bangs and face-framing steps.

>> Keep masculine cuts angular.

>> Go easy on cutting graduated (beveled) ends on mid-length haircuts (see Chapter 7 and Chapter 13) or you could end up giving a Little Lord Fauntleroy haircut.

>> If you want to add layers, make sure the hair has enough body (waves or manageable curls) to rock these layers without outside intervention (heated styling tools or round brushes).

WARNING

Beware of thinning hair. All haircutting tutorials in this chapter do not take hair loss into consideration because hair loss varies from person to person. If you encounter hair thinning when checking the hair and scalp before doing a haircut (usually along the front hairline, the top of the head, or at the crown), always create a plan that includes cutting these areas separately. Specific tips for cutting thinning hair are covered in Chapter 24.

The following sections cover basic men's haircuts that will definitely build your barber cutting skills, stat!

Negotiating a Standard Business cut

Moderate

Tools you'll need for this haircut include a blow-dryer, scissors, trimmers, styling or vent brush, and a cutting comb.

The most common men's hair design is a *basic business cut* (see Figure 15-2), ranging from 2 to 3 inches (5 to 7.6 centimeters) on top and tapering down to ½ inch to ⅛ inch (1.3 to 0.3 centimeters) at the hairline, depending how short you want the hair to be. It requires a complete haircut every 3 or 4 weeks, based on how fussy the wearer is about their hair. (Chapter 11 shares how to touch up a basic business cut to extend the time between barber or salon appointments.)

WARNING

The length directions for this tutorial are based on fine and medium hair textures (see Chapter 4). Coarser hair textures may need additional length to avoid creating what I refer to as a pop-up porcupine cut.

FIGURE 15-2:
The Standard Business cut looks great and requires minimal daily styling.

Photographer: Tom Carson. Hairstyling: American Male, Reading, PA

To try your hand at the Standard Business cut, follow these steps:

1. **Mist the hair with water and comb it straight back and down to the bottom hairline.**

2. **Using trimmers, clip the neckline to the desired length and shape.**

   TIP

   To ensure accuracy, work from the center of the neckline to each of the outside corners.

3. **Using trimmers to clip the sides of the neck area, start at the corner of the neckline and work your way up to the back of the ear.**

4. **Following the hairline, use either scissors or trimmers (whichever tool you're most comfortable using) to cut the perimeter line around the ears (see Figure 15-3b).**

   REMEMBER

   Always bend the ears forward to keep them out of harm's way while creating a larger cutting space.

5. **Using your comb, part out the top section by identifying the four corners at the top of the head (see Figure 15-3a). (Chapter 5 explains how this is done.)**

   When finished, the top section should be in the shape of a rectangle.

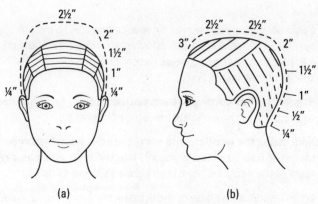

FIGURE 15-3:
How to cut a masculine business cut.

(a)   (b)

© John Wiley & Sons, Inc.; Illustration by Rashell Smith

6. Paralleling the hairline, separate a ¼-inch deep (0.6 centimeter) subsection of hair between the front two corners created in step 5.

7. Using the wide-spaced teeth on a cutting comb, comb this hair straight down on the forehead without applying tension. Cut the hair to 3 inches (7.6 centimeters) in length. (Depending on the hair type and growth direction, you may or may not need to shorten this length once the entire cut has been done.)

8. Addressing the top section, make a ¼-inch wide by ½-inch (0.6 by 1.3 centimeters) long, back-to-front subsection at the top/back perimeter.

9. Comb the hair to a 90-degree elevation away from the scalp. Cut this subsection at a horizontal angle to 2.5 inches (6.4 centimeters) in length. This is now your first traveling guide (see Figure 15-3b). (Reference Chapter 5 for information about elevations, angles, and traveling guides.)

10. Borrow a thin slice of hair from the guide subsection you cut in step 9 and create a back-to-front subsection right in front of this subsection (see Figure 15-3b).

Following your guide, cut it to the same elevation, length, and angle.

11. Repeat this haircutting pattern up to the front perimeter subsection that you cut in step 7.

Repeat this cutting pattern until the entire top has been cut.

12. Addressing the back of the head, take a ½ inch wide by 1½ inch long (1.3 by 3.8 centimeters) vertical subsection, starting at the top/back perimeter line and moving straight down the head. Include a strand of hair from the perimeter line to act as your guide (see Figure 15-3b).

13. Comb the hair straight out from the scalp at a 90-degree elevation. Cutting at a downward diagonal angle, gradually shorten the hair from 2.5 inches to 2 inches (6.4 to 5 centimeters) in length (see Figure 15-3b).

Continue angling and shortening your cutting line, so the hair gradually becomes 1 inch (2.5 centimeters) in length at the crest of the *occipital bone.* (Chapter 5 shares how to locate the occipital bone. Figure 15-3b illustrates the specific cutting instructions.)

14. **Repeat this haircutting pattern until the entire back has been cut down to the crest of the occipital bone (see Chapter 5).**

15. **Addressing the neckline and using the scissors-over-comb technique, taper the hair so that it gradually lengthens to 1 inch as it reaches the crest of the occipital bone (see Figure 15-1 and 15-3b).**

When you reach the base of the occipital bone, slowly begin angling the teeth of the comb toward you as you move up the head. This will gradually lengthen the hair until it's the same length where the two cutting lengths meet.

16. **Continue working your way up the back of the head, using the scissors-over-comb technique, until the entire area has been cut (see Figures 15-1 and 15-3b).**

Check the entire back area for length and blending. Use the scissors-over-comb technique to blend all areas that don't smoothly transition from one length to another (see Figure 15-1).

17. **Addressing the side of the head, separate a ½-inch-wide by 2-inch-long (1.3 by 5 centimeters) vertical subsection, starting at the top/back perimeter line and moving down the side of the head (see Figure 15-3a). Cut the hair at a 90-degree elevation and at a diagonal cutting angle to progressively shorten the hair from 2½ inches to ½ inch at the hairline.**

Make sure the hair is still wet. If you detect any dryness, re-mist the hair.

18. **(Optional) Beginning at the side/bottom hairline you just cut in step 17, use the scissors-over-comb technique to gradually taper the hair from ¼ inch up to ½ inch in length when you're about ½ inch above the ears (see Figure 15-3a).**

If the hair is coarse and sticks up when cut too short, skip this step. The same is true of overly large or protruding ears.

19. **Place the cutting comb teeth side up at the hairline above the middle of the ear to 1 inch behind the ear. Using the scissors-over-comb technique, taper the ends at a diagonal angle to blend where the side and back lengths meet.**

Repeat this cutting pattern until both sides are done.

Carefully check the entire haircut for length and blending.

20. **Use your trimmers to shorten the bottom perimeter of the sideburns to the desired length and adjust the angle, if needed. Using the**

scissors-over-comb technique, layer the sideburns. Connect the back corner perimeter line of the sideburns with your perimeter cutting line that ends right in front of the ear.

TIP

Because most men shave numerous times between haircuts, they tend to whittle away at the shape of their sideburns. Always take extra care to reshape the sideburns in order to make your cut pop.

21. **Use trimmers to sharpen your perimeter lines and clip any stray hairs on the neck.**

Buzz Skill clipper cut

Tools you'll need to complete this tutorial include clippers or trimmers, cutting comb, clips, and a barber pencil.

The "Boys Next Door" clipper tutorial in Chapter 16 is the same haircut as the Buzz Skill cut in this chapter (shown in Figure 15-4), with the exception of the front hairline. A hard, front hairline is popular for many trendy masculine cuts because it adds a sharp-looking detail to even the simplest of cuts.

TIP

The technique used to create a precision hairline is the same as the hard part technique that's mentioned in "Parting the hard way" in this chapter.

FIGURE 15-4:
You can elevate a one-length buzz cut by adding a front hairline design.

© drbimages/Getty Images

To guide the front hairline design, use a white barber pencil (a.k.a. barber chalk) to trace the natural hairline. Then, using trimmers or clippers, clip the front hairline following the pencil lines. Make sure your lines are crisp and clean. The latter usually requires clipping the lines more than once.

Barber pencils are available at beauty supply and some mass-merchandise stores, and on their respective websites.

Fading away

The mechanics of creating a fade cut are the same as a taper cut (see Figure 15-5).

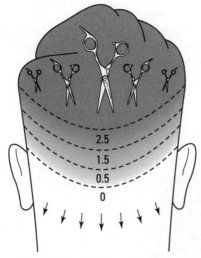

FIGURE 15-5:
Fade cuts are barber mainstays for their more youthful clients and all fashion-focused customers.

TIP

Fade cuts range from low to mid and high fades:

>> Low fades are shortest around the hairline up to the middle of the occipital bone (see Chapter 5).

>> Mid fades are shortest from the hairline up to the top of the occipital bone.

>> High fades can stop at the recession areas of the forehead or go as high as the side perimeters of the top section.

Kicking back with a Trendy Casual cut

Moderate

Tools you'll need for this haircut include a blow-dryer, scissors, clippers, Nos. 1–4 clipper guides, trimmers, cutting comb, and a vent brush.

While traditional business cuts (see "Negotiating a Standard Business cut" earlier in this chapter) remain a very common request, the Trendy Casual cut shown in Figure 15-6 is a classic cut among younger and young-at-heart clients. Doubling as a casual and business cut, this design uses both scissors and clippers to achieve a clean and modern look.

FIGURE 15-6: This casual style can also double as a more youthful business cut.

Photographer: Tom Carson (www.tomcarsonphoto.com); Hair: Alexandra Harris and Alicia Petti; Makeup: Chelsea Police; Michael Christopher Salon, Cleveland, Ohio

The following steps walk you through this cut:

1. **Working on wet (not dripping wet) hair, locate the four corners and separate the top section of hair as explained in Chapter 5. Then, beginning and ending at the back two corners of the top section, create a curved back section as shown in Figure 15-7a. Secure both sections to avoid cutting confusion.**

Make sure the parting for the lower section goes below the crown area and slightly above the top of the occipital bone.

2. **Addressing the back of the head, use trimmers to define the shape of the neckline, as well as the back/side hairline up to the back of the ears. Remove unwanted neck hair (see Figure 15-7a).**

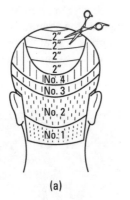 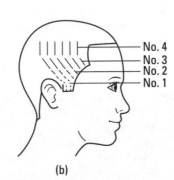

(a)   (b)

© *John Wiley & Sons, Inc.; Illustration by Rashell Smith*

FIGURE 15-7:
How to cut a
Trendy
Casual cut.

3. **Using clippers with a No. 1 guide, clip the hair from the neckline up to the bottom of the occipital bone (see Chapter 5). Arc (rock) the clippers toward you (see Chapter 8) when you reach the bottom of the occipital bone to slightly lengthen the hair (see Figure 15-7a).**

4. **Attach a No. 2 guide to your clippers. Clip the hair from the bottom of the occipital bone (where you left off) to the top of the occipital bone, arcing the clippers as you reach your stopping point (see Figure 15-7a).**

5. **Attach a No. 3 guide to your clippers. Clip the hair to within 2 inches (5 centimeters) of your top section.**

6. **Attach a No. 4 guide to your clippers. Clip the hair up to the back curved section (see Figure 15-7a).**

   Pay particular attention to the areas where you changed guide sizes. If needed, blend the hair using the clippers-over-comb technique by tilting your comb toward you to gradually lengthen the hair and seamlessly blend the two lengths.

7. **Run your comb, teeth side up and in different directions, over the hair you cut in steps 3–6. Use the clippers-over-comb technique to shorten any hair that was missed on your first pass.**

8. **Addressing the sides of the head, attach a No. 2 guide to your clippers. Clip the hair from the side/bottom hairline to midway between the bottom hairline and the top section (see Figure 15-7b).**

9. **Switch to a No. 3 clipper guide. Clip the hair up to 1 inch away from the top section perimeter line.**

10. **Switch to a No. 4 clipper guide and clip the hair up to the top perimeter line.**

11. **Addressing the top/back perimeter, create a thin, side-to-side subsection. Hold the hair at a 90-degree elevation. Using scissors, cut the hair at a horizontal angle and 2 to 3 inches (5 to 7.6 centimeters) in length (your choice). This is now your top traveling guide. Take an identical side-to-side subsection in front of this subsection, identify your guide and repeat the cutting pattern (see Figure 15-7a).**

    Continue cutting the top section until it is trimmed within ¼-inch (0.6 centimeter) of the hairline. Addressing the very front section you just omitted, cut it at a diagonal to lengthen the hair an extra ⅓ inch (0.9 centimeter) (see Chapter 5).

    If the person has recessions along the hairline, cut the hair along the perimeters of these recessions separately. (See Chapter 24 for tips on how to cut thin and receding areas.)

12. **If sideburns are present, shape the outline of the sideburns using trimmers, and then shorten the interior hair by using the trimmers-over-comb technique.**

TIP

Using a vent brush, blow-dry the hair straight back. Once dry, part the hair and run a slick of light-hold wax or pomade (ends and mid-shafts only) to create a more structured style. For casual wear, brush the hair back or to the side, apply a flexible pomade, and lightly tousle the hair with your fingers.

» Cutting designs with girlish panache

» Cutting no-fuss boyish styles

Chapter 16

Getting Snippy with Children's Styles

Tools you'll need for this chapter include scissors, clippers and No. 2 clipper guard, trimmers, blow-dryer, clips, vent brush, soft styling brush, tail comb, pick (pic) comb, and cutting comb.

If you're a parent, your first foray into haircutting is usually with children's hair. Although this task may seem like an easy place to start, performing a haircut on youngsters often takes all the patience and skill you can muster. The good news? By following along with this chapter cutting times will be shorter; results will be better; and kids will look forward to all the goodies — okay, bribes — you have in store for them.

Kids' cuts are much easier for those who have a knack for good planning. If you're an inspirational cutter who never knows exactly what you'll be doing until several minutes after your young charges have been sitting in your chair, you may be in trouble. Preplanning your designs, having all your tools and supplies at the ready, and making sure that you're using your youngest kids' best hours to your advantage will give you a much better chance to have a fairytale ending.

TIP

Chapter 22 gives you loads of information about keeping your tykes calm, safe, and happy while you're tackling their mops. If you're dealing with fidgety, impatient, or grumpy kids, I recommend that you read Chapter 22 first and then return here for my adorable haircutting tutorials.

Getting Practical with Your Pint-Sized Peeps

While children may look like life-sized dolls, their personalities and preferences can shatter that impression within five minutes of sitting in your chair. Many children staunchly defend their right to wear short, long, stylish, or radical hairstyles. Other children are oblivious to how they look, but they're still death on time. When my son was young, for instance, he was so unaware of his appearance that he actually liked to wear his school uniform on weekends and couldn't care less if his haircut had holes in it. Like many impatient children, his biggest demand was getting his hair done pronto, a goal that I've set for every haircut in this chapter.

In all cases it's very important to choose simple styles that also match the child's hair capabilities. If your child has straight hair, for instance, curling the hair every day isn't practical. If your child has curly hair, it's equally unrealistic to choose a style that's typically worn straight. In all cases, the haircuts you do for your wee ones should take into consideration how to keep their hair away from their face. This is important because face-hanging hair obscures their vision and tends to dip into things like finger paint, glue, and ice cream.

TIP

The tutorials in this chapter are for children ranging in age from 2 years old to primary school age. I've limited the tutorials to this age range because once a child hits the double digits, the tutorials in Chapters 12–15 are usually more appropriate.

WARNING

Frequently styling children's hair in tight ponytails or tight braids can cause hair loss due to a condition called *traction alopecia* (extreme or constant pulling on the hair roots). While this hair loss may be temporary, if the hair roots become irrevocably damaged, it's a permanent condition.

TIP

You can test the growth pattern of kids' hair by combing it straight back from the front hairline and letting the hair fall naturally. The way it falls is the direction of its growth. Even easier is observing the direction of the hair at the end of the day. If you always comb the hair to the side and it ends up lying forward, the natural growth pattern is trumping your sense of style. By going with the flow or leaving longer layers on top, you'll have the best chance of creating a manageable haircut that can be combed into place in a matter of seconds and remain that way through playground antics, games, and naps.

Girly Cue Cuts

Petite feminine hairstyles can be short, mid-length, or long. In this section, I share detailed tutorials on how to cut carefree shorter and mid-length styles. I've done this because long hair on youngsters only requires end trims and the occasional hunt for split ends. Both of these techniques are covered in Chapter 10. Bang trims are covered in Chapter 9. If you have a long-haired beauty, the most important thing you can do is to keep their hair healthy and tangle-free. Chapter 17 gives great advice on how to care for their hair.

Petite Chic cut

Moderate

Tools you'll need for this haircut include scissors, blow-dryer, soft styling brush, clips, and cutting comb.

The Petite Chic cut is for toddlers who still have some vellus (baby) hair, as opposed to terminal (mature) hair that begins to appear on the scalp at about 2 years of age. The model in Figure 16-1 has a combination of terminal hair (fringe area) and vellus hair (the balance of the hair).

The Petite Chic cut is ideal for straight or wavy hair.

To complete the Petite Chic cut, follow these steps:

1. **Mist the hair with warm water until the hair is wet, but not dripping wet.**

2. **Separate the hair in half by parting the hair from the crown to behind each ear (see Figure 16-2). Pin away the front half of the hair.**

   Check out Chapter 5 to locate different areas of the head. See Chapter 6 to review different sectioning patterns.

3. **Comb the back section down to a 0-degree elevation (see Chapter 5). Place the side of your non-cutting hand or finger (depending on the head size) about 1 inch (2.5 centimeters) above where you plan to cut the hair to prevent it from moving. Cut the bottom hair straight across to 1 inch past the hairline.**

   If the existing hair is quite long and/or thick, separate the hair into 1-inch-deep horizontal partings.

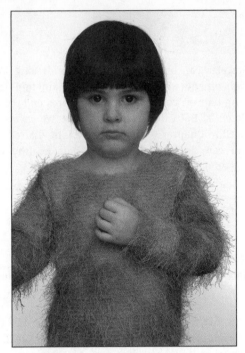

FIGURE 16-1:
Designing kid's cuts that go with the flow of the natural hair growth will keep their hair in place all day.

Photographer: Tom Carson (www.tomcarsonphoto.com);
Hair: Ladies & Gentlemen Salon, Mentor, Ohio

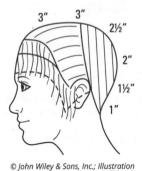

FIGURE 16-2:
How to cut the Petite Chic cut.

© John Wiley & Sons, Inc.; Illustration
by Rashell Smith

4. **Comb the hair at the back/side area straight down. You will be cutting the hair 1 inch in length at the side hairline, which will put your cutting angle at a diagonal (see Figure 16-2). Place the side of your non-cutting hand along the side hairline. Starting at the bottom outside corner of the back hairline and ending at mid-ear level, follow the hairline while cutting the hair to 1 inch in length.**

5. **Repeat step 4 on the opposite side of the head.**

    Always check the length and angle of both sides to make sure they match. If they don't, adjust the cut before proceeding to the front half of the hair.

6. Addressing the front half of the hair that you created in step 2, separate a top section by locating the four corners at the top of the head. (Chapter 5 shows how this is done.) Secure the top section with a clip.

This will create a top section and two side sections.

7. Addressing one side section, comb the hair straight down. Part out a ¼-inch-deep (0.6 centimeter) horizontal section (see Figure 16-2). Pin away the balance of this subsection to avoid cutting confusion.

8. Comb the subsection you separated in step 7 straight down to a 0-degree elevation (see Chapter 5). Without applying tension, cut the hair at a diagonal starting at the midpoint between the jawline and the cheekbone and back to the mid-ear (see Figure 16-2).

To determine the correct angle before cutting the hair, place the back of your cutting comb starting midway between the jawline and cheekbone back to the mid-ear. The hair at the mid-ear should be 1 inch long.

This subsection is now the guide for the balance of the side section.

9. Comb the balance of the side section straight down at a 0-degree elevation. Carefully following your guide that you cut in step 8, cut the balance of the side section.

If the side sections are thick (unusual for toddlers, but still possible), separate and cut the side sections in two or more horizontal subsections.

Repeat steps 8–9 on the other side.

10. Addressing the top section that you created in step 6, separate a ¼-inch-deep front parting that parallels the hairline all along the width of the top section (see Chapter 5). Comb all the hair you just separated to the center of the nose and cut the ends to just below the eyebrows or below the eyes, depending on the desired length (see Chapter 9). This is now your guide to create the fringe shown in Figure 16-1.

If you want the top section (fringe area) to be slightly wider, create a wider parting on each side of the top section, moving diagonally from the back of the top section to the hairline on each side.

Comb the hair over the forehead and view your handiwork. The hair should be slightly longer on each side. If needed, snip any errant ends. Also check the sides to ensure they are exactly the same length.

This is now your fringe guide for the balance of the top section.

11. Unpin the rest of the top section and comb it forward over the forehead and into its finished style position (see Figure 16-1). If the hair is still thin on top, you will be able to see the guide you cut in step 10 through the hair. If you cannot easily see the guide, separate the top section into two horizontal (side-to-side) sections.

12. After combing the hair into the finished style position, cut the ends following your guide.

TIP

To style the Petite Chic haircut, use a soft-bristle styling brush to brush the hair into the desired style position while you blow-dry the hair on a low-heat setting. After completing the blow-dry, apply a thin slick of soft-hold pomade on the front tips you created when diagonally cutting the front/sides of the hair (see Figure 16-1).

Lollipop Kids cut

Moderate

Tools you'll need for this haircut include scissors, blow-dryer, vent brush, clips, cutting comb, and tail comb.

The curly hairstyle seen in Figure 16-3 is actually a layered bob that angles up toward the face to softly frame the jawline. It's moderately difficult to cut, but it's simple to manage because the style can be air-dried or blown straight and looks fantastic with pretty head bands or barrettes. If you really want to go all out for special occasions, bring on the curling iron or flat iron (discussed in Chapter 19 and Chapter 20).

The Lollipop Kids cut works best for children in their early elementary school days. It's most fabulous on Type 2c to Type 3c (wavy to curly) hair (see Chapter 4). This range of hair types has lift and waves or curls that effortlessly provide volume and movement.

The tutorial for the Lollipop Kids cut is broken into two parts: (A) perimeter and (B) layering. If you take this cut one step at a time and work carefully, you'll create a standout style.

Part A: Perimeter cut

The perimeter shape for this cut sets the stage for an overall darling look that curves along the back area and then vertically hugs the jawline. While following the perimeter cut directions, always remain aware of where you are cutting in relationship to the face, jawline, and the side of the neck.

1. Detangle and then mist the hair with warm water until it's wet, but not dripping wet.

2. Part out and secure the hair into six sections: four back and two front/side sections.

FIGURE 16-3:
This girlish style
involves cutting
long layers and a
jaw-hugging
perimeter.

Photographer: Tom Carson (www.tomcarsonphoto.com);
Hair: Ladies & Gentleman Salon, Mentor, Ohio

Chapter 6 includes information and illustrations on several sectioning patterns, including the one you'll be using for this cut.

3. **Part out a horizontal, ¼-inch-deep (0.6 centimeter) subsection from both of the back/bottom sections.**

4. **Without using tension on the hair, trim the back perimeter in a curved line and to the desired length (see Figure 16-4). This is now your first cutting guide. (Chapter 5 explains and illustrates cutting guides.)**

   Carefully check your guide before cutting any more subsections. Make sure that the length on both sides matches perfectly and you're satisfied with the curved perimeter shape. If you need to correct the guide, drop a second ¼-inch horizontal subsection and adjust the length and/or shape. You can only do this one time without it becoming apparent, so give it your best shot.

5. **Increasing the size of your subsections to ½-inch deep (1.3 centimeters), continue dropping subsections and cutting the ends to your guide until the entire back of the head has been cut (see Figure 16-4).**

   Make sure to never lose sight of your guide.

   Always follow the curvature of the head. (Chapter 5 discusses head shapes.)

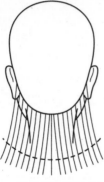

FIGURE 16-4:
How to shape the
perimeter of the
Lollipop Kids cut.

6. **Once the back area of the hair has been cut, comb it straight down and into its finished style position.**

   Check the hair to ensure it is the same length on both sides. If it's not cut correctly, re-pin the back into four sections. Part out horizontal, ½-inch subsections from both back sections until you discover where you lost your guide. Starting at this point, correct the cut discrepancy by retrimming the balance of the back area.

   Pin the back section away from the side sections to avoid cutting confusion.

7. **Unpin one of your side sections and dampen the hair with a fine misting of warm water.**

8. **Part out a horizontal, ½-inch-deep subsection right above one ear and re-pin the balance of this section to prevent cutting confusion. Borrow a strand from the adjacent back section to act as your guide (see Figure 16-5).**

   Chapter 5 provides complete information regarding guides.

9. **Comb this subsection straight down to a 0-degree elevation (see Chapter 5 for elevation information). Following your guide, cut the ends at a horizontal (straight across) angle to the front of the ear. Then start curving the line upward to just below the jawline (see Figure 16-5).**

   Notice how the perimeter line shown in Figure 16-4b only has a slight curve until it reaches the front of the neck. This is important because if you cut a curved angle too soon, it will create a gap in the haircut when dried.

Part B: Layering

The key to a great layered haircut is to create layering that lifts the hair while still blending with the rest of the hair. By carefully following the directions in this section, you create blended layers that are part of, and not separate from, the total style.

10. **Separate the top section by using the four corners at the top of the head to create a rectangular shape. (Chapter 5 walks you through this procedure.) Then divide this section in half by creating a middle, back-to-front part (see Figure 16-5).**

    Pin away the balance of the hair to prevent it from intermingling with your top section and causing cutting confusion.

11. **To figure out where the top layer of the haircut will fall, separate a strand of hair at the back of the top section. Move the strand down the back of the head. Snip the ends when you reach the mid-occipital area (see Chapter 5).**

    This is now your guide for your first top cutting subsection.

12. **Separate a 2-inch-long by ¼-inch-wide (5 centimeters by 0.6 centimeter) subsection on each side of the middle part, including the guide you cut in step 11. Comb the hair from both subsections straight up to a 90-degree elevation above the middle part (see Figure 16-5). Cut the hair at a diagonal angle so that it lengthens as you cut toward the back of the section.**

    This is now your stable guide.

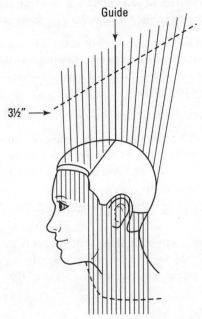

FIGURE 16-5:
How to create long layers for the Lollipop Kids cut.

© John Wiley & Sons, Inc.; Illustration by Rashell Smith

13. **Take all of the hair in the top section and comb it up to your guide that you cut in step 11. Following your guide, cut the top section.**

If the hair is thick or quite a bit longer than your guide, comb the hair up to your guide in more manageable size subsections. You can do this by parting out thinner back-to-front sections and combing them up to your guide.

14. **Comb the hair on both side sections up to your guide. Following the guide line, trim the hair (see Figure 16-5).**

If the hair is too unwieldly to do this, cut one side of the head at a time.

15. **Addressing the back of the head and using a tail comb, divide the hair into two horizontal sections (side-to-side partings).**

16. **Starting at the top/back perimeter line and using the guide that you created in step 11, separate a ¼-inch-wide by 1½-inch-long (0.6 centimeter by 3.8 centimeters) subsection, moving down the back of the head. Comb this section up to a 180-degree elevation (see Chapter 5 for information on degrees of elevation). Starting with your guide, hold your fingers at a diagonal angle and trim the hair to the desired length (reference Figure 16-5).**

This is now your traveling guide.

17. **Comb the back/top section up to your guide line and trim the hair. If the hair is too thick or unmanageable, comb and trim smaller subsections.**

18. **Unpin the back/bottom section. Lightly re-mist the hair with warm water, if necessary. Comb the hair section up to the guide line and, following your guide, cut the hair. If the hair is unmanageable, divide and cut the hair into smaller sections.**

You will have hair that's too short to reach the guideline. Leave this hair as is.

19. **Part out a ⅓-inch deep (0.9 centimeter), shallow, semicircular parting along the hairline between the front two corners of the top section. Comb the hair down without tension and cut the hair to the desired bang shape and length (see Chapter 9).**

Chapter 9 features several fringe tutorials, including the one in step 19.

TIP

To create a dressy style, apply a light styling spray before blow-drying the hair. Curl the hair afterward with a 1-inch (2.5 centimeters) curling iron. (Chapter 19 shares great information about curling irons. Styling tips are covered in Chapter 20.)

BOBBING FOR KIDS CUT

Many adult haircuts are for kids, too. One of the easiest and most practical haircuts you can give a child is a classic bob (see Chapter 13 for bob haircut tutorials). Unlike the old-fashioned kids' bob that screams practicality without a whisper of style, modern bobs are more eye-catching since the bangs are often designed to frame the eyes and/or face, and the perimeters are cut at different angles, depending on which bob style you choose to cut.

The only difference between bobs for adults and bobs for children is the length used when framing the face. For young children, the goal for every haircut should be to keep the hair off their face and out of their eyes. This means cutting the fringe and perimeter lines around the face shorter than directed in Chapter 13.

A straight bob is perfect for children of all ages who have straight Type 1 and Type 2 hair.

Bountiful Curls cut

Moderate

Tools you'll need for this haircut include clips, scissors, and a pick comb.

If the kiddo in your chair has Type 4, mid-length hair (when dry) and wears their hair in a natural style, Bountiful Curls is a dry cut that's sure to please both of you (see Figure 16-6).

Trimming Type 4 hair can be done on dry or wet hair, with curly-hair experts equally divided between which of the two cutting methods is best. (Chapter 4 discusses hair types.) The following tutorial is a dry cut, which I personally prefer when doing light trims on coily hair.

Dry cutting natural Type 4 hair is done by sculpting the hair using shape (outline or silhouette) and form (depth or dimension). It's done on hair that has been shampooed and conditioned two to three days prior to the haircut. This waiting period gives each curl time to completely revert back to its natural shape.

If the hair hasn't been trimmed in three or more months, it will need a serious reshaping. Any time this is the case, I recommend that you have a beauty professional cut the hair. This will create a perfect template to follow when trimming the hair at home.

FIGURE 16-6:
Natural hair trim for coily hair.

© len4foto/Adobe Stock

Follow these steps for the Bountiful Curls cut:

1. **Use your fingers to check for tangles and matting, and lightly lift the hair away from the scalp.**

   - If mild tangles are present, use your fingers to gently separate the curls at the scalp and midshafts.

   - If matting is present, do not proceed with the service. Matting is a sign of neglect and must be dealt with by a beauty professional who specializes in Type 4 hair.

   - Insert a pick comb and lift the hair at the scalp only.

   - If the hair is still somewhat packed down at the scalp, insert your fingertips and gently move the hair back and forth at the scalp only.

2. **Study the shape of the hair.**

   - **First study the shape of the sides of the hair while looking directly at the person's face.** Do the sides need to be reshaped in some areas? Are the bottom areas of the sides that are behind and in front of the ears too voluminous? Are there curls that are significantly longer than the desired hair shape?

   - **Check the outline of the hair by directly facing each side of the head.** Study the shape of the hair from the crown to the back hairline. Does the hair need to be reshaped in some places?

- **Face the back of the head.** Study the sides from that viewpoint and note any regularities that need to be addressed.

- **Inspect the top of the head.** Has it collapsed or does it still have the desired shape?

- **Look for dips (recessed areas) in the style.** Gently pull on the curls in these areas and observe how fast they recoil back to their original shape.

    A strong recoil means that the curls are tighter and have more elasticity than the surrounding hair.

    A weak recoil means the curls are looser and have less elasticity.

    If you pull on them and they remain in the desired style position, it's most likely a styling issue.

3. **Address the sides of the hair. Facing the front of the head, begin sculpting the sides of the hair shape by trimming curls that noticeably fall outside of the desired haircut silhouette (see Figure 16-7). When you reach the side area from the back of the ear down, slightly taper the hair by shaping it at a diagonal cutting angle (see Chapter 5). Doing so will allow the hair to gently curve toward the neck.**

    Any time you see curls that are significantly outside the hair shape, make sure that they aren't positioned in the wrong place before cutting them.

REMEMBER

When you're trimming curls to reshape the hair, less is always more in terms of results.

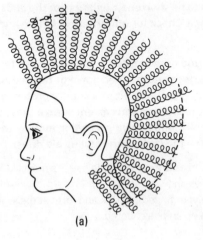
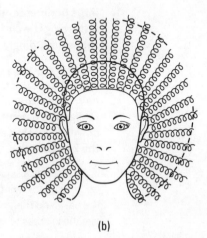

FIGURE 16-7:
How to trim a full, natural hairstyle.

(a)

(b)

© John Wiley & Sons, Inc.; Illustration by Rashell Smith

4. **Repeat step 3 while facing each of the sides of the head. Focus on reshaping the back of the hair from the crown down to the back hairline (see Figure 16-7b).**

5. **Facing the back of the head, trim the side sections that you did not reach when facing directly at the person in your chair. Blend all areas of the sides to ensure a seamless cut and that you have created the desired shape.**

6. **Address the top of the hair. Has it flattened out? To restore some fullness, use your fingers to lightly separate thin, horizontal (side-to-side) subsections of hair throughout the top section. Lift each of these subsections up to a 90-degree elevation without applying tension (see Figure 16-7a). Snip ¼ inch to ½ inch (0.6 centimeter to 1.3 centimeters) off the ends of the curls. Using your fingertips, gently move the hair back and forth at the scalp to encourage lift.**

   Remember that overgrown, flat hair at the top of the head has probably dried flat. Once the hair has been shampooed and conditioned again, lift the hair to encourage more fullness.

   If the hair still resists lifting to your satisfaction, it's time for a professional haircut.

7. **Always check to make sure that you haven't created a step (non-blended line) between the top and the sides or back of the hair. If you have, pick up the curls right along the line of separation. Lightly trim the ends at a diagonal angle (longer toward the back or the sides) to remove the separation line (see Figure 16-7b).**

8. **If the perimeter needs to be shortened, lightly trim the ends without disturbing the curl shape. Check for uniformity of length and adjust the shape accordingly.**

9. **Address any gaps that you noted in step 2. Anywhere you found spring-loaded curls and the curls are not packed down or tangled with other hair, they either need to grow out a bit or a beauty professional needs to realign the haircut. In the interim, you can encourage these curls to calm down by lightly dampening and applying a styling mousse to areas where the hair recesses. Stretch the curls as the styling aid dries.**

   If the hair has a similar curl as the surrounding hair, it's most likely a styling issue. Look for hair tangles and separate them. Take a pick and lift the hair at the base and then move your fingertips back and forth at the scalp to encourage these areas to stand up and be counted.

To style the hair away from the face, slightly dampen and apply a styling gel or mousse to a 1-inch to 1½-inch (2.5 centimeters to 3.8 centimeters) margin around the front hairline and comb the hair back and flat to the head. Using tension, place a paper wrap or neck strip across this area and secure it with clips at the top of each ear. Do not disturb the hair until it is completely dry.

Getting into Boyish Styles

Give your active little ones (and yourself) a break by keeping their hair short enough to look good even though they've spent the better part of the day rolling in the grass.

Boyish cuts can be done with scissors or clippers. In this section, I have included short, traditional styles that use both of these tools to get the job done. There are also several cuts in Chapter 15 that are carefree and appropriate for little ones in need of 20-minute haircuts that require little or no styling.

The Basic Boyish cut

Moderate

Tools you'll need for this haircut include scissors, trimmers, blow-dryer, pick comb, and cutting comb.

The Basic Boyish cut looks good for all hair types but is really exceptional on Type 3 hair (see Chapter 4 to learn more about hair types). My son has Type 3A curls and wears this cut especially well. It's also a fuss-free cut that requires little attention once the curls have been placed after each shampoo (see Figure 16-8). (See Chapter 4 for more information on hair types.)

REMEMBER

If you're dealing with straight Type 1 hair, you'll need to cut the hair a bit shorter. For very curly or coily hair, you'll need to adjust the lengths according to the amount of shrinkage the hair will have after it dries.

Follow these steps for the Basic Boyish cut:

1. **Mist the hair with warm water until the hair is damp. If the hair is curly or coily, use a pick comb (see Chapter 2) to lift and separate the hair.**

FIGURE 16-8:
The benchmark for a Basic Boyish cut is to shape the hair in such a way that the natural curls or waves are free to move and still look great.

© FatCamera/Getty Images

2. Using a cutting comb, comb the hair below the occipital bone straight down to a 0-degree elevation (see Chapter 5). Hold the hair in place about 1 inch (2.5 centimeters) above your cutting line with the side of your non-cutting hand or the teeth of your cutting comb. Following Figure 16-9, cut the back/bottom neckline straight across.

3. Addressing the back/side neckline, comb the hair to the opposite side of where you'll be cutting (for example, if you are cutting the hair on the left side, comb the hair toward the right side).

   Starting at the corner of the neckline, separate a ½-inch-wide (1.3 centimeters) section that parallels the side hairline. Comb the hair down at a 0-degree elevation. Moving from the corner of the bottom hairline up to just behind each ear, cut the hair to 1 inch in length (see Figure 16-9).

   Continue cutting the hair over the ear at a 0-degree elevation while maintaining a 1 inch hair length (see Figure 16-9).

   Repeat step 3 on the other side of the head.

4. Moving to the top of the head, separate the top section by identifying the four corners. (Chapter 5 provides detailed information on how to do this.)

   When done correctly, the top section will be the shape of a rectangle.

   Pin away the hair surrounding the top section to avoid cutting confusion.

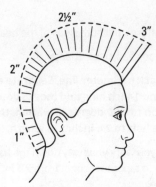

FIGURE 16-9:
How to do a Basic Boyish cut.

© John Wiley & Sons, Inc.; Illustration by Rashell Smith

5. **Working within this rectangular section, make a ½-inch-wide, back-to-front parting, starting at the center/back area of the top section (see Figure 16-9). Cut the hair to 2½ inches (6.4 centimeters) in length.**

   Chapter 5 shares in-depth information about haircutting angles.

   The top section will gradually lengthen from 2½ inches at the back of the top section to 3 inches (7.6 centimeters) at the front hairline.

6. **Borrowing a thin section of hair to use as your cutting guide, make an identical parting in front of the subsection you created in step 5. Using a diagonal cutting angle, cut the hair so that it gradually lengthens to 3 inches at the front hairline.**

   Continue cutting the top section at a diagonal cutting angle and moving from back to front.

7. **Vertically separate the hair from the back corner of the top section down to behind each ear. Pin away the back section to avoid cutting confusion.**

8. **Moving to the top of the vertical parting you created in step 7, separate a vertical subsection that's ½-inch wide and 1 inch long that moves down the side of the head.**

9. **Holding the hair at a 90-degree elevation away from the scalp, cut this section at a vertical (straight down) angle to 2½ inches in length. This is now your new traveling guide.**

   Chapter 5 discusses and illustrates all cutting angles.

10. **Continue separating vertical subsections as you move from your first traveling guide down to the ear. While doing this, use a curved cutting line that gradually tapers the hair from 2½ inches to 1 inch in length at the back hairline.**

    Chapter 5 discusses curved cutting lines.

Continue repeating this cutting pattern until both sides of the head are cut.

Make sure to always follow the head shape (see Chapter 5).

11. **Move to the center of the top/back perimeter line. Separate a vertical subsection that's ½-inch wide and 1-inch long and moves down the back of the head. Comb the subsection to a 90-degree elevation. Using a horizontal cutting angle, cut the hair to 2½ inches in length.**

Repeat this haircutting pattern as you work your way down the back of the head, using a diagonal cutting line to taper the length from 2½ inches at the top to 1 inch at the bottom hairline.

Continue cutting the back of the head, following the instructions in step 11.

12. **Remove stray hairs on the back of the neck (the nape) with trimmers. Check the hair around the ears and snip any stray hairs.**

TIP

Warm up a few drops of a styling tonic in the palms of your hands and run your hands through the hair to enhance the curls.

Boys Next Door buzz cut

Easy

Tools you will need for this haircut include clippers, No. 2 guide, trimmers, blow-dryer, and cutting comb.

The most common boyish cut is the No. 2 buzz cut. You can see a picture of this cut if you flip back to Figure 8-5 in Chapter 8. The Boys Next door buzz cut doesn't need to be combed to stay in place; it has plenty of style longevity as long as you keep the perimeter trimmed; and it's also easy to cut and maintain at home, saving you both time and money. This boyish cut is also tied to two important events in every young person's life: summer vacation and heading back to school.

TIP

A word to the wise: The best way to remove embedded snippets of hair that are part and parcel of every clipper cut is to use a blow-dryer. The problem in doing this is the snippets are blown several feet away, even when using a low-velocity air setting. One option is to clip the hair outdoors. If that isn't possible, I suggest combing out the snippets with the fine-tooth side of a comb, and then sending your youngsters to the bathroom to rinse their hair in the shower once the haircut is done.

Follow these steps for the Boys Next Door buzz cut:

1. **Check the direction of the hair growth all over the head by using your fingers and a cutting comb.**

   Always clip the hair against the grain (growth direction).

2. **Using clippers with a No. 2 guide, begin your clipper cut at the back/bottom hairline. Clip the hair in short strokes and an upward direction. (Chapter 8 covers the basics of clipper cutting.)**

   If you're using clippers with a taper lever, adjust it to clip at ¼ inch (0.6 centimeter) in length.

   Remove embedded snippets with a blow-dryer or the fine-tooth side of your comb.

   For a little more personality, separate the front/center hairline. Trim and point cut this area using scissors after you have clipped the rest of the hair.

3. **Return to your original clipping area at the back/bottom of the hair. This time clip the hair sideways and then diagonally. Once the entire head has been reclipped, run your cutting comb against the hair growth and throughout the hair. If you see snippets that have escaped your clippers, re-clip thee areas.**

   If you want the hair to be longer at the front/center hairline, trim this area now by cutting it to 1 inch (2.5 centimeters) in length. If the hair is thick, lightly point cut the tips of the hair.

4. **Using trimmers, shorten, shape, and crisp up the neckline. Crisp up the lines on the sides of the neck up to the ears. Bending the ear to avoid a cutting mishap, crisp the hairline around the ear and to the front/bottom hairline.**

   View illustrations in Chapter 8. Chapter 15 includes instructions and visuals on how to sharpen the hairline.

5 Making Your Haircuts Shine

Keep hair healthy by choosing the best shampoos and conditioners.

Choose the right styling products for the perfect look.

Get the lowdown on the heat styling tools you need in your haircutting toolkit.

Discover the styling tricks that the pros use.

Chapter **17**

Setting the Stage for Cuts and Styles: Caring for the Hair and Scalp

As a kitchen beautician, you probably won't be shampooing and conditioning every person's hair you cut, but that doesn't mean that proper shampooing and conditioning aren't important to your finished hairstyles. Like anything you create, if the material you're working with is subpar, the end result will suffer.

The information in this chapter is invaluable for your hair and your family's hair. For small children, make sure you use the right hair care products. For adults and teens in your household, stocking their bathrooms with the correct products will give them the best defense against dry, damaged, poofy, frizzy, or limp-as-lettuce hair. Along the way, there are plenty of tips on how to deal with everything from an oily scalp to ways you could unknowingly be harming the hair.

TIP

Before reading this chapter, I suggest that you review Chapter 4, which discusses different hair types — your first clues about what the hair requires to remain healthy and looking its best. (Pssst. I've left some mini explanations throughout this chapter for those who prefer to move forward and never look back.)

THE BEST OFFENSE IS A GOOD DEFENSE

One common misconception is that you always have a second chance to be nicer to your hair. An array of moisturizers and strengtheners are available to help the hair look healthier, but as soon as these products wash out, you're stuck with the same old damaged goods you had before you treated the hair. Hair is mostly made of dead keratin cells; it can't "heal" like your skin. At best, hair care products provide a temporary bandage. This is why practicing prevention is hugely important. When you first notice hair becoming dry on the ends, for instance, you need to assess and treat the condition immediately.

Doing No Harm to the Hair

Although you see a lot of marketing hype about wellness these days, you never really hear much about what a detrimental lifestyle can do to your hair. Hair damage is a big deal. When it becomes damaged, every day can be a bad hair day — something that most people find depressing. Before investing in a new hair care regimen, though, you should look at how you or your family members may be unknowingly harming their hair.

What you're doing *to* your hair is just as important as what you're doing *for* your hair. The following are some common lifestyle habits that damage the hair and how to avoid them.

>> **Frolicking under UV rays:** No matter whether you or your loved ones are cavorting at the beach, lounging by the pool, or catching some rays at your local tanning salon, UV rays fade hair color and cause dryness and brittleness to the point that the only practical solution is to cut off the damage. Sun streaks in the hair, by the way, are a sure sign of sun damage.

   To minimize sun damage, apply a leave-in conditioner that contains a UV ray protectant and, if the hair is long enough, wrap it up in a bun. Not long enough for a bun? Cover the hair with a hat, bandana, or head wrap.

>> **Taking too many shortcuts:** Overly committed people who don't have time to do things right often become their hair's worst enemy. They take shortcuts, such as blasting the hair with hot air to make it dry faster, roughly combing through the hair while it's still tangled, and not conditioning properly for the sake of saving a little time.

Blow-dry damage can be minimized by wrapping the hair in a towel until it's at least 50 percent dry (75 percent is better). While the miracle of absorption is happening, get busy with other things like applying your makeup, shaving, or eating a warm croissant with local honey dribbling down your chin. Then, and only then, dry and style the hair.

>> **Cruising the coast in a convertible sans scarf:** Not only does this activity expose the hair to too much heat and sun, the wind also literally beats it up, creating roughness and *split ends* — the forked little devils that develop on unhealthy strands and ends.

This type of damage can be prevented by simply wearing a protective scarf and, if the hair's long enough, also securing it in a bun to protect the fragile ends from whipping about.

If a motorcycle and helmet are involved, always put a scarf on the hair first to prevent the lining from tearing the hair.

>> **Being a chemical junkie:** The too-frequent use of hair color, hair lightener (bleach), relaxers, or permanent wave solutions is extremely detrimental to the hair. In short, chemical junkies literally burn — sometimes even melt — their hair. The first signs of chemical abuse are dry, dull hair. If chemical abuse continues, it leads to a noticeably rougher hair texture, quick-fading color, the inability to hold a style, and breakage.

Much of this damage can be avoided by refraining from dramatically changing hair colors every month — going from red to blonde, for instance, which requires extra stripping of the existing hair color — and never overlapping hair chemicals when doing *color touch-ups* (treating the new growth at the roots only). Letting the hair grow out at least ½ inch (1.3 centimeters) before retouching the hair color makes it easier to avoid overlapping applications. This same advice applies to chemical relaxers.

If you or someone you know is having serious hair loss or breakage caused by harsh chemical services, do not touch the hair. Instead, always recommend that they book a consultation with a stylist that is a certified *trichologist* (certified specialist in hair health). If the scalp is irritated or injured, you should recommend that they seek the help of a dermatologist right away.

>> **Restless sleeping:** A little bit of tossing and turning is okay, but when restless sleeping becomes a daily gymnastic event, the hair can become worn to the point that it looks like a frayed rope.

If this sounds like you, while you're waiting for your nerves to settle down, rest your head on a satin pillowcase to allow the hair to glide easily across the fabric. If your hair is Type 3C or any Type 4 texture, always pin up or wrap your hair to preserve the style and wear a satin hair bonnet while sleeping.

WILD AND WOOLY MOTORCYCLE RIDES

A true example of the unforgiving nature of hair happened to a stylist that I once knew. She was so obsessed with her hair that we nicknamed her Goldilocks. Every conversation you had with this woman ended up being about her hair, and when she grew tired of talking about it, she encouraged others to pick up the thread and share their thoughts. One hot day, a handsome client came to our salon and offered her a ride on his motorcycle. Impulsively, she hopped on the back and away they went. One hour later, she returned with her hair standing on end and — I swear — a head full of split ends. I was stunned to see how fast the heat and wind beat up her hair. It happens like that sometimes, so never take a chance by treating your hair badly even once in a while.

TIP

To find out if someone has hair breakage, ask them to wear a shirt that's the opposite lightness or darkness of their hair. If you're dealing with blond hair, for instance, ask them to wear something black. If you're evaluating dark hair, ask them to wear something white. Then, brush through the hair when it's dry. If you see broken bits of hair on the fabric, the hair is in need of more moisture and hydration. You should also suggest that they use more appropriate haircare products, turn down the heat on their styling tools, and offer to do a thorough split-end cut (see Chapter 10). If they're willing to lose a couple inches of length, do a complete haircut too.

AUTHOR
SAYS

The one hair treatment that I use and recommend for weak, dry, and brittle hair is the K18 Leave-In Molecular Repair Hair Mask. It's a miracle worker when it comes to strengthening and re-balancing stressed hair.

Avoiding the Overuse of Hair Products

Dull hair has a one-dimensional quality due to its lack of *shine*. When trying to decide why someone's hair is dull, the first thing you should look for is any coating that's clinging to the hair shaft. This is especially important when the hair feels normal — no roughness, breakage, or split ends — but does feel coated and looks incredibly dull.

REMEMBER

The four telltale signs that there's product buildup on the hair:

» Hair is dull and lackluster, despite being in good condition.

» It doesn't feel clean after being shampooed.

>> It's limper than usual.

>> The hair is stringy (strands cling together).

Most often, a coating builds up on the hair when people regularly use too much of any product, use the wrong product formulations, or are not properly rinsing their hair. Finding out which shampoos and conditioners people are using and how they shampoo their hair at home usually reveals at least part of the problem. If they're using a rich formula for dry hair, for instance, but their hair is normal, the hair can look dull and dirty soon after being shampooed.

Overuse of styling aids also creates a coating on the hair. Styling sprays and hair sprays (fixatives) are meant to be sprayed 10 inches (25.4 centimeters) or more away from the head, to create a diffused application (see Chapter 18 for more information).

The above advice also pertains to lazy days spent swimming in lakes and rivers, which are chock–full of minerals that attach to the hair.

POOL HAIR, *DO* CARE

If you have a little mermaid or merman on your hands who loves spending every summer swimming in the pool, you need to deal with those nasty stains that turn blonde hair into a putrid shade of green and make darker hair colors look dull and ashen. This greenish hue comes from chlorine oxidizing the copper in the water, which then binds this metal to the hair. Fortunately, swimmers don't have to choose between having fun and being beautiful. Beating swimmers' stains and damage is as easy as developing some sensible hair care habits, along with purchasing special products to permanently defeat the green.

You can find numerous swimmer shampoos that are sold through retail outlets, beauty supply stores, and salons. For my clients, I recommend Malibu C Swimmer's Wellness products that leave the hair stain-free, soft, and in good (even better) condition.

- Before jumping in the water, rinse the hair for 60 seconds to ensure that it's wet through and through. Thoroughly wetting the hair prevents it from absorbing as much chlorine or other undesirable elements found in the water.

- If the hair's long enough, put it in a bun to protect the ends from too much sun exposure. Sun exposure creates *hair porosity,* rendering it unable to retain a healthy moisture level or hair color. Porous hair also lacks sufficient elasticity, making it more susceptible to breaking.

(continued)

(continued)

- Encourage people close to you (including you) to cover their hair any time they're not in the water.

- Everyone should rinse their hair immediately after getting out of the water — even if they're only taking a rest.

- At the end of swimming, immediately shampoo and condition the hair.

- Look for any signs of buildup — dull, ashy ends, green hair, or even a stained scalp. Whip out the swimmer's shampoo the moment you suspect that pool water may be getting the upper hand.

- Have swimmers step up their deep-conditioning schedule to once a week. Deep conditioners include products like intense moisturizers, protein treatments, or a combination of the two to protect the health of their hair. These products are easy to spot because they're clearly labeled on the front of the jar or bottle. Marketing words typically used to describe these products are *strengthener, reconstructor, and deep treatment.*

- Always have your family use hair care products with sunscreen and antioxidant benefits. The right products list these benefits on their labels, and usually include rich antioxidant and UV filters such as vitamins C and E, sunflower seed oil, or ginseng.

Testing Hair Porosity

Whether shopping for a conditioner, leave-in conditioner, or deep conditioning treatment, it's important to first determine the porosity of the hair. In simple terms, *hair porosity* is the degree that your hair accepts and retains moisture (oil) and hydration (water). The less porous the hair is, the more tightly the cuticle layer adheres to the hair, making it susceptible to thick coatings of products and natural sebum. The more porous the hair is, the drier it will be because it has less ability to retain moisture and hydration. If you or someone in your family has medium porosity hair, which accepts and retains healthy amounts of moisture and hydration, welcome to the golden circle of hair.

To test for porosity, pluck out a hair from the front, back, and both sides of the head, put them in a bowl of tepid water, and leave them there for five minutes. (Testing strands from different areas of the head will let you know whether the hair has a uniform porosity or not.)

>> **Low porosity:**

- Floats on the surface of the water

- Has a tight cuticle that resists absorption

- Takes forever to dry

- Ideal porosity for light spray-on conditioners

- A gentle clarifying shampoo should be used once a month (or as needed) to remove buildup on the cuticle layer.

>> **Medium porosity:**

- Takes a long time to sink to the bottom

- Has a slightly open cuticle

- Looks its best when treated with conditioners that contain light plant-based oils such as argan, grapeseed, or jojoba

- Benefits from the application of a light leave-in conditioner between regular conditioning applications

>> **High porosity:**

- Quickly sinks to the bottom

- Has a wide-open cuticle

WHAT IS SEBUM AND WHY IS IT IMPORTANT?

I mention sebum throughout this chapter because it's an important factor in whether most people are having a good or bad hair day. Any time the scalp is greasy or dry and itchy, there is too much or too little sebum present on the skin.

Sebum is an oily, waxy substance that is produced by our body's sebaceous glands, which are found in abundance on the scalp. It's a mixture of fatty acids, waxes, sugars, and other natural chemicals that combine to form a protective barrier to prevent skin dehydration. Because of its sticky consistency, it also contains sweat, dead skin cells, and tiny particles of whatever is floating in the air. A growing number of scientists suspect that sebum may also have antimicrobial and antioxidant capabilities. If true, sebum may be one of the first barriers against harmful bacteria and protect the skin against free radical activity that's caused by environmental pollutants, UV rays, and other nasties that can damage the skin.

- Hydration quickly enters and exits interior of the hair

- Ideal for cream-based conditioners that increase the level of hydration in the interior of the hair and moisture to help seal the cuticle layer

- Needs deep conditioning treatments (weekly or bi-weekly) formulated for damaged or curly/coily hair

Perfecting Your Family's Hair Care Routine

Shampooing and conditioning the hair is a routine task that all of us have done thousands of times in our lives. So, what could I possibly share that you don't know already? For many people, the short answer is, "plenty."

Avoiding common cleansing missteps

Hair is a dead material. The condition of the hair largely depends on what is done to it between the time it sprouts out of the scalp to when it's cut off. The following list covers ways to make sure you're shampooing and conditioning properly to avoid common missteps.

>> **Use warm, never hot, water.** Hot water strips the hair of protective oils, leaving it susceptible to dehydration, brittleness, and breakage. It also dehydrates the scalp, causing the skin to become sensitive, itchy, and flaky.

>> **Thoroughly wet the hair.** Before applying shampoo, make sure the hair is thoroughly drenched with water right down to the scalp. If the hair is short and thin, this will only take a few seconds, but if the hair is super-thick and oily, it could take 30 seconds or more. This is important because water helps to equally distribute the shampoo throughout the hair.

>> **Use the correct amount of shampoo.** Applying a palmful of shampoo is way too much for even the thickest hair. Doing this will coat the hair because it's almost impossible to completely rinse out, especially when it contains conditioning ingredients. For nearly all shampoos, a dime-sized dollop is more than enough for thin or short hair, and a quarter-sized dollop is an ample amount for longer and thicker hair.

>> **Emulsify the shampoo.** Slapping shampoo on the back of the head and then trying to distribute it throughout the hair is a bad habit that usually starts in childhood when kids first start shampooing their own hair. (One of the best grooming habits you can teach your kids is how to properly cleanse their hair.) Once the hair is thoroughly drenched and the proper amount of shampoo has

been dispensed on one palm, always emulsify the product by rubbing both palms together until the shampoo expands.

>> **Cleanse the hair strands last.** The first place that should be shampooed is the scalp. Sebum is concentrated in this area, and because it's a sticky substance, it collects a lot of bacteria, debris, and styling aids. Because the scalp skin tends to be sensitive, removing impurities also helps to prevent inflammation. Once the scalp has been lightly massaged with the fingertips — not the fingernails — in a circular motion (to help prevent tangling), start working the product down the strands. Shampoo the hair by gently squeezing it to aid in the cleansing process without roughing up the cuticle. If there is a load of styling aids on the hair, also leave the shampoo on the hair for an extra minute before rinsing.

>> **Thoroughly rinse the hair.** Starting at the top/front, rinse the hair thoroughly. (Rinsing the top area last reintroduces shampoo to areas that have already been rinsed.) Once the hair is rinsed, repeat this process one more time.

>> **Apply the conditioner strategically.** Always apply the conditioner in layers. Emulsify a dime-sized dollop of conditioner by rubbing the palms together and then applying it to the driest areas first (usually the ends and the outside layers of the hair). After the conditioner has been applied, gently squeeze the hair to encourage better product distribution and absorption. If the hair still feels dry and rough after a minute, dispense another dime-sized dollop and apply it to these same areas. Dispense another dime-sized dollop of conditioner and massage the product through the rest of the strands. Repeat if necessary. Unless the scalp is naturally dry, avoid applying conditioner right next the scalp. Thoroughly rinse the hair, starting at the front/top of the hair.

How often should you shampoo your hair?

That's a million-dollar question. While there isn't a single answer to this question, there is a right answer for each person. How often you shampoo your hair depends on how much or how little sebum your scalp produces, the amount and types of styling aids you use, whether you participate in vigorous workouts or outdoor activities, or any time your hair smells stale and dirty.

Speaking of stinky hair, certain medications can cause odors on the scalp, as well as where you spend the majority of your day. If you work at or near a cosmetic counter, for instance, your hair could smell like a mixture of lavender dreams and earthy wonderland until you shampoo your hair. Too, when a buildup of perspiration mixes with the bacteria on your scalp, it starts releasing an odor that smells like a combination of a wet German shepherd dog and musty body odor (truth).

TRAINING HAIR TO GO LONGER BETWEEN SHAMPOOS?

This claim refers to controlling oily hair. The problem with this belief is that you can't train your hair to go longer between shampoos because it doesn't produce sebum (see the sidebar "What is sebum and why is it important?" in this chapter). The trend of stretching the time between shampoos should be claiming, "You can train your *sebaceous glands* to reduce the production of sebum."

Our body is an incredible human factory that removes waste, repairs damaged skin, and replenishes protective substances produced by the body, including sebum. The over-production of sebum can be caused by hormonal activity, heat, exercise, stress, using harsh products, or genetics, to name just a few oily culprits.

The process of training the sebaceous glands to chill out claims to be done by gradually extending the time between shampooing the hair. If someone normally shampoos their hair five times a week, for instance, they would gradually lengthen that time to four times a week, then three times a week, and so forth until they reach their goal of one shampoo per week, per month, or never. Being an oily-haired person, I tried this "system" a few months ago, but my personal oil factory just kept working overtime. However, I've read glowing reviews by people who claim that it works.

Personally, I think this fad could cause more harm than good because the scalp needs frequent TLC. To better manage oily hair, see "Special tips for oily scalp and hair" later in this chapter.

Caring for Dry and Oily Scalps

If you have what's commonly referred to as a "normal" scalp, you probably never pay attention to it. It doesn't itch, flake, or feel as tight as an old-fashioned swimming cap. But if you have a dry or oily scalp, your appearance and physical comfort require constant attention to keep it as healthy as possible and do what you can to help balance the production of sebum.

Special tips for dry scalp and hair

Chronic dry scalp is a condition that's caused by insufficient sebum covering the scalp. Dry scalp can be genetic or caused by poor nutrition, overall body dehydration, low humidity, hormonal fluctuations, stress, food sensitivities, using harsh haircare products, and much more.

If anyone is unsure about why their scalp is dry, they should consider seeking the help of a naturopathic physician, as a dry scalp is very often caused by vitamin and fatty acid deficiencies. This same type of physician can also order hormone tests, blood work, and check for other internal and external factors that may be contributing to a parched scalp.

The following tips help to retain moisture on the scalp and maintain moist and supple locks:

>> Use mild, rich shampoos and conditioners. Alternate regular shampoos with a gentle co-washing product (see "Getting Clean with Co-Washing" in this chapter.)

>> Gently wash and thoroughly rinse the hair with cool water.

>> Apply a natural-based scalp oil every other day or as needed. My current favorites are Alikay Naturals Essential 17 Hair Growth Oil and Eden Bodyworks Papaya Castor Scalp Massaging Serum. Both are quickly absorbed by the scalp, are non-greasy, and relieve itchiness.

>> If the scalp is tight, massage the scalp right after you apply the serum.

>> Use a scalp scrub (see "Giving the Scalp a Scrub-a-Dub-Dub" later in this chapter to clear away flakes and coatings at least once a month.

>> Do a deep conditioning treatment once a week. I personally love Kerastase Paris Nutritive Masquintense for Type 1 and Type 2 hair; Jessicurl Deep Conditioning Treatment for Type 3 hair; and TGIN Honey Miracle Mask for Type 4 hair. (See Chapter 4 for more information on hair types.)

TIP

Because there are many quality conditioning products on the market, shop around before settling on a single product. (Hint: If available, purchase travel-size products to try a variety of conditioning treatments without breaking your budget.)

>> Apply a leave-in conditioner to seal down the cuticle and keep the hair moist and hydrated. For Type 4 hair, I love Alikay Naturals Lemongrass Leave-In Conditioner. For a lighter leave-in conditioner, Aveda Nutriplenish Leave-In Conditioner is my go-to product. The latter has a natural scent that's to die for, and the conditioning benefits last for up to three days.

Special tips for oily scalp and hair

The following tips can help manage what I call "oily head syndrome":

TIP

>> Use shampoos that claim to be volumizing, strengthening, or balancing, which are less moisturizing and more effective at removing excess oil without stripping the scalp bare.

>> Wash and condition your hair using warm — never hot — water. If you're heartier than I am, use tepid or even cold water for better results.

   If you're like me, you're probably wondering how to tell that you're using tepid water. Tepid water is neither cool nor hot to the touch and only slightly warmer than body temperature.

>> Because most people with an oily scalp and mid-length or longer hair have two separate conditions — also called combination hair (oily scalp and dry midshafts and ends) — treat these two areas separately by applying a hydrating and moisturizing conditioner on dry hair away from the scalp and a light conditioner (or none at all) next to the scalp.

>> For anyone who shampoos daily or every other day, only cleanse the scalp and then rinse the shampoo through the rest of the hair.

>> After cleansing and conditioning, rinse the hair with tepid or cool water for 60 to 90 seconds to prevent products from building up on your strands and to discourage the release of additional sebum.

>> If the fringe area becomes oily in no time at all, wet or dry shampoo this area separately between full shampoos and use blotting tissues on the forehead a few times a day. I personally use Boscia Black Charcoal Blotting Linens because they're made from 100 percent natural abaca tree fiber (a.k.a. Manila hemp) and are free of synthetic fragrances or other known irritants like methylparaben.

>> Avoid excess heat when blow-drying the hair.

>> Refrain from frequently touching or running your fingers through the hair.

>> Clean all used hairbrushes and combs on a weekly basis to avoid reintroducing styling gunk and oils onto the scalp and strands.

>> Resist brushing the hair at the scalp any more than is necessary as this stimulates the release of sebum.

>> Change pillowcases at least once every three days to prevent the sebum and styling aid residue that's absorbed by these coverings from being reintroduced to the hair.

LIVING IN BALANCE: HAIR AND SCALP pH

The pH scale ranges from 0 to 14 with 0 to 6 being acidic, 7 being neutral, and 8 to 14 being alkaline. Neutral substances like water have a pH of 7. The natural pH of hair, scalp, and sebum is between 4.5 and 5.5. This natural acidity prevents fungi and bacteria from growing on the scalp. It also keeps the cuticle layer closed and the interior layers of the hair in good condition. The packaging or literature accompanying hair care products should state the pH level of the product. If the product only claims to be pH balanced, keep in mind that it may have a pH of up to 7.

So how do you maintain the normal pH of your hair and scalp? The DIY solution is old-fashioned vinegar. You can make your own vinegar rinse by adding two tablespoons of apple cider vinegar to one cup of warm water. After you conclude your shower hair care routine, pour this homemade vinegar rinse on your hair, leave it on for a minute or two, and then rinse with cool water. The one big drawback is that a homemade vinegar rinse can dry the hair and deposit a sharp, pungent odor. A better alternative is to use a product that's made to balance and restore the pH of hair. My go-to pH balancing product is the Color Extend Vinegar Rinse by Redken, which doesn't leave the hair dry or smelling like pickled beets.

Selecting Shampoos and Conditioners Based on Hair Types and Conditions

The following information is based on hair types (review Chapter 4) and hair conditions, including damaged hair that feels rough when you pinch and then slide your fingers toward the ends; chips off at the ends when you brush or comb through the hair; has widespread split ends; or feels dry and brittle.

Before putting even one toe inside a store or accessing a beauty site with the intention of buying a shampoo and conditioner, you should know the particular hair type and condition of your hair and your family members' hair.

The following list includes recommended hair care based on hair types. Keep in mind that if the hair has been treated with permanent color, permanent wave solution, permanent relaxer, or lightener (bleach), it should always be treated as fragile hair.

» **Type 1A and Type 1B (straight, fine hair):** Avoid rich, conditioning shampoos and conditioners as they will weigh down the hair and also risk coating it with silicones or oils that cause what little body the hair has to collapse.

» **Type 1C (straight, fine/medium texture hair):** Use a shampoo for normal hair and a moderately rich conditioner, especially on the very top (outside) layers and ends of the hair. Many products that claim they are formulated for normal to dry hair also will work for this hair type.

» **Type 2A (loose waves that lack definition):** Follow the care instructions for Type 1C, except after applying the conditioner throughout the hair, apply extra conditioner around the hairline, on the ends, and anywhere else the hair tends to frizz.

» **Type 2B (more defined waves, greater tendency to frizz):** Use a shampoo and conditioner for dry hair. During the conditioning phase, apply throughout the hair and then directly add a dab to all areas that tend to frizz, including the hairline and the ends. Press your fingers onto the targeted hair and smooth it from root to end.

» **Type 2C (strong waves, loves to frizz):** Quite often, Type 2C has a slightly coarser texture, which requires hair care products with more weight and richness. For shampoos, alternate between curly and dry hair formulas, and always use a conditioner for dry, frizzy hair. Like Type 2B, reapply dabs of conditioner in all areas that are prone to develop a rough texture or frizz and press the product onto the hair, moving from root to end. Make sure to leave the conditioner on the hair for a couple of minutes, or about the same amount of time that it takes to sing your favorite shower tune.

» **Type 3A to Type 3C (curly, loves to frizz, tends to be chronically dry):** Use rich shampoos made for curly hair. Conditioners should be highly hydrating and moisturizing. Massage the product onto the hair by separating 1-to 2-inch (2.5 to 5 centimeters) sections, and then pressing the conditioning product onto the hair from root to end. After the hair is rinsed and towel-blotted, apply a lightweight, leave-in conditioner throughout the hair, with added product along the hairline and ends. I recommend that these hair types also be treated with a rich moisturizing and hydrating mask at least once every two weeks. Curly hair types can benefit from co-washing between regular weekly shampoos.

» **Type 4A to Type 4C (coily, fragile, chronically dry and frizzy):** Type 4 hair is the neediest and most fragile hair type, but with proper care, it can be gorgeous and shapely. In general, co-washing the hair every week will leave the hair moist, fresh, and ready to spring into action. Applying a daily leave-in conditioner keeps the co-wash results fresh. Even so, washing the hair with a very gentle shampoo should be done every two weeks to one month. See the sections "Special Tips for Dry Scalp and Hair" and "Getting Clean with Co-Washing" in this chapter.

Hair products should always be made specifically for coily hair, and a deep conditioning and hydrating treatment should be done on a weekly to bi-weekly basis. Also, pay particular attention to the condition of the scalp, which can develop flakiness, itchiness, and tightness if not properly cared for with the regular application of a scalp oil — pure botanical oils work best — and a monthly scalp scrub (see "Giving the Scalp a Scrub-a-Dub-Dub" in this chapter).

The manufacturing processes and plastic packaging required for liquid shampoos and conditioners are incompatible with a pure green lifestyle. If these factors concern you, see "Sidling Up to the Bar" — the next section in this chapter.

Sidling Up to the Bar

Like all products, there are great, not-so-great, and awful bar shampoos and conditioners. However, with so many of these products on the market, there are probably more than a few that could be just right for your needs.

In terms of packaging, bar hair care only requires minimal, biodegradable packaging and no plastic or petroleum packaging of any kind. They are also typically free of potentially harmful chemicals such as aldehydes, propylene glycol, and sodium hydroxide. Some natural shampoo bars contain naturally occurring sulfates that may or may not cause sensitivities with prolonged use. I don't recommend buying a specific hair care bar unless it only contains natural fragrances (synthetic-free) and essential oils (to help purify the scalp).

Like any new habit, it takes time and patience to find the best hair care bars for your hair and lifestyle. If you don't find shampoo and conditioner bars that you love on your first try, pass them on to your family members to try and purchase a different brand/formulation for your hair.

TIP

Shampoo and conditioner bars are great for backpacking and camping (less weight), and while going through the tedious process of airport screenings.

Generally speaking, shampoo and conditioner bars are available in three categories:

>> **Cold-pressed bars** are the most natural and rely on ingredients such as olive oil to balance the moisture content of the hair.

>> **Glycerin-based bars** produce the least amount of lather and are extremely gentle to the scalp and hair.

>> **Surfactant bars (shampoos)** produce the best lather and may contain sodium lauryl sulfate (SLS) or sodium laureth sulfate (SLES), or a gentler surfactant like decyl glucoside (a glucose-based surfactant).

Because hair care bars tend to be waxier than their bottled alternatives, using these bars directly on the hair can cause a progressive buildup. Instead, rub the wet bar between the palms and apply it like a traditional shampoo. If you feel a buildup in your hair, use an apple cider rinse (see "Living in balance: Hair and scalp pH" in this chapter).

Getting Clean with Co-Washing

Co-washing refers to a cleansing conditioner that's used in lieu of a traditional shampoo. It's ideal for Type 4 hair and can also be suitable for Type 3 hair that tends to become dry and brittle on day 2 or 3 after a traditional cleansing.

REMEMBER

When co-washing the hair, it's important to focus mainly on the scalp by massaging this tender skin with the fingertips — never the fingernails — for at least 90 seconds. This will help to better cleanse and relax the scalp and increase the microcirculation to encourage a healthier scalp.

The challenging part of this cleansing method is finding the right product for the hair and scalp and establishing a routine that keeps the hair fresh and moist without ever looking dull and greasy. Although many people use their favorite conditioner to co-wash their hair, I don't recommend doing this. Preferred co-wash products contain mild cleansers to lightly cleanse the scalp and slow the buildup of flakes and product residue, as well as dirt and grime that naturally accumulate on our hair as we go about daily life. Co-washing products are available in foaming and non-foaming formulas.

TIP

Two co-washing products that I particularly love are Oribe Cleansing Crème for Moisture & Control (energizes the scalp and restores moisture balance) and Joico Co+Wash Whipped Cleansing Conditioner (reduces frizz, defines curls, and does not leave a greasy coating).

Leave-In Conditioners: Giving Hair Frequent Sips of Water and Moisture

Setting the stage for styling often requires the regular application of a leave-in conditioner, especially on Type 3 and all Type 4 hair. Even the occasional use of a leave-in conditioner on Type 1 and Type 2 hair can be beneficial on days when there's low humidity or the hair has been challenged in some way (see "Doing No Harm to Your Hair" earlier in this chapter).

Leave-in conditioners are designed to hydrate and lock in moisture, and to keep the hair silky, soft, and pH balanced (see "Living in balance: Hair and scalp pH" earlier in this chapter). They should also contain a heat shield to slow the burn when using heat styling tools, as well as UV filters to protect the hair from sun damage.

You should only buy leave-in conditioner that offer these six benefits:

» Re-hydrates the hair

» Locks in hydration with lightweight oils like argan and jojoba

» Refreshes the overall appearance of the hair

» Discourages flyaways, frizz, and static electricity

» Protects the hair from detrimental UV rays and high-heat damage

» Does not build up on the hair

Giving the Scalp a Scrub-a-Dub-Dub

You exfoliate your face and your body, but did you know that you should also exfoliate your scalp? Scalp scrubs remove dead skin cells and product buildup and contain skin-nourishing ingredients the scalp craves. The info in this section can help you hack your way through a jungle of marketing gibberish and focus on proven benefits.

While scrub materials vary, they do have one shared goal: to remove the accumulation of dead skin cells and clingy product residue without damaging the scalp. Some of the most common scrub materials are Himalayan or sea salt, sugar crystals, plant-based exfoliating beads, oatmeal, or finely crushed apricot kernels. Some scrubs contain papaya or pineapple enzymes that break down dead skin cells so they can be washed away. Salicylic and alpha hydroxy acids can also be included for this same reason.

Scalp scrubs should also contain nourishing and soothing ingredients, such as almond or jojoba oil; moisture-retentive ingredients like coconut or olive oil; and *humectants* like panthenol or aloe vera, which also help to calm the scalp and keep it moist. Many also contain energizing ingredients such as peppermint or caffeine to stimulate the microcirculation and refresh the scalp.

My current scalp scrubbing favorites are R+Co Crown Scalp Scrub for oily scalps (that's me), which contains non-irritating salicylic acid and kaolin clay, and Philip B. Peppermint Avocado Scalp Scrub (for all my family members) that exfoliates, attracts water to the skin, and naturally purifies the scalp with eucalyptus oil.

WARNING

While this type of product is categorized as a "scrub," you shouldn't vigorously scrub the scalp while using a scalp scrub. Confusing, right? Any time you cleanse or scrub your scalp only use your finger pads or a special scalp brush and apply light pressure while gently massaging the scalp.

REMEMBER

Make sure to read the label before buying any scalp scrub. If you have a sensitive scalp, only buy products that are made for sensitive skin.

WARNING

Overusing scalp scrubs can cause scalp irritation and increase flaking. On a normal scalp, you shouldn't use a scalp scrub more than once a week, with two weeks being preferable; sensitive scalps should be scrubbed no more than once a month. Choose your products carefully to avoid irritating your scalp!

To achieve the best results, follow these three easy steps:

1. **On damp hair, apply the scrub directly on the scalp in sections: top, sides, and back. Do your best to avoid overlapping the scrub onto your hair.**

2. **Gently massage your scalp for up to two minutes, using your fingertips or a soft scalp brush with rounded bristle tips. Massage the scalp in small circular motions to prevent tangling the hair.**

3. **Rinse thoroughly with cool water.**

Refreshing the Hair with Dry Shampoos and Conditioners

If you want to add a few more days to your style longevity before using a wet shampoo and conditioner, this section is perfect for your needs. Dry shampoos and conditioners are available in spray and powder forms. Sprays work best on fine or thin hair. Those with coarser hair types may find that powder is more effective because of the added density at the scalp. Some dry shampoos go for the great sop, while others absorb oil while giving the hair a piecey texture — a big deal for fine hair types. Dry shampoos and conditioners help to moisturize, fight frizz, and boost shine. Both are meant to be used between wet shampoos and conditioners.

Dry shampoos: Sopping up sebum and uninvited debris

Dry shampoo sops up perspiration and excess oils on the scalp that can seep onto the first couple inches of the hair, as well as environmental impurities and odors. Unlike regular shampoo that's formulated with water and cleansing agents that rinse away oils and impurities, dry shampoo's active ingredients are made up of alcohol (spray form), along with various starches, clay, talc, or crushed minerals — including tourmaline. Some dry shampoos also boast having micro-sponges that absorb oil, sweat, and dirt, while making the hair smell fresh and clean.

Speaking of smelling fresh, because of the various scents used in dry shampoos to deal with stale-smelling hair, make sure that you choose a product with a scent you wouldn't mind "wearing" for a day or even longer.

REMEMBER

Dry shampoos *refresh* rather than *cleanse* the hair. The only way to cleanse the hair is with a liquid or bar shampoo. And as nifty as dry shampoos are, they aren't meant to replace cleansing shampoos. Overuse of dry shampoos can not only make the hair dry, dull, and stringy, but it also can create an unhealthy scalp environment that could lead to everything from an itchy scalp to actual medical conditions.

WARNING

Safety concerns about talc have been discussed and tested by countless researchers since 1972. While the jury is still out regarding whether talc contributes to certain cancers, I believe that when in doubt, don't do it. Because of this concern, I avoid talc-based dry shampoos and recommend that you do too.

Reading hair care instructions only as a last resort can create a bad hair day. Instead, check out my four dry shampoo tips to live by, and I promise you'll love the way your hair looks and feels:

>> Dry shampoos should only be used on dry — never wet — hair.

>> They don't replace traditional cleansing shampoos.

>> They're not recommended for very dry hair or scalp.

>> Using too much dry shampoo in one sitting can cause a white powdery film to accumulate on the hair, make the hair look dull and stringy, and prevent the product from working as intended.

TIP

If you find that using dry shampoos makes your scalp dry or itchy, there are waterless shampoos that contain soothing ingredients. Two such products are One More Day (with zinc) by Philip Kingsley and Klorane Dry Shampoo with Oat Milk.

Dry conditioners: Replacing lost moisture and shine

Dry conditioners can be used to hydrate dry hair and refresh dry strands any time between wet conditionings. They can also combat frizz and add shine. Using a dry shampoo on the roots and a dry conditioner on the midshafts and ends is a great style cheat on days you're due to cleanse and condition your hair, but you'd rather be doing (insert your favorite activity) instead.

The lightweight oils that are typically found in dry conditioners include sunflower seed extract (UV filter), panthenol (humectant), and seed butters (moisture). Several dry conditioners can even cancel frizz and flyaway parties that seem to have a social life of their own. Many also include lightweight silicones for slip and shine. Depending on the products, they can also add texture while doing good by the hair.

Unlike dry shampoos, dry conditioners are suitable for all hair types, including coily hair.

WARNING

Before purchasing a dry shampoo or conditioner, carefully study the ingredient label. Pure powders have fewer ingredients than spray powders, which require alcohol and propellants to dispense the product. Some contain methylparabens (preservative with a risk for allergic reactions), aluminum, and synthetic (as opposed to physical) sunscreens that are reactive and could irritate the skin.

REMEMBER

If you have a normal or oily scalp, never spray a dry conditioner on the root area. Instead, start the application 3 inches (7.6 centimeters) away from the scalp.

How to dry shampoo and condition hair

Dry shampooing and conditioning can work great or just so-so, depending on whether you take all the steps needed to absorb as much oil as possible and condition the hair right down to the tips where dryness usually exists.

By following these seven steps, you have the best chance of refreshing your hair and style and stretch the inevitable need to wet wash and condition your strands by up to a few days.

1. Separate your hair into rough partings as you apply the dry shampoo at the scalp to dry hair.

2. If you're using a spray, hold the product about 6 inches (15.3 centimeters) away from the hair. If you are using a powder, hold the product a couple of inches (about 5 centimeters) from the head and lightly sprinkle the powder onto your scalp. If the oil line (where the oiliness stops) extends a couple of inches down the hair shaft, apply there as well.

3. Allow the product to remain on the scalp untouched for five minutes.

4. Use a warm (not hot) blow-dryer set on a low air velocity for an additional few minutes to encourage maximum absorption.

5. After the product has had time to sop up the oil and debris, use your fingertips to massage the scalp to ensure complete absorption.

6. Gently brush your hair with a soft (preferably boar bristle) brush to remove excess product.

7. Tip the head upside down and lightly spray a dry conditioner through the mid-lengths and ends. Apply heat using a blow-dryer to add texture and distribute the product throughout the hair. Make sure your ends are thoroughly conditioned and keep the conditioner away from the scalp area.

TIP

For extra oily or coated hair, apply a dry shampoo and then put the hair in a bun or wrap it with a scarf right before bedtime. Brush the product out of the hair after getting your beauty rest and then apply the dry conditioner as detailed in step 7.

> » Achieving greater texture, lift, and volume
>
> » Using texture powders for volume, double density, and hold
>
> » Mastering mousses, custards, and puddings for hair

Chapter **18**

Handling the Sticky Stuff

Without a doubt, it's rare to pass a person on the street or watch a single YouTuber who isn't propping up or calming down their hair with multiple styling aids. Without a doubt, we are obsessed with making our hair behave in ways that it would never do on its own.

I suggest that you keep this short and sweet chapter handy, as it will not only tell you which products do what, but also the styling aids that take on starring roles in different situations. Stick with me (pun intended), and you'll make the best choices for each head of hair in every situation.

BE A HAIR CONSERVATIVE

TIP

For those with liberal tendencies — if one is good, three are better — it's important to show some restraint when applying styling aids. Conservatively applying these wonder products in light layers is always your best bet for achieving the hold and volume you want. Too-generous applications can not only defeat your styling goals, but also leave the hair sticky, hard, flaky, dull, drenched with oil, and looking downright dirty.

Becoming a Styling Aid Connoisseur

Enter any store or access any website that carries a wide array of beauty goods, and you risk going down the rabbit hole and staying there for days. There are so many styling products that want to leap off the shelves and into your shopping cart. To avoid buying interlopers that you won't like and don't want, check out the different categories of styling aids that I share below. I promise it will bring clarity to what you need to style your hair and your family's hair.

Mousse is more than a dessert

Mousses are applied to wet or damp hair and come in a variety of formulations, with one being just right for your hair. Dispensed like whipped cream, lightweight mousses do not weigh down fine hair. Specific formulas are also beneficial for thick or curly hair by helping to define and revive curl definition and put frisky frizz in its place. There are also mousses made especially for roller sets and hair wraps, and to form finger waves. Many of these products add shine and have moisturizing benefits for the hair and scalp. They're also available in hard-hold formulas, which I personally still dislike, because I prefer not to see or feel styling aids on the hair. If you're the same way, stick with soft-hold products.

Getting a grip on hair gels

You may have bid farewell to your hair gel after your awkward high school days, but ditching this type of styling aid altogether may be a styling mistake. Unlike the days of high school football games and hair gel helmets, there are several products on the market that have a firm hold while keeping the hair pliable. Most often, gels are applied to wet or damp hair. However, some of the lighter formulas can be used to finish a hairstyle by using a tiny amount and lightly running it through the midshafts and ends.

TIP

Instead of plopping a blob of gel on the head and then trying to distribute it through the hair, dispense a small amount in the palms of your hands and rub them together to warm and expand the product. Lightly apply the gel where needed. Continue layering gel applications until you're happy with the results.

Gels are made for different hairstyle goals, so read the labels carefully before buying. Gel products are available to:

>> Shape and sculpt hair

>> Define curls

>> Elongate curls

>> Provide a soft, medium, firm, or extreme hold

>> Smooth frizz

>> Provide a matte or shiny finish

Shimmying up the barber pole

If you are cutting or touching up a classic barber cut, the hair is almost always layered — especially on the top of the head. The challenge is how to keep these top layers in some sort of style, as opposed to lying flat or standing on end. There are five categories of styling aids that will enhance barber styles: pomades, pastes, clays, styling creams, and waxes.

>> **Hair pomades** are soft, gel-like, or waxy styling products that deliver a range of holds and shines, depending on the formula you're using. You can apply the product to towel-dried hair, or to completely dry hair. Although blow-drying the hair is optional, I recommended placing the hair and then blow-drying it on a low heat setting to set the pomade. By using your fingertips to lift the hair while blow-drying, you can create a believably voluminous style.

>> **Styling pastes** have a thicker consistency than pomades, with a viscosity ranging from craft glue to toothpaste. They're lightweight and pliable, can control the shape, and add definition to hair. They're formulated to create a shiny or matte finish. Styling pastes can be used on all lengths and hair types. They can be applied on damp hair to create better hold, and on dry hair to create tousled hair styles.

>> **Hair clays** provide a high-hold, matte finish. They will keep your hairstyle in place for the whole day and sop up natural oils and greasiness. Remember that once the clay is set, it's not moving, so make sure your hair looks just the way you like it right after applying the clay and then allow the hair (and clay) to dry naturally or use a low-heat blow-dryer.

>> **Styling creams** are very mild. They feel like a lotion or light face cream, act like a moisturizer, provide a bit of definition, and offer minimum hold. You can apply the styling cream on damp hair before blow-drying, or apply a slick of the cream after the hair is dry and has been placed in the finished style.

>> **Hair waxes** are either water-based (water is the top ingredient with waxes being listed further down the ingredient deck), or wax-based (waterless formulas that contain solid petrolatum, wax, and oil). Water-based formulas are the easiest to shampoo out of the hair. Wax-based products require multiple washings to completely remove all traces of the product. Both types of products are primarily used to create retro styles, like those shown in the movie *Grease*.

Know when to hold 'em

Texture (working) sprays are used after the hair has been dried. These versatile stylers can lift the root area and add texture to the hair. To use a texture spray to your best advantage, separate sections, hold the hair up, and spray the targeted area about 10 inches (about 25 centimeters) away from root area. You can also use a warm blow-dryer with minimum airflow to dry and set the product. As amazing as this product works, I find it incredible that you can easily brush it out of the hair and start over.

Hairsprays have been used since the 1950s to freeze hair into place and, as all college students know, to kill scary bugs that take up residence in their dorm rooms. Today's hairsprays range from soft to hard hold and are always the last product applied to the hair after it has been styled. Do not hot iron the hair after applying hairspray as it can damage the hair, coat the barrel or plates, and even stain lighter hair colors.

REMEMBER

Hairsprays are *fixatives,* as opposed to texture or working sprays, so once you apply hairspray, you should consider the hair set.

While modern hairsprays don't leave the hair looking like it's frozen in time, some cheaply made hairsprays will make the hair feel crunchy. If the hairspray you're holding in your hand right now does this, it's time to go shopping. Look for hairsprays that are formulated with UV-ray filters. This is important because UV rays can deteriorate the health of the hair and accelerate color fade.

Taking a hair powder

Like physics, volume powders focus on volume, density, and mass. They can reform the behavior of fine, collapsible hair, and visually double the thickness of all hair textures. Most volume powders are packaged in shaker form, although a few brands offer aerosol versions. As an added bonus, volume powders can absorb scalp oils until not even a scintilla of sebum is left behind. They are well suited for hair Types 1 and 2, work well on healthy Type 3 hair, but can be disastrous for Type 4 (coily) hair. (See Chapter 4 for more information on hair types.)

Aside from lifting hair at the root area and creating extreme volume and greater density, volume powder is used to make braided styles and updos bigger, thicker, and more defined; create piecey effects for cropped, spiked cuts; and turn long-layered hair into a *mane* event.

Like all extreme products, volume powders do have a few drawbacks. They tend to dry the hair, leave a dry coating behind, and create an extremely matte finish. Because they absorb oil on the scalp, always avoid using volume powders on dry or sensitive scalps. Also, because volume powders refuse to leave on their own accord, they must be shampooed out of the hair. I suggest the *occasional* use of volume powders. All hair lovers should have a volume powder on hand for special occasions and any time they want to their hair to have a lot of oomph.

TIP

You can partly counteract the drying effect of volume powders by conditioning your hair the night before or designating the next day as your wash-and-care day. If you love your shiny hair, apply the volume powder where it doesn't show, like underneath braids or the underlayers of your hair.

Smooth around the edges

Edge tamers are a must for those with curly hair, and especially for Type 4 (coily) hair. They can also be used on any hair type with a fuzzy hairline that's ruled by baby hairs that need to calm down. Edge tamers come in a variety of formulations. Watch for those that offer moisturizing benefits to keep frizz at bay and keep edges slick and smooth all day. Also look for products that require minimum product to achieve maximum results and have absolutely no issue with product flaking.

TIP

My go-to styling tools for edging include a toothbrush or a disposable mascara wand, and a tail comb. Apply the product to the brush or wand and then style the edges of the hairline. I sometimes follow up with a tail comb to swirl the hair even more and finish the end placement.

Lunch is served: Nutritious oils and serums

Hair oils and serums have become must-have products for all hair types. They can be applied by dispensing drops on the palms of the hands and rubbing them together before applying the product to the hair. Some are available in pump form. Most hair oils and serums tout benefits derived from seed oils, including argan, macadamia, and moringa. However, the first ingredient in many of these products is dimethicone — or one of its chemical cousins. When it comes to hair oils and serums, this isn't a bad thing, as dimethicone leaves the hair shiny and discourages frizz. If oils and serums are applied too frequently, they can make fine, straight hair look and feel oily.

Pure plant-based hair oils and serums are excellent for Type 4 hair, as they're made with vegetable oils — as opposed to dimethicone — that moisturize and condition the scalp and discourage hair breakage.

Four Specialty Styling Aids for Coily Hair

Type 4 hair benefits from special products that maintain curls on a daily basis. In addition to a light application of leave-in conditioner, consider the following products for natural hairstyles:

>> **Hair juice, hair mist, and hair quench** products are basically made of fruit or herbal waters. Most also contain humectants — such as aloe vera, panthenol, or honey — to draw moisture from the environment, as well as light oils to condition and protect the hair. All three are excellent for lightly moisturizing and refreshing natural curls, and most can be used daily or as needed without weighing down or distorting curls. Look for products that also add natural shine to the hair.

>> **Butters and whipped butters** will often contain thick seed oils — including shea or coconut oils — as their first ingredients. Whipped versions have a softer texture that make them easier to apply and spread through the hair. Creams, butters, and whipped butters help maintain curl definition and give hair texture a boost. They're known for their nourishing, anti-frizz, and soft-hold benefits, while not making the hair look greasy or feel crunchy. Butters are recommended for twist-outs, braid-outs, rod sets, and wash-and-go styles.

>> **Defining and nourishing creams include puddings, custards, meringues, and smoothies.** Each of these names describes the consistency, weight, and hold of the product, which is extremely helpful when choosing one for your hair. All provide intense nourishing benefits that treat the hair while encouraging a smooth cuticle and healthy curl shape. Nourishing creams are matches made in heaven for 4A to 4C coils and excel when used for braid-outs and twist-outs.

>> **Cream gels** are a combination of moisturizing creams or hair butters and gels. Providing the hold of a light-to-medium gel and the softness of a cream-based product, they add curl definition and style retention, which makes them the perfect choice for twisting or braiding styles, discouraging flyaways, and preventing frizz. Cream gels also allow coily curls to bounce and move, making this product a must-have for very curly and coily hair.

Chapter 19

Everything You Need to Know about Heat-Styling Tools

While the bulk of this book focuses on haircutting, styling the hair after a cut adds a new dimension to what you can do for others and yourself! But just like you wouldn't use a child's plastic shovel to dig in the garden, successfully styling hair starts and ends with using the right tools. This chapter gives you eye-opening information on how to choose the right tools for your needs, sidestep sketchy marketing claims, and safely use and store all your corded tools. (Check out Chapter 20 for great styling tips on straight, wavy, curly, and coily hair.)

TIP

Hair types are mentioned throughout this chapter, so you definitely need to be familiar with them in order to get the most out of the upcoming information. If you need a refresher, refer to Chapter 4.

Brushing Up on Heat-Styling Brushes

Shopping for heat-styling brushes can be so confusing that many people end up buying them based on their color and snappy design. If this sounds like you, you've got plenty of company. Because the brush business is incredibly competitive, marketers use every trick possible to grab your attention and make their tools end up in your shopping cart. This is why everyone should become savvy on different brush types and in which steps of the styling phase their abilities truly shine.

Key brush types used for heat styling

Check out Table 19-1 for information about different types of heat-styling brushes and what they're used for. The table includes images to help you visually identify each brush type. To get the most out of this chapter, have your current brushes laid out in front of you. After reviewing them with a more informed eye, are you all set, or do you need to go brush shopping?

TIP Many brushes have anti-static benefits. If you don't have an anti-static brush on hand, grab a fabric softener sheet and a styling brush with stiff bristles. Push the sheet through the bristles and brush the hair. Boom! Bye-bye static.

TABLE 19-1 **Brush Types and Their Unique Roles When Heat-Styling Hair**

Type	Tension	Uses
Vent brush	Mild	Rough-drying (drying the hair in a controlled manner, but not actually styling it); messy non-specific styles; speeds up drying times; can loosen waves or curls when mild tension is applied
Paddle brush	Moderate	Gently smooths while detangling, brushing, and blow-drying longer hair

Type	Tension	Uses
7-row styling brush	Firm	Smooths hair from root to end during the blow-dry process; shapes ends straight; prepares hair for flat-ironing
9-row styling brush	Firm	Smooths hair from root to end during the blow-dry process; makes hair slightly fuller; cups ends under for a more finished look *Tip:* If you must choose one styling brush (7-row versus 9-row), purchase the 9-row styling brush.
Round brushes	Light to Firm	Creates shapely body, soft waves or curls; makes curling iron work easier and faster *Note:* The larger the round brush diameter, the looser the blow-dried shape will be.
Wet and dry brushes	Light	Gently removes tangles on wet hair; can be used as a styler for light control

Photos courtesy of Spornette

Giving your brushes a checkup

To ensure that you're only using damage-free brushes, give them a thorough checkup once a month, or any time one starts snagging the hair.

Keep the following in mind:

>> **Vent brushes and most air-cushioned brushes** have nylon bristles with ball tips to prevent snagging the hair and scratching the scalp. Even though it may

seem wasteful, if your ball-tipped brush has even one ball missing, you should toss it and buy a replacement.

>> **Hard rubber-like cushioned styling brushes** are frequently subjected to high heat and strong tension. Because of how they are used, the cushions tend to crack or lift away from the brush head. The first time you feel a single hair snag or snap, you should carefully examine the brush. If the cushion has deteriorated, toss the brush. You can avoid this situation for many years by purchasing a good quality tool. (I use and recommend Denman 7-row and 9-row stylers. Sam Villa brushes are also very durable.)

COZYING UP TO IONS AND FAR-INFRARED HEAT

While the rule that opposites attract is true for magnets, did you know that it's also the case for hair? Dry, damaged hair has a positive ionic charge that lifts the cuticle layer, causing the hair to feel rough, look dull, have a halo of frizz, and encourage static electricity. Showering the hair with negative ions has the opposite effect by closing the cuticle layer (outside layer of the hair), making the hair look shinier, calming down frizz, and preventing static-filled hair.

- **Ionic generator** is a catchall claim for all styling tool materials that generate negative ions. This is important because negative ions break up water molecules on the surface of the hair to dry the hair faster, smooth the cuticle, and minimize frizz.

- **Ceramic** releases negative ions when heated. It also evenly heats the base, barrel, or plates of styling tools and retains heat longer than other materials. Ceramic composites are used for flat iron plates to promote even heating, as well as on the inside workings of blow-dryers for this same purpose.

  Many ceramic tools also claim *far-infrared properties,* which means they heat the hair from the inside out and dry the hair faster at a lower heat setting. Far-infrared heat also traps hydration in the interior of the hair by closing the cuticle layer and effectively sealing the hair.

- **Tourmaline** is a semi-precious mineral that produces the most negative ions of all materials used for styling tools. It's often combined with ceramic to release a significantly higher number of negative ions.

Warning: If the hair you are dealing with tends to be naturally limp and clingy, tools that produce negative ions may leave it in a droopy, noodle-like state.

>> **Round brushes** are fantastic tools to shape the hair, but some definitely have a few drawbacks. Round brushes with metal or ceramic-coated metal barrels are prone to snagging strands of hair. This is caused by either a loosened cap at the tip of the barrel or where the barrel is attached to the handle. When this happens, it's important to keep the hair away from the edges of the barrel while blow-drying until you can replace the brush. If the barrel is wobbly, it's toast and should be tossed right away. (I use Spornette round brushes, which are moderately priced and last a long time. Other great brands are by CHI and brushes made by Conair's professional division.)

Information on how to sanitize and disinfect brushes is covered in Chapter 21.

Choosing the Best Blow-Dryer for You

Blow-dryers can either be your BFF or your worst frenemy, depending on the type of hair you're heat styling, and the tool's heat and air velocity settings, weight, and attachments that fit the nozzle. Because most quality blow-dryers last for years in a home setting, it's important to purchase the very best one you can afford.

New technology is always being introduced to the beauty market. One example is the new digital motor technology, which is lighter than most hair dryers and produces more air pressure and less heat to dry the hair. Blow-dryers with digital motor technology are made by many companies, including Conair. Dyson has developed its own digital motor technology that moves air up to 430 miles per hour to speed up drying times, adds more shine, and helps to reduce heat damage. Always keep in mind that tools that embody more advanced hair-dryer technology can be much more expensive than those that rely on scientific know-how that's been around for years. For your purposes, a traditional dryer will probably be just fine. Of course, if you have extra jingle in your pocket, go for it!

Style-worthy blow-dryer features

Before buying your next blow-dryer, or while studying the one you currently own, compare your tool(s) with these features and benefits. (Also reference Figure 19-1 to view many of the features found on quality blow-dryers.)

>> **Blow-dryer wattage** is usually prominently listed on the front of the packaging and often on the tool itself. (Watts measure the amount of electrical power used by the blow-dryer motor.) Blow-worthy dryers use from 1200 to 2200 watts. Unless you're drying a super thick, super long head of hair, anything over 1875 watts is overkill.

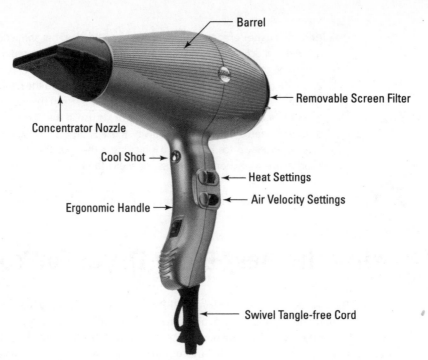

Barrel

Removable Screen Filter

Concentrator Nozzle

Cool Shot →

Heat Settings

Air Velocity Settings

Ergonomic Handle →

Swivel Tangle-free Cord

FIGURE 19-1:
Key blow-dryer features that improve the drying experience and enhance styling results.

Stylecraft Gamma+ Italia

>> **Weight** is a critical factor when blow-drying hair. If your arms tire easily or you want to preserve the health of your wrists, elbows, and shoulders, choose a lighter-weight blow-dryer that still has plenty of punch.

>> **AC, DC, and digital motors** impact the power, longevity, and weight of blow-dryers. AC (alternate current) motors are stronger, heavier, and last almost twice as long as most DC (direct current) motors. Blow-dryers with digital motors are lightweight, produce a powerful air velocity, and have a much longer lifespan than either AC or DC motors.

>> **Ergonomic handles** are more comfortable to grip and give you more control when grasping and maneuvering a blow-dryer. A bonus feature would be a cushioned ergonomic handle for even greater comfort.

>> **Barrel length** is an important factor when purchasing a new blow-dryer. You should choose a length according to your arm length and height. Whether you're short, tall, or somewhere between, the ideal barrel length will allow you to keep your arm in a natural downward position to avoid stressing your upper arm and shoulder.

>> **Heat, cool (sometimes labeled "cold"), and air velocity** switches or buttons should be included in your blow-dryer design. At the very minimum, your blow-dryer should have two heat settings, two air velocity settings, and one cool-shot setting. (See Chapter 20 for blow-drying tips using these features.)

» **Blow-dryer attachments** can be packaged with the blow-dryer or sold separately. Either way, only use attachments that are made specifically for your blow-dryer model to ensure an exact nozzle fit.

Attachments you need to dry and style all types of hair include an air-concentrator nozzle (not flared or open at the sides); a wide, flared air-concentrator nozzle to *rough-dry* (dry the hair in a controlled manner, but not into a specific style) longer, thicker hair (optional), an air diffuser with fingers or nubs to dry and lift the hair at the scalp; and a pick (also spelled pik) attachment to significantly lift very curly hair at the scalp and shape the style.

» **Tangle-free, swivel cords** prevent cord damage and persistent twisting that forces you to play tug-of-war with the cord while blow-drying the hair. Some blow-dryers have a retractable cord feature that helps to keep it twist-free and make it easier to store the blow-dryer between uses. The biggest drawback with the latter is the cord is usually six feet or less.

» **Ionic and far-infrared** properties are touted by many blow-dryer companies to separate their products from others that may or may not offer the same thing. (See sidebar, "Cozying up to ions and far-infrared heat," in this chapter for more information.)

WARNING

Beware of false claims when shopping for tools with ionic technology. Many brands use this claim to sell styling tools that generate a puny number of negative ions. Remember that the proof is always in the pudding.

AUTHOR SAYS

I recommend that you test your new ionic tool against your existing blow-dryer. To do this, separate your hair in half from the middle of your forehead back to the bottom hairline. Twist and firmly secure one section. Dry the other half with your old/existing dryer. Once dry, twist and re-pin the hair and then unpin the other section. Dry this half with your new dryer. Does the ionic tool noticeably smooth the cuticle, make your hair shinier, leave it free of static electricity, and dry your hair in considerably less time? If not, I suggest that you return the tool, especially if you paid a higher price for nothing more than marketing features.

Maintaining your blow-dryer

You should always do a complete checkup on your blow-dryer at least once a month, as well as any time it isn't acting quite right, such as periodically stopping while blow-drying or emitting an acrid smell.

Here are some checkpoints you should pay attention to when examining your blow-dryer. If you detect any of these problems, you should stop using this tool immediately and either have it professionally repaired (locally or by the manufacturer) or toss it in the trash.

HOW TO PROPERLY STORE CORDED STYLING TOOLS

When not in use, all electric styling tools should be stored in a drawer or container where they are shielded from dust and debris. Equally important is how you handle the cords. Many people either don't secure the cord or, worse yet, tightly loop the cord around the blow-dryer or styling iron to keep it "safe." Wrong. To avoid damaging the wires inside the cord or molding the cord into a spiral shape, loosely gather up the cord the same way you would a garden hose by holding it up at the base and then gathering the cord in relaxed loops. Once this is done, secure the looped cord with a Velcro strap.

>> **Examine the cord to ensure it is properly attached at the base of the blow-dryer.** Loose cords can expose wires and give you a terrible shock.

>> **Examine the electrical plug to ensure it is properly attached to the cord.** Poorly attached plugs with exposed wires can cause serious bodily injury and increase the risk of fire.

>> **After running the blow-dryer for a few minutes, disconnect it from the outlet and touch the plug to see if it's hot, as opposed to being room temperature or slightly warm.** Overheated plugs are serious signs of electrical problems with either your blow-dryer or the wall outlet.

>> **Clean the filter (screen).** It's extremely important to keep your filter free of hair and fuzz because blow-dryers suck air into the back of the unit, move the air over a heating coil, and then blow the heated air out of the end of the nozzle (see Figure 19-1). If the filter is clogged, your blow-dryer won't receive enough air to perform properly. As you can imagine, a clogged filter also shortens the life of this pricey tool.

To clean the filter, remove it from the back of the blow-dryer (see Figure 19-1). Use a small metal brush or a stiff nylon brush to scrub and remove the debris clinging to the screen. If there are fine fibers still embedded in the screen, wash it with hot, soapy water and use a stiff brush to remove all remaining debris. Rinse and allow the screen to completely dry before reattaching it to the blow dryer.

Choosing the Best Styling Irons for You

There is a dizzying array of curling and smoothing irons on the market, but when you sort them into categories, choosing the ones that are perfect for your needs is relatively easy. Styling iron categories include curling irons, flat irons (smoothing irons), and a trendy catchall category of unnecessary electric styling tools that are fun to use but aren't essential for styling the hair.

This section arms you with what you need to know about heated styling tools, including their various uses and which ones work best for different types of hair.

Types of curling irons and wands

Curling irons come in different barrel sizes, as well as hand-clamp (Marcel) curling irons, spring-clamp curling irons, and clipless (clampless) curling wands. The following is a quick explanation of your options:

>> **Curling iron with Marcel handle:** Reshapes hair into curls or waves; clamp (also called a shell) is manually controlled

>> **Curling iron with spring clamp:** Reshapes hair into curls or waves; clamp automatically grips the hair

>> **Curling wand:** Does not have a clamp to hold the hair; wand (barrel) can be conical or straight

AUTHOR SAYS

To create standard curls, I recommend that you purchase irons with spring clamps because they're the easiest to handle and pose the least amount of risk of burning yourself or someone you love.

WARNING

There is a category of non-electric curling irons that are heated by an outside source, such as a gas stove or an electric heating unit. These are primarily used on Type 4 hair (see Chapter 4). These tools can be heated up to 850 degrees Fahrenheit (454 degrees Celsius), which is twice the temperature of most electric irons. These tools are not covered in this chapter because in the hands of novices, using these special curling irons (commonly referred to as tongs) can go terribly wrong. If you want to use non-electric styling irons, I strongly suggest that you seek out specialty hands-on training by a professional who uses these tools on a regular basis. When handled correctly, they can produce amazing results.

Curling iron bells-and-whistles

Companies that market styling irons face the daunting challenge of making their tools stand out in an overcrowded market. While it would be great if their focus was on improving the features and benefits, quite often, companies focus on marketing gobbledygook that makes no sense to those who know just a thing or two about styling irons. To bring clarity to your search for the perfect electric curling irons, consider the following features and benefits (and see Figure 19-2):

>> **Traditional spring clamp irons are easier and safer to use.** Many beauty professionals use this type of iron, and you should too.

>> **Rapid heat-up and constant heat technologies are blessings for anyone curling hair.** They eliminate the need to wait for the iron to reach the desired temperature and prevent it from cooling down mid-styling.

>> **Automatic shutoff is a bell you'll want to ring.** When this added feature is present, the iron shuts off after it's been idle for a certain number of minutes. This safety feature prevents everything from shortening the life of your iron to the threat of fire.

>> **Barrel lengths vary to accommodate different lengths of hair.** Short, often chubby barrels work well for short or mid-length hair, but they aren't that great when curling longer hair because you can run out of barrel before you reach the ends of the hair.

>> **Barrel sizes for spring clamp irons typically vary from ½ inch to 2 inches (1.3 to 5 centimeters) in size.** Some companies also make barrels as small as a teeny tiny ⅜-inch (0.9 centimeter) barrel. In all cases, the smaller the barrel, the tighter the curl, as you can see in Figure 19-3.

If you need a variety of sizes, I suggest that you purchase a curling iron set with assorted barrel sizes that you plug in to a special curling iron handle. (One of the nicest and most affordable curling iron sets is made by Hot Tools Professional. A pricier option is the T3 set, which is elegant in design and dependable in function.)

>> **Digital temperature settings and readouts allow you to precisely set and check the temperature of your iron.**

>> **Electric styling iron heat capabilities usually range from 0 degrees up to 450 degrees Fahrenheit (–17 to 232 degrees Celsius).** Reference Table 19-2 for temperature guidelines based on textures and hair conditions.

>> **Cool tips on spring clamp irons are optional but are still highly recommended.** This feature gives you the added benefit of controlling your iron with both hands.

>> **Tangle-free, swivel cords prevent cord damage and persistent twists that force you to play tug-of-war with the cord while ironing the hair.**

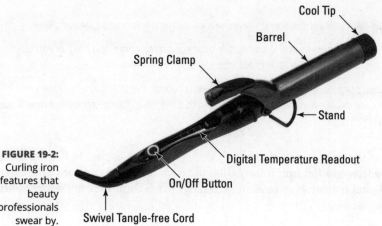

Cool Tip

Barrel

Spring Clamp

Stand

Digital Temperature Readout

On/Off Button

Swivel Tangle-free Cord

FIGURE 19-2:
Curling iron features that beauty professionals swear by.

CHI LAVA Curling Iron

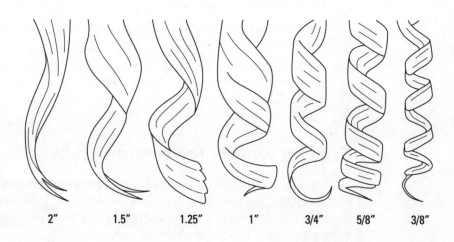

FIGURE 19-3:
Different barrel sizes give you different curls.

2"   1.5"   1.25"   1"   3/4"   5/8"   3/8"

© John Wiley & Sons, Inc.; Illustration by Rashell Smith

Finding your perfect flat iron

Flat irons can be used to smooth, straighten, and even curl the hair (see Chapter 20). If you're planning on styling your family's hair, you'll probably want to have at least one flat iron in your styling arsenal.

Flat irons are available in a variety of plate sizes, materials, and different shaped edges. The plate size is determined by the diameter (side-to-side) measurement of the plates. They can be used to smooth, straighten, and even curl the hair. (See Chapter 20 for flat iron tips and tricks.)

>> 2-inch (5 centimeters) plates are best for long hair because they cover more surface area in less time.

>> 1½-inch (3.8 centimeters) plates work well for thick, coarse, or curly hair.

>> 1-inch (2.5 centimeters) plates are best suited for short and mid-length hair. This is the most popular plate size.

>> Mini plates are used for very short areas (like a short fringe) to smooth or create details around the hairline and to smooth isolated strands of rebellious hair.

Much of the information shared for curling irons also applies to flat irons. Shared curling iron and flat iron information includes rapid and constant heat capabilities, digital temperature readout, and tangle-free cord. Here are a few additional tips for flat irons.

>> The plates can have *squared edges* (straight styles) and *beveled edges* (curved to create a slight bend in the hair).

>> The plates must be smooth and flawlessly polished for a snag-free styling experience.

>> Flat irons can be thick and somewhat bulky or have a sleek, slender design. I prefer slender flat irons because they are easier to use and do the same job as their bulkier cousins.

Curling wands for trendy styles

All styling wands make it easy to create rockin' curls. Some styling wands come with a cool tip, which allows you to grab the end of the barrel (the tip) for additional control. You control the iron and hair by wearing a heat-resistant glove and using your fingers to wrap and hold the hair.

Like all hair tools, beauty innovators continue to release new curling wand designs. Today you can find straight, tapered, reversed taper designs, and more. My advice is to have a traditional tapered wand on hand to create unstructured beachy waves and skip the more specialized models.

Note: The features covered in the "Curling iron bells-and-whistles" section also pertains to curling wands.

Nifty, nonessential heat styling tools

Once you have your basic arsenal of styling tools, you may want to add a few tools that are cool to use but not needed to complete any hairstyle. These tools include, but aren't limited to, electric brushes that dry and shape the hair in one step;

air-wrap tools that automatically wrap the hair around the outside of a barrel to dry and curl each section in one action; and steam styling irons (which I do not recommend because they risk damaging the hair).

The most used nonessential professional tool is a crimping iron, which goes in and out of vogue as a finished look but is always in style for creating volume on the underneath layers of the hair (see Chapter 20 for crimping tips).

The list goes on and on from there because new, trendy, and gimmicky tools are being introduced all the time. My advice is to focus on your basic tools and master the skills needed to use them properly. Then, if you're curious about nonessential styling tools, purchase one or two of them and start playing.

Temperature Guidelines for Heat Styling

AUTHOR SAYS

I first saw heat damage in real time when I was in beauty school back when dinosaurs roamed the earth. It's odd how that memory comes flooding back any time I talk about potential heat damage, and not in a good way. It was summer, and the doors to the school were open for ventilation. I was sitting at my station enjoying the breeze while watching a student across from me ironing a beautiful head of lightened and highlighted blonde hair. The student wrapped her iron around the first section next to the ear and kept it there while she talked about her boyfriend. I started squirming in my seat after noticing that the hair nearest the scalp was turning gold. Before I could utter a word, the whole section of hair broke off near the scalp and was dangling around the barrel of the iron and the smell of burnt hair filled the air. As a witness to this debacle, it taught me a lifelong respect for heat-styling tools without ever having to go through that experience myself. I want to do the same for you.

Heat styling hair doesn't include a one-size-fits-all temperature. Every hair type and condition require different heat temperatures to safely curl or smooth the hair. Table 19-2 lays it all out for you.

TIP

Always choose the heat styling temperature for the most fragile area of the hair. If the hair has been highlighted, for instance, you should set the temperature for fragile hair.

TABLE 19-2 ## Temperature Guidelines for Different Hair Textures

Hair Texture	Fahrenheit	Celsius
Fine, chemically treated with lightener, permanent hair dye (mixed with a developer), lye or no-lye straighteners, perm solutions, or damaged and naturally fragile hair regardless of the cause	275 to 325 degrees	135 to 163 degrees
Medium hair textures	300 to 350 degrees	149 to 177 degrees
Coarse hair textures	375 to 400 degrees	191 to 204 degrees
Extremely curly/coily hair (all textures)	400 to 450 degrees	204 to 232 degrees

> » **Blow-drying like a pro**
>
> » **Creating poppin' curls**
>
> » **Ironing out the kinks**
>
> » **Solving common styling issues**

Chapter 20

Styling Tips and Tricks

A special satisfaction comes from styling your own haircut. The lift you planned for the top area or the details you cut around the face suddenly come to life. It also teaches you a lot about haircutting. When blow-drying, for instance, hair can shrink right before your eyes, making you a better judge of length the next time you cut someone's hair. It also improves your texture techniques, your precision work, and shows you better ways to create beautifully blended looks.

Even so, styling is a personal thing. Some haircutters' eyes will literally glaze over at the thought of their scissors being at rest for 30 minutes while they labor over wet hair, while others find styling to be the best part of the experience. Whichever side of the fence you're on, you should at least brush the hair into the finished style and loosely (sans brush) blow-dry it following every cut.

TIP

Because hair has a way of shifting and pulling little tricks on you as it goes from wet to dry, blow-drying the hair gives you one final opportunity to inspect your handiwork and make sure that everything has come together as planned.

They Went That-a-Way: Directional Styling and Lift

If you take the wrong approach when wanting a toddler to do something they don't want to do (like eating their broccoli), you know that even if you do prevail, the results could still be disastrous. Styling hair works the same way. The only way to seamlessly create a style that's free of angst is to use the correct styling directions and lifting techniques to achieve your styling goals. Fortunately, once you understand directional partings and volume-control techniques, getting hair to move and lift is (usually) a breeze.

Directing the style

Hair partings control the direction of the hair for every style (see Figure 20-1). When you part the hair in the correct direction, you have a much better chance of styling success, even when the hair you're dealing with seems to have a mind of its own.

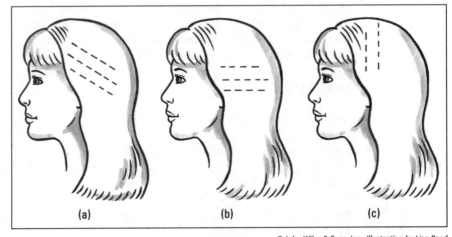

FIGURE 20-1:
Partings that direct the hair in specific directions include (a) diagonal, (b) horizontal, and (c) vertical.

© John Wiley & Sons, Inc.; Illustration by Lisa Reed

TIP

Directional style partings are the same as the haircutting angles covered in Chapter 5. If you've skipped that chapter, or it's been awhile since you've read it, now is the time to give the section on angles a quick read.

Here are the three most important directional partings you make when styling hair:

>> Diagonal partings allow the hair to follow the curvature of the head. Instead of creating a straight back or straight forward direction, the hair gently curves in these same directions (see Figure 20-1a and Figure 20-2).

>> Horizontal partings are used for areas where the hair is supposed to lie down. A one-length bob is a good example of when you would use horizontal partings (refer to Figure 20-1b).

>> Vertical partings are used to make the hair go straight back or straight forward (see Figure 20-1c and Figure 20-3). Many longer styles use vertical partings, as well as hair that's blown or curled away from the face.

FIGURE 20-2:
To create maximum, natural-looking movement for this short hairstyle, the sides have been swept back in a diagonal direction.

Photographer: Tom Carson (www.tomcarsonphoto.com);
Hair, Cut and Style: Liza; Makeup: Roi;
Barbaria Salon, Foster City, California

FIGURE 20-3:
The front area of
this style has
been vertically
curled back to put
the spotlight on
the model's face
and bone
structure.

Photographer: Tom Carson (www.tomcarsonphoto.com);
Hair: Bridgette Hardy; Makeup: Shelley Beal;
Cloud 9 Salon and Spa, Martins Ferry, Ohio

Learning the base-ics

This section shares information about three directions you can use to create less, moderate, or maximum volume. It all has to do with directing the *base* of the section — the hair that's right next to the scalp (see Figure 20-4). When you combine controlling the volume with directional parting for movement, you have a great style in the making.

Taking it down a notch

Some people can't get their hair to stand up, while others can't get it to lie down. If you're dealing with hair that has too much volume, or you just want the hair to hug the scalp for a specific style (like the one in Figure 20-5), you can use drying and styling techniques to make the hair calm down.

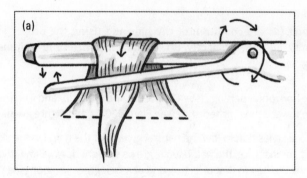

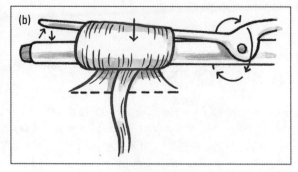

FIGURE 20-4:
(a) Styling the hair *off base* in the same direction as the style reduces volume; styling the hair off base in the opposite the direction of the style increases volume; (b) styling the hair *on base* creates moderate fullness.

© John Wiley & Sons, Inc.; Illustration by Lisa Reed

FIGURE 20-5:
Styling hair off base in the same direction as the finished style encourages the hair to lie close to the scalp.

Photographer: Tom Carson (www.tomcarsonphoto.com);
Color and cut: Liza; Style: Courtney; Makeup: Roi; Barbaria
Salon, Foster City, California

TIP

After caring for the condition of the hair and using the proper styling aids (see Chapters 17 and 18, respectively), focus on controlling volume by doing the following.

>> Take horizontal partings (see Chapter 5) and blow-dry and iron the hair off base toward the finished style (see Figure 20-4a and Figure 20-5).

>> Choose styles that follow the natural growth of the hair. On the sides of the head, for instance, the hair usually grows straight down. Blow-drying and ironing the hair in that direction and at a 0-degree elevation (see Chapter 5) will create a much sleeker style.

BEING A BIG TEASE

Teasing the hair can build a little or a lot of volume. The trick is to tease the hair in such a way that your handiwork creates the exact lift you want while still being invisible in the finished style. To achieve this, always tease the underside of the hair sections to keep it hidden from view.

For lift at the scalp — either overall or in specific areas of the head — separate one small blow-dried or ironed section at a time and do the following.

1. Hold the section at a 90-degree to 180-degree elevation, depending on the amount of lift you want. (See Chapter 5 for degrees of elevation.)

2. Insert the bristles of a teasing brush or the teeth of a styling comb through the underside of the section 1 inch to 1½ inches (2.5 to 3.8 centimeters) away from the scalp.

3. Holding the hair taut, push the brush or comb straight toward the scalp. Repeat this action until the hair is lightly packed at the scalp. If the hair is quite limp or resistant, apply a working spray at the root area as you go.

4. Once you've finished teasing the hair, use your comb or brush to lightly smooth the top strands or layers over the teasing.

For overall volume, tease the hair from the base to the mid-lengths of the hair:

1. Separate the hair into sections as you work through the hair.

2. Lift each section and use a teasing brush, wide-tooth comb, or your fingers to lightly tease the underside of each section from the root area down to the mid-lengths of the hair.

3. Lift the teased sections and spray the underside with a working spray.

4. Style the hair with your fingers without disturbing the light teasing.

>> Use a classic styling brush right next to the scalp and exert more tension on the hair as you dry the hair at a 0-degree elevation. (Chapter 5 discusses elevations; Chapter 19 provides details about styling brushes.)

Taking it up a notch

To create styles with overall volume, additional lift at the top or crown area, or to fluff up fine, limp hair, always use volumizing styling products and direct the base of the hair.

Keep the following tips in mind when you want to give hair some lift:

>> On longer hair, flip the hair over the head and blow-dry the base of the hair in the opposite direction it will be styled. This is a less structured way of overdirecting the base.

>> On shorter hair, lift the hair with your fingers while you dry the root area.

>> Blow-dry and iron the hair on base (see Figure 20-4b) for moderate volume, or off base (away from the finished style) for greater volume (see Figure 20-6).

FIGURE 20-6: To create more fullness on top, this style has been curled off base in the opposite direction of the finished style.

Photographer: Tom Carson (www.tomcarsonphoto.com); Color and cut: Liza; Style: Terry; Makeup: Roi; Barbaria Salon, Foster City, California

>> For straight hairstyles lift strands of hair with your fingers and apply a styling spray to the underside of the hair at the root area.

Blowing Them Away with Your Drying Techniques

To ensure that you always create an on-point style, your blow-dryer must always follow the downward growth of the cuticle layer (root to end). When the cuticle layer is closed tight against the hair shaft, the outside of the hair is ultra-smooth and shiny.

WARNING

Blowing the hair in the wrong direction opens the cuticle layer, leaving the hair vulnerable to dehydration, brittleness, dullness, and color fading.

Sectioning the hair

Although it may seem like overkill to section and secure the hair for blow-drying, until you become adept at controlling unclipped hair, pinning is the way to go. You can then easily control the hair, while you put your full effort into getting your brush, blow-dryer and hands all going in the right direction (as discussed in Chapter 6).

Working with tension

The finished hair — straight, wavy, or curly — is created by the amount of tension that you exert on the hair. If you want the hair to be straight, for instance, you need to apply more tension (pull) on the hair during the drying process. If you want it to be curly, little or no tension should be used.

TIP

Tension should always be evenly applied to the hair and in a controlled manner. It should never be strong enough to damage the hair or the hair root.

Seriously breathtaking blow-dry sets

In addition to preparing the hair for curling or flat iron stylings, using different blow-dryer techniques can create full, fluffy styles; loosely structured looks; sleek finishes; soft waves; or stronger, more defined curls. (For basic blow-drying techniques, refer to the beginning of this section.)

Blow-dry setting techniques

Casually tossed long hair with just a bit of curl can be achieved by using a blow-dryer and a medium-to-large round brush. For shorter styles, blow-drying the hair with a smaller diameter round brush can set the hair in a softly curled style.

Check out these blow-dry round brush techniques that can be used for many different styles:

>> **Lifting the top and crown with round brushes:** Blow-dry the hair by overdirecting the hair for volume (see "Learning the base-ics" in this chapter). Apply a working spray at the base of each blow-dry section and then all over each section when the hair is almost dry.

>> **Spot lifting:** After round-brushing the top and crown area (see Chapter 5), apply a working spray and large-to-jumbo rollers in these same areas to create even more lift. Allow the curls to set for a few minutes before removing the rollers.

>> **Creating a full, curly style with round brushes:** Use the appropriate size round brush and styling aids to dry the hair on base or overdirect the hair for lift (refer to Figure 20-4). Start at the bottom hairline and work your way up to the top of the head. Pin each curl as you go and apply a light layer of working spray before moving on to the next section. Allow the set to remain undisturbed for up to 20 minutes.

>> **Creating a wavy style with round brushes:** Follow the directions for a full, curly style set. If you don't want a lot of height on top, round brush the top layers off base (refer to Figure 20-4a). After you release and break up the curls with your fingers, use a soft brush (boar bristle is best) to lightly brush the hair straight down and at a 0-degree elevation (see Chapter 5). Also use this same brush to gently brush the waves into place. Dispense a couple of drops of smoothing serum onto your palm, run your palms together and lightly skim your hands over the top layers of the hair.

TIP

When styling waves, control the curls by keeping your hand flat against the hair right above the brush as you move from the base down to the ends of the hair.

Scrunch styling for movement and curl

Scrunching (see Figure 20-7) will give straight hair more movement and wavy or curly hair a stronger shape and better definition. In terms of heat styles, hair scrunching is also the ideal way to create an eye-pleasing, unstructured look.

FIGURE 20-7:
Hair scrunching
produces
maximum
natural curl.

Photographer: Tom Carson (www.tomcarsonphoto.com);
Hair: Jordan David; Makeup: Betty Mekonnen; Wardrobe:
JBat Boutique; Douglas Carroll Salon & Spa, Raleigh,
North Carolina

Hair scrunching on damp hair is done right after the hair has been shampooed, conditioned, blotted, and prepped with styling aids. When scrunch-styling hair, volumizing products are helpful for straight hair; curl-enhancing products will make curls and waves pop, and smoothing products are excellent for super-curly, frizz-prone hair.

TIP

To avoid creating crunchy 1980s curls for anything other than a Halloween party, only use lightweight, flexible gels or sprays when scrunching the hair.

AUTHOR SAYS

If you're a curly wannabe like me, scrunching is the perfect solution. Using my hair as an example, without scrunching or using any styling aids, my hair is a type 1C (refer to Chapter 4 for more on hair types). However, when I scrunch it with curl-enhancing products, it jumps to a 2B (wavy with some loose curls).

Once the hair has been prepped for scrunching, do the following:

1. **If the hair is more than 4 inches (10.2 centimeters) past the shoulders, use a styling or paddle brush to remove all tangles (see Chapter 19 for more information on brushes). Flip the hair over the head and bend forward until the hair is hanging straight toward the floor.**

(See directions on how to scrunch shorter hair at the end of this tutorial.)

2. **Using your fingers, rake through the hair to make sure that all strands are lying in the same forward/down direction.**

3. **Using a blow-dryer and a diffuser attachment (see Chapter 19), begin scrunching the hair by placing your palm below the ends of the hair and then moving your hand up to where you want the tighter curls to begin.**

   This will make the hair pool in the palm of your hand.

   If the hair is too bulky to easily fit in the palm of your hand — which can cause less curl definition — scrunch smaller sections of hair.

4. **Open and close your fingers to scrunch the hair while applying heat to the scrunched-up curls and the hair above it.**

5. **Do this throughout the hair until it's 90-percent dry.**

6. **Lightly spritz a working spray or a lightweight spray gel throughout the hair without disturbing the curls or waves you worked so hard to create. Then give the curls one more scrunch.**

7. **Allow the hair to remain undisturbed until completely dry.**

TIP

On short hair, scrunch the hair while sitting upright. Select small sections of hair and, going all the way to the scalp, scrunch the strands with your fingers.

Curling Irons: Spiraling in Control

Knowing how to use a curling iron or wand like a professional allows you to give a beautiful finish to many different hairstyles. In this section, you'll learn more than one way to create everything from springy curls to waves. In order to get plenty of experience before curling a live person, I recommend practicing your moves on your ever-patient mannequin.

Perfecting poppin' curls

Curling hair is a skill that, once perfected, will make your hairstyles come to life (see Figure 20-8). If you follow the directions in this chapter, as well as Chapter 19, I promise that you'll be able to ace this styling task.

FIGURE 20-8:
Using a 1-inch (2.5 centimeters) curling iron creates bouncy, curly styles.

Photographer: Tom Carson (www.tomcarsonphoto.com);
Hair: Danny DuBose; Make-up: Ashley Nicole Pugh;
Bob Steele Salon, Atlanta, Georgia

Follow these top tips on how to successfully curl the hair:

» Set the stage with a great directional blow-dry based on your planned style (see "Blowing Them Away with Your Drying Techniques" earlier in this chapter).

» Preheat the iron to the desired temperature (see Chapter 19).

» When ironing the hair, always make directional partings (see "They Went That-a-Way: Directional Styling and Lift" at the beginning of this chapter).

» Take sections of hair that are thin enough to evenly heat the hair from root to end.

» Preheat each hair section by running the iron through it a couple of times before actually curling the hair.

» If you do not have a constant heat feature on your iron, frequently check the curling iron temperature.

WARNING

Never heat style extremely damaged hair. If it looks like cotton candy, resembles a frayed rope, has been chemically damaged, or breaks while the hair is being brushed (see Chapter 17), always cool-set the hair (see "Heat-Free Styling Tips" later in this chapter).

Curling wands: Creating loose and unstructured styles

Curling wands are clip-free irons with a tapered barrel that starts wider at the *hilt* (nearest the hand) and narrower at the tip. The firmness of the curls is controlled by how much manual tension you apply to the strands, and how thick the sections are during the curling process. Curling wands work best for looser curls or waves. They're not designed to create volume.

TIP

Information about curling wands is covered in Chapter 19. The different types of materials used for curling wands are the same as for curling irons, which are also covered in this same chapter.

REMEMBER

Because your fingers are very close to the heated wand, always use a heat-resistant styling glove that effectively shields your skin from being burned while never interfering with the dexterity of your fingers. Heat-resistant gloves are commonly included with the purchase of a styling wand and are also sold separately.

Here are several tips on how to curl the hair with a curling wand.

>> Unlike the sections you create when using a curling iron, I find that 1-inch-square (2.5 centimeters) sections work best when using this tool.

>> To avoid burning your hand or forearm — and achieving the best curl shape possible — hold the curling wand tip side down and vertical to the floor.

>> Unless you're ambidextrous, always use your dominant hand to wind the hair around the wand.

>> Begin wrapping the hair around the wand off base (see Figure 20-4a) and where you want the curl to begin.

>> Use your fingers to control the tension of the hair.

>> For beachy curls, pinch (compress) the hair together using your thumb and index finger and then wind it around the wand.

>> For traditional curls, wrap the hair flat around the wand.

>> If you find the curls are too tight, pull one time on the ends of each curl while the hair is still warm.

Curling wands are wonderful tools, but they can be tricky to use. Practice using a curling wand on a warm setting until you're more comfortable curling the hair.

Flattening the Curve: Straightening Irons

Flat irons are used to straighten or smooth the hair (see Figure 20-9), create springy curls, and produce a sleek finish to the hair strands. Temperature guidelines for flat irons are shared in Chapter 19, and the different materials used for flat iron plates are the same, whether you're using a round brush, curling iron, or flat iron. However, there are some differences that you should know about before flat-ironing hair.

Becoming a smooth beauty operator

Once the hair has been shampooed and conditioned, and the correct styling aids have been applied (see Chapters 17 and 18), dry the hair by following along with "Blowing Them Away with Your Drying Techniques" earlier in this chapter.

Once the blow-dry is complete, re-section and pin the hair. Starting at the back/bottom section and working your way up the head, take ½-inch (1.3 centimeters) subsections and do the following.

>> **Straight, sleek styles:** Iron the hair straight down at a 0-degree elevation (see Figure 20-9).

>> **Smooth, full styles:** Iron the hair at a 45-degree or 90-degree elevation.

>> **Smooth, more voluminous styles:** Overdirect the base of the hair in the opposite direction it will be styled.

>> **Smooth styles on curly hair:** Iron the base of the hair separately a couple of times before smoothing the rest of each subsection.

Once you start gliding the iron down a section of hair, never stop until it has been completely ironed. If you pause at any point along the way, you risk damaging or even breaking the hair.

The curlier and coarser the hair is, the more passes you'll need to make with your iron. Fine, straight hair may require a single pass of the iron, for instance, while coarse, curly hair may require up to three passes.

FIGURE 20-9:
Flat-ironing
straight hair
creates a sleek,
more polished
style.

Photographer: Tom Carson (www.tomcarsonphoto.com);
Haircut and Style: Sonia Gur; Color: Ava Gardner; Makeup:
Jen Blalock; Planet 21 Salons, Charlotte, North Carolina

TIP

Smoothed styles that start to revert to frizzy curls within hours of straightening or smoothing the hair are referred to as *curl reversion*. Curl reversion can be caused by improperly prepping or blow-drying the hair, insufficient iron passes, perspiration, or environmental factors such as fog, rain, or humidity.

Curling hair with a flat iron

Flat irons can also be used to create curls (see Figure 20-10), which can be loose, tight, or irregular, depending on how you flat-iron the hair.

Flat-ironing ribbons and curls

After prepping the hair with hair care and styling aid products that encourage curl, blow-dry the hair with a round brush. Section the hair into four or six sections (depending on the length and thickness of the hair) (see Chapter 6). Separate 1-inch-square (2.5 centimeters) sections and curl the hair as follows:

1. Iron the hair straight down until you reach the point where you want the hair to curl.

2. Without stopping your downward movement, turn the iron 180 degrees either toward or away from you.

FIGURE 20-10:
This particular style can be created by flat-ironing curls and making some ends straight and smooth.

Photographer: Tom Carson (www.tomcarsonphoto.com);
Hair and Makeup: Macy Cordy; Cloud 9 Salon and Spa,
Martins Ferry, Ohio

3. **With the hair still between the plates, wrap the rest of the hair one time around the outside of the iron/plates. Slide your fingers toward the ends and grasp the hair for control and tension.**

4. **While maintaining moderate tension on the hair, continue moving the iron down the section until all of the hair has been ironed.**

5. **Repeat steps 1–4. Alternate curling the ends and ironing them straight.**

TIP

The faster you move through each subsection, the looser the curl will be. By ironing the hair at different rates, you can vary the tightness of the curls for a less structured style.

WARNING

If a flat iron is left in one spot for even a few seconds, you risk severely damaging the hair. When curling the hair, practice the turning movement in steps 2–4 on a mannequin, which never cries when your first few attempts don't create perfectly shaped curls or there's the smell of burnt hair in the air.

Heat-Free Styling Tips

There's a special joy in styling curls in their natural shape without damaging this delicate fabric. Because heat-free styling is the healthiest way to style curly and coily hair, this section is devoted to natural ways you can shape curly styles without using a blow-dryer or any outside source of heat.

TIP

It's rare for anyone to have uniform curls throughout their head. When creating a natural hairstyle, you may find a few straight or barely wavy strands, or random curls that are so tight they create recessions (holes) in the hairstyle. Any time you encounter these situations, wait until the hair is completely dried and styled. Then, use a curling iron to curl straight pieces or apply a styling aid and stretch super-tight curls.

Plopping for curl perfection

Curl plopping is an alternative to scrunch-drying curls that can be done with or without heat. Plopping allows curls to dry in their natural shapes.

All you need to plop the hair is a worn cotton T-shirt and some styling aids. A cotton T-shirt soaks up moisture without creating frizz while the hair dries, and significantly cuts down on the drying time. An alternative to the T-shirt is an official hair plopping microfiber towel. My go-to towel for hair plopping is the Curly Tee Towel because it's easy to use and comes with a drawstring to better secure the wrap. Even so, my favorite way to plop hair is still using a worn-out T-shirt.

WARNING

Avoid using a terry cotton towel. Because these towels are designed to absorb as much water and moisture as possible, they will leave the hair parched. They also rough-up the cuticle layer, which causes the hair to frizz.

Here's how to properly plop and retain gorgeous curls.

1. **Start with wet, freshly washed and conditioned hair.**

2. **Squeeze out excess water and apply a leave-in conditioner and your go-to oil and styling aids. Apply a little more product than you normally would to compensate for the absorption by the T-shirt.**

3. **Use your fingers to arrange the curls in the shape you want them to dry.**

4. **Lay out a T-shirt on a counter or chair with the neck of the T-shirt nearest you.**

5. **Flip the hair over the center of the T-shirt by bending your head and torso. Lower your head directly down on the T-shirt to form compressed curls (imagine a Slinky and you're on the right track).**

6. **With your head still bent in the same position, grab the hem of the T-shirt and place it on the back of your neck.**

7. **Grabbing the sleeves of the T-shirt, bring them up to the front of the head, twist the sleeves together and then tie the cuffs together to form a secure turban wrap.**

8. **For a heatless set, leave the hair in the wrap while getting your beauty sleep or until the hair is bone dry.**

   (Optional) Leave the hair wrapped for 15 to 20 minutes, remove the T-shirt, and using a blow-dryer with a diffuser attachment, scrunch the hair dry.

Twirly curly finger styles

Curly and coily hair, as shown in Figure 20-11, can be shaped with your fingers or a tail comb. But, before getting your digits busy twirling curls, make sure the hair has been properly prepped with styling aids.

1. **Addressing each curl, apply a flexible gel or styling mousse, and comb through the curls with a fine-toothed comb to smooth the cuticle layer.**

2. **Smooth each curl with your fingers by pinching the hair and moving from root to end.**

3. **Twirl each curl around and around your index finger.**

   (Optional) Use a comb with a space between the teeth and the end of the comb.

4. **Place the base of the curl in this space and twirl the comb.**

Place a loose net over the hair to ensure the curls aren't disturbed. Do not touch the hair until it's 100-percent dry.

Curling super-fragile-istic hair

Fragile, damaged hair will break off in a heartbeat, making it the most delicate fabric you'll ever encounter. Whether you're brushing or styling the hair, it needs to be handled like vintage lace that could fall apart if handled too roughly. Any time you encounter fragile hair, cool sets are the way to go. This is also true of anyone who doesn't want heat applied to their hair.

FIGURE 20-11:
The finger-curling technique is used to define and shape curls for natural styling.

*Photographer: Tom Carson (www.tomcarsonphoto.com);
Hair: Calena Hopkins; Makeup: Chelsea Wallis; Currie Hair,
Skin and Nail Salon, Glen Mills, Pennsylvania*

New-fashioned roller sets

Here is a great way to achieve a modern look with old-fashioned rollers that your grandma may still be using to set her hair.

1. **Apply a lightweight gel, flexible setting spray, or mousse on damp hair, paying particular attention to the ends.**

2. **Set the hair with plastic rollers in the directions you want the hair to go. (See "They Went That-a-Way: Directional Styling and Lift" earlier in this chapter.)**

3. **Roll the hair according to the amount of lift you want for the style. (See "Learning the base-ics" earlier in this chapter.)**

4. **Use a fine-tooth comb to comb the ends flat on the roller.**

5. **Allow the hair to air dry. If time is a problem, use a blow-dryer with a diffuser attachment to speed up the drying process.**

Handling Styling Conundrums

What if you've tried your best, and something still doesn't go right with the hair? Table 20-1 shows some common troubleshooting situations that can see you through most mishaps.

TABLE 20-1   **Styling Problems Solved**

Problem	Reasons/Solutions
Failure to rise. You want the hair to flip, and instead it flops.	You're asking the hair to do something it physically can't do — ultra-fine fairy hair, for instance, playing the starring role in an updo. The wrong styling aids were used. Too little or too much product was applied. The hair wasn't dried on base or overdirected in the opposite direction of the end style.
Overblown hair. Dry, dull styling results are generally caused by over-drying the hair.	Refrain from drying the hair on the highest heat setting. Check each section for dryness more frequently. Use a thermal protectant to ensure that the hair isn't exposed to too much heat. Use a leave-in conditioner prior to blowing the hair dry.
Fuzzy finishes. You want to avoid fuzzy, rough textures of hair because they're considered the antithesis of beauty.	Any moisture left in the hair will cause the hair to frizz. Always point the blow-dryer toward the ends of the hair. Use a little more tension on the hair while blow-drying. Shampoo and condition the hair with anti-frizz products. Use a leave-in conditioner prior to blow-drying. Apply a styling aid that promises sleek, smooth results. Finish the hair with a flat iron.
Limp curls. Laboring over a style only to see the curls roll over and die is disheartening to say the least.	Shampoo and condition the hair with body-enhancing properties. Make sure the hair is dry before styling. Use stronger styling aids to create a crisper finish to the hair. Use a leave-in conditioner that emphasizes proteins to give the hair more body. Use a moderate-hold finishing spray to keep your work intact.

Problem	Reasons/Solutions
Midday fallout. When your hair betrays you midday, you have a real problem on your hands.	Shampoo and condition the hair with products containing body-enhancing properties.
	Use stronger styling aids.
	Use a protein-based leave-in conditioner to provide more "oomph" to the hair.
	Use a strong-hold finishing spray right after styling the hair.
	Use a moderate-hold finishing spray to do a midday touch-up on the hair.

Chapter **21**

Cleaning Up Your Act

Although learning about sanitizing and disinfecting procedures may seem about as interesting as perfecting the art of housework, it's your only assurance that your haircutting area and implements are not harboring nasty little beasties like flu and cold germs or bloodborne diseases like hepatitis C.

This chapter contains tips on how to keep your family and friends safer while receiving a haircut, and for you to be more protected while cutting hair. It also includes insider information about how to spot a clean or dirty salon or stylist.

Sanitizers versus Disinfectants

Before we dig into what you can do to keep your cutting space safe, I want to clarify two important product categories that I refer to throughout this chapter: *sanitizer* and *disinfectant*. While many people use these terms interchangeably, they're actually used in two different steps that work together to wipe off and then wipe out *pathogens*.

» Sanitizers are used during the cleaning phase. They remove debris and eliminate germs with a soap or household cleaner. The goal of sanitizing is to lower the number of germs to a safe level.

>> Disinfectants do not clean surfaces. Their only job is to kill up to 99.9 percent of all bacteria and viruses.

REMEMBER

You should always use a hospital-grade disinfectant with an Environmental Protection Agency (EPA) registration number on the container. This is important because hospital-grade disinfectants are virucidal, bactericidal, tuberculocidal (a particularly resistant bacteria), and fungicidal. Two household disinfectants that have hospital-grade properties are Lysol® and bleach-free Clorox® Disinfecting Wipes.

WARNING

Disinfectants are regulated as pesticides by the EPA. Never purchase a "disinfectant" that does not have an EPA registered number on the packaging. When using disinfectants, wear latex or nitrile gloves to prevent product absorption through the gloves and onto your hands.

For those who adhere to the "When all else fails, read the instructions" approach to life, please know that it doesn't apply to disinfectants. You should always follow all directions included on the packaging for your own safety and the safety of others.

Treating Your Haircutting Space

Your first step to creating a safer cutting space is to sanitize and disinfect all work surfaces. This includes your work counter, cutting chair, and containers. If you have an entry door into your cutting space, also sanitize and disinfect the doorknobs. Finish your cleaning with an aerosol disinfectant to eliminate the danger of infectious airborne droplets.

REMEMBER

If you are one of the rare home haircutters who has a shampoo setup, you should also sanitize and disinfect the sink and chair after each use. When doing so, don't forget to include the hose and nozzle (the most forgotten parts!).

Disinfecting Towels and Capes

If you're only cutting your family's hair, you may think that disinfecting towels and capes is going a little overboard. While this may seem to be the case, I suggest that you actually take this a bit further by always washing and disinfecting all towels, washcloths, and bedding used by your family. You can do this by adding the recommended amount of a hospital-grade disinfectant to the wash. This step is important because washing machines for home use rarely get hot enough to kill certain harmful germs.

TIP

Wash all cutting capes with Velcro fasteners in a lingerie laundry bag to prevent them from becoming entangled with other items that are being laundered at the same time.

Disinfecting Combs and Brushes

When it comes to combs and brushes, sharing is not caring. The human scalp can harbor nasty germs and debris. Once you use a brush or comb on anyone's hair, it should be sanitized and disinfected before using it on another person.

Here's my recommended supply list for sanitizing and disinfecting combs and brushes:

>> Two plastic containers with lids that are large enough to completely immerse the combs and brushes

>> Shampoo or dish soap

>> Quaternary ammonium compound (QUATS) concentrate (sold in beauty supply stores and online) or other hospital-grade liquid disinfectant

>> Firm toothbrush or stiff nail brush

>> Scissors (not your good haircutting scissors) (optional item)

>> Thick salon or hand towels

>> Nitrile or latex gloves

How to sanitize and disinfect your combs and brushes, stat!

1. **Remove all loose hairs.**

2. **Fill a plastic container with hot water and a squirt of shampoo or dish soap. Completely immerse the brushes and combs.**

3. **Place the plastic lid on top of the container and allow the brushes and combs to soak for at least 30 minutes.**

TIP

Cleaning alternative: After removing the debris from your brushes and combs, place them on the top tray of your dishwasher and wash them on the sanitizing cycle. If your dishwasher doesn't have a sanitizing cycle, skip this tip!

SAFELY STORING CLEAN AND DIRTY COMBS AND BRUSHES

One of the most important things you can do to keep your work environment safe is to always store your clean and dirty combs and brushes in separate, closed containers. You can do this by using rectangular containers with lids. You can also store your tools in gallon-sized plastic freezer bags. Either way, I recommend that you mark your containers "clean" and "soiled."

4. Remove and rinse the tools.

5. Using a stiff plastic brush, scrub away the remaining debris and styling aid residue.

6. Wearing latex or nitrile gloves, fill the second container with water and add a disinfectant solution according to the label instructions.

7. Place the cleaned combs and brushes in the plastic container.

8. Soak the tools for the recommended amount of time (usually 10 minutes).

9. Wearing gloves, remove the tools from the solution, rinse them, and place them on a clean towel.

10. Place another clean towel over the tools and roll them up in a bundle. Rock the bundle back and forth to release any liquid trapped in the brushes. Allow them to dry completely before using.

Cleaning and Disinfecting Scissors

Most stylists are concerned about disinfectants ruining their haircutting scissors, including yours truly. Fortunately, there is a safe way to disinfect scissors without soaking them in a strong disinfectant solution by doing the following:

1. Sanitize them using a soft brush and soapy water.

2. Rinse and pat dry.

3. Apply a disinfectant scissor spray with the blades wide open.

   One spray made specifically for scissors is Kasho Scissor Spray, which disinfects and lubricates your scissors at the same time.

Disinfecting your scissors helps to prevent the spread of many different diseases, including more serious ones that are transmitted by blood.

Sanitizing and Disinfecting Trimmers and Clippers

Just like scissors, cleaning and disinfecting clippers and trimmers go a long way in preventing the spread of pathogens. Here is an easy and safe method for ridding your buzzing buddies of nasty germs and trapped snippets of hair.

To properly clean and disinfect trimmers and clippers, you need the following items:

>> Firm toothbrush

>> Pipe cleaner

>> Disinfectant spray for trimmers and clippers

>> Disinfectant wipes for the casings

>> Lubricating oil made specifically for trimmers and clippers

>> Latex or nitrile gloves

Sanitizing and disinfecting clippers and trimmers in five easy steps:

1. **Use a firm toothbrush to remove hair snippets from the sides of the cutting blade.**

2. **Fold a pipe cleaner in half and slide it between the blades (clippers only). Move the pipe cleaner back and forth to loosen and remove bits of hair.**

3. **Wipe down the casing with a disinfectant towelette.**

4. **Turn on your clippers or trimmers. Tilt the tool slightly downward and spray a clipper and trimmer disinfectant on the blades.**

    I use disinfectant spray products made by Wahl and Andis.

5. **Lubricate the blades with a clipper and trimmer oil in the same way you applied the disinfectant in step 4.**

Sanitizing and Disinfecting Sundries

Hair-related sundries include items such as hair clips and clamps, hair pins, small plastic spatulas for dispensing cream-based products, and neck and face brushes. Some sundries — such as plastic spatulas — are designed for a one-time use only, while others can be sanitized and disinfected.

>> **Neck and face brushes** can be sanitized by first washing them in warm, soapy water (swirling them in the palm of your hand works great). After thoroughly rinsing the brushes, saturate the bristles only (not the ferrule, which attaches the bristles to the brush) with 70-percent alcohol for 30 seconds. Then rinse, shape the bristles and set them out to dry.

>> **Pins, clips, and clamps** can be sanitized by washing them with warm, soapy water and then disinfecting them with a disinfectant spray.

Scalp Encounters of the Third Kind

Most people have perfectly healthy scalps, but occasionally you'll encounter someone who does not. Because it's the "do nots" that you need to be concerned about, always check the scalp while you check the hair before every haircut, whether it's a 3-year-old family member or your best friend. A healthy scalp should be free of redness, sores, blisters, or cuts (no matter how small).

I categorize unhealthy scalp conditions into two categories: contagious and non-contagious.

>> **Scalp conditions are not contagious.** They can be as benign as dry, flaky skin or dandruff (larger, usually oily flakes) to psoriasis (scaly, silvery skin patches). Conditions also include alopecia areata (patchy hair loss) and sudden hair thinning.

>> **Scalp infections and infestations are contagious.** They include fungal infections like *tinea capitis* (ringworm) and bacterial infections like *impetigo* caused by staph or strep bacteria (red sores that burst and form a yellow-brown crust). The most common scalp infestation is *Pediculus humanus capitis* (head lice).

AUTHOR SAYS

The singular name for lice is louse. Calling someone a louse or saying you feel lousy dates back to olden times when head and body lice infestations were extremely common.

THE ONLY GOOD LOUSE IS A DEAD LOUSE

Although people seem to feel great shame about having an infestation of head lice, these little critters are actually not finicky about their choice of human hosts. They will homestead on anyone's head whether they're a minister, attorney, teacher, or pampered child. Small children are most likely to get a head lice infestation because they love to roll around on the floor together, rub heads, use each other's hairbrushes, and trade hats for the day.

You can spot a head lice infestation by checking for oval-shaped white specks that cling to the hair at the root area (called nits) and parting the hair in different areas to look for red (right after feeding), tan, or off-white insects about the size of a sesame seed. Sometimes you can also see movement. The scalp is also typically red and itchy.

If you discover a case of head ice, decline or stop the haircut immediately. If it's one of your family members, treat the hair and scalp with a commercial pediculicide and use a nit comb to remove the nits (lice eggs) from the scalp area. Disinfect your cutting area and wash and disinfect the person's bedding and clothing. If you haven't dealt with this situation before, I strongly recommend that you ask your family doctor or nurse practitioner for their pediculicide brand recommendations and specific instructions on what you should do to eradicate the infestation.

How to Spot a Clean or Dirty Stylist and Salon

Understanding the importance of disinfection when cutting hair also gives you the know-how to protect your own health when visiting a salon. Are you relaxing in a clean environment as you have your head rubbed and scrubbed, or are your lovely locks being immersed in a sea of nasty critters that could give you anything from the stomach flu to serious liver damage caused by hepatitis C?

Is your stylist clean or dirty?

Here are some clues to look for before and during your appointment, starting by observing the stylist in action who will be doing your hair.

>> Are their mirror and station surfaces clean? What about their styling chair?

>> Are clips and clamps used and then tossed into a drawer as opposed to a container marked soiled?

» Do they use a neck or face brush and put it anywhere but in a soiled container?

» After they have finished with the previous client, do they sanitize and disinfect their station and chair? Equally important, do they sanitize and disinfect their station with the same towels they used for their previous client or use a fresh cleaning cloth or towelette?

» Do they put their scissors back in their case without sanitizing and disinfecting them first?

» Do they gather up their combs and brushes and toss them in a drawer, or do they put them in a soiled container? (Some states allow stylists to place their soiled and clean brushes and combs in separate drawers, but this practice isn't ideal.)

» What happens to the cape used for the previous client? Do they remove it from their station, or do they keep it at their station to drape you too?

» Do they sanitize their hands before inviting you to sit in their chair?

» While sitting at their station, be nosy by subtly looking in their drawers any time they're opened. This is important because, honestly, I have seen everything from a layer of dead skin flakes at the bottom of drawers to a mix of dirty and clean brushes. I have even seen stylists use the cleanest of their dirty brushes on clients.

» Are you offered a freshly laundered robe to wear during the service?

» Do you have a fresh towel, neck strip, and cape around your neck?

» Do they sweep after cutting and before they blow-dry your hair?

Is the salon clean or dirty?

You should also be using your powers of observation to detect whether you're in a clean or dirty salon. I suggest you do the following.

» If there's a reception desk, take a peek at the area where the receptionist is working to see if it's dirty, cluttered, or otherwise messy.

» Are the retail and reception areas dust-free? Is the glass free of fingerprints and smudges?

» Are the salon floors clean and well maintained? Any dust or hair collecting in the corners?

» Are you offered a beverage in a disposable or glass cup? Only accept a beverage in a disposable cup, as dishes used by the salon are usually washed by hand and rarely in a commercial dishwasher.

» Subtly but thoroughly inspect the shampoo room. Have the chair and sink been sanitized and disinfected? (If it doesn't look like it, always ask for it to be cleaned/recleaned.) Is the backbar area where hair care products are kept clean and well organized? Has the trash been emptied lately? Are there used and dirty tint bottles or bowls and brushes present? Is there a hair critter (loose hair) or multiple colors of hair wrapped around the sink strainer?

» Always visit the restroom. Look for cleanliness overall, as well as the presence of hand sanitizer and antibacterial soap in pump containers. Toilet seat covers should be available in a sanitary dispenser. Having a touchless towel dispenser is a bonus.

» If the salon launders towels, capes, and gowns on the premises, don't hesitate to ask if they're disinfected during the wash cycle. If you still feel uneasy, look for a salon that uses a professional laundry service.

6

The Part of Tens

IN THIS PART . . .

Engage young children for a happy haircutting experience.

Recognize styling fails and find out how to fix them.

Get advice on dealing with thinning hair.

Chapter **22**

Ten Slices of Advice on Cutting Kids' Hair

Most children are far less enthusiastic about getting their hair cut than you are about transforming their locks into neat little works of art. Five minutes seems like a long time to a young child — and 20 minutes like an eternity. Coaxing them to happily stay put for an entire haircut means using every trick in the book. In a sentence, you need to provide an experience that's fast, fun, tasty, and filled with kid-size activities.

REMEMBER

Before you plunge headlong into cutting kids' hair, make sure you have these tools, supplies, and equipment at the ready:

» Chair (preferably a styling chair or barstool with a back and low arms)

» Child-size beanbag pillow

» Child-size cutting cape

» Thin, small towels or dish towels

» Large, fluffy face brush

» Cornstarch

» Spray bottle filled with warm water

- » Hair conditioner
- » Quality combs and soft brushes
- » Haircutting scissors
- » Small toys
- » Entertainment
- » Healthy snacks
- » Rewards for good behavior

Good Timing

You can minimize the time children must spend getting their hair cut by being completely organized before having them sit in your chair. Having your tools at the ready and knowing exactly what you plan to do with the hair prevents kids from having to sit through a lot of preparation.

REMEMBER

Setting your mental timer is also essential. When you hit that crucial 15-minute mark, you should be heading toward the homestretch of your haircut. (Check out quick haircuts for kids in Chapter 16.)

Having good timing also means choosing your children's hour of power when they're most likely to be patient. Sandwiching a haircut between dinner and bed-time, or during their regular naptime, may be good for your schedule, but it could be the worst time for the child. What's their best time of day? Choosing this magic window of opportunity to do your haircutting wizardry gives you the best chance for pulling off a stress-free experience.

Secure Seating

WARNING

I've seen children get their hair cut while sitting on lawn chairs stacked on top of regular chairs, and even a bench set atop a table. Although the elevation may be right for the haircutter, these unsteady setups jeopardize kids' safety by giving them dangerous opportunities for spinning, hopping, and toppling out of their seats while you're cutting their hair. Proper seating for adults and squirmy little ones, who are typically bursting with energy, is covered in Chapter 1.

If you're reading this book because you want to focus on children's haircuts, there are children's styling chairs that are fun, colorful, and come in a variety of designs. New children's hairstyling chairs are sold by online salon equipment distributors, but you can find used chairs (many in pristine condition) for sale by salons that are remodeling, as well as private sellers who no longer need a children's styling chair because their youngest kids are now adult-size teens.

REMEMBER

Follow these three steps to safely seat a small child:

1. **Place the beanbag on the chair seat.**

2. **Put the child on the beanbag.**

3. **Watch the little tyke become mired in the fabric — no wiggling, no spinning, and no nipped ears caused by doing a tuck jump even though they're still a month away from their third birthday.**

Curbing Curiosity

If you have heated tools in the vicinity of your cutting chair, make sure they're cool to the touch, unplugged, and the cords are off the floor. Also, keep all styling products out of reach and preferably out of sight. If you have sharp tools that you aren't using for this haircut, put them in a drawer or a closed container.

Covering Up

Because children have extra-sensitive skin, hair clippings drive them wild. You can help prevent itching and scratching by purchasing a child's haircutting cape from a beauty supply store. Or online. In terms of comfort and durability, the most ideal capes are made out of water-resistant cloth and are secured at the neck with a Velcro fastener. This type of fastener allows you to precisely adjust the cape so it's never too small or too loose. Other options are children's plastic shampoo capes with Velcro, snaps, or metal fasteners. Capes with engaging prints are particularly big hits with the petite set.

You can also protect children's backs from major hair invasions by putting a thin, soft towel underneath the cutting cape to catch stray bits of hair. An oldie-but-goodie hand towel, or even a dishtowel, will do. Using these two items together (one under the cape and one over the cape) enables you to create a protective draping.

TIP

Draping involves placing the towel horizontally across and around the shoulders, while keeping it flat to prevent it from interfering with the haircut. Put the haircutting cape over the towel, allowing ½ inch (1.3 centimeters) of the fabric to peek out around the sides and back of the neck. Sensitive youngsters are then safely protected from marauding hairs that would otherwise be creeping down their necks and backs, and sometimes burrowing their way into the waistband of their pants.

Brushing Up

Having a fluffy *face brush* on hand to use during and after their haircuts is a must. I've always called it a *tickle brush* for my youngest clients. Wee ones love getting "tickled" and can't stop giggling while I efficiently remove hair snippets from their face and neck.

After you've finished cutting the hair, lightly apply cornstarch to the brush, tap it to remove the excess, and brush away any remaining snippets to stop the "itchy-hair syndrome" dead in its tracks.

Spiking the Waters

Having a spray bottle at the ready is a must because children's hair typically dries in a heartbeat. You can avoid any vigorous protests over being sprayed with a strong blast of cold water by using a spray bottle with a mist setting and filling it with warm water. To create an even better haircutting experience, mix a small amount of conditioner — no more than a capful — into the warm water to painlessly remove any tangles as you go. You can score extra points by using a children's conditioner that has a bubble gum, grape, or some other candy-inspired fragrance.

Banishing Tears

Besides misting the hair with a detangling spray (if needed), avoiding painful haircutting experiences means using a soft boar bristle brush (which you can read more about in Chapter 19) on children who are under the age of 3. Because the softness of these brushes varies — many manufacturers add nylon bristles to make their brushes sturdier — testing for softness before committing to a purchase ensures that you end up with one that's made for sensitive little scalps.

The same holds true for combs. Believing that all combs are alike has gotten more than a few haircutters in trouble. Poorly made combs have sharp, rough teeth that feel as though they're tearing their way through the hair and scraping the scalp. These problems can be remedied by using carbon or hard rubber-like combs. Manufacturers that use these upgraded materials generally take extra smoothing steps that make their combs effortlessly glide through the hair without scratching the scalp.

Getting a Grip

Doing some hand jive of your own also ensures that little eyes, noses, and ears remain intact while you're creating your masterpiece. Whenever two hands aren't needed to cut the hair, place your free hand squarely over the top of the child's head. Squeeze just tight enough to stop any movement. You can then go about your business knowing that you're safely snipping areas that are close to the skin while positioning the head to enhance the haircut.

Entertaining

So far, the only things missing from this happy occasion are toys, healthy snacks, and cartoons. Giving your child snacks like grapes or carrot sticks in a sandwich bag to keep them safe from falling hair, having a few small toys (preferably ones that they haven't seen before) at the ready to plop on their lap at the first sign of impatience, or hitting the play button to watch their favorite movie can buy you several additional minutes when cutting their hair.

TIP

To keep toddlers' hands out of danger, stylists have a sneaky trick they play on their youngest clients. After they have been secured in the chair, safely draped, and have had a little teasing with the tickle brush, ask them, "Can you help me by holding these so I don't drop them?" *These* could be a clean, colorful hair clip (preferably with sparkles) for one hand and a neck brush or another clip for the other hand. Most kids clamp their little mitts around each of these items and hold them for several minutes. Some will even grip them for the duration of the haircut.

Ensuring a Good Time

As an extra insurance policy, adding some sort of small reward at the end of children's haircuts really pays off. I always praise little tykes for being good by adorning their ears with "sticky" earrings (self-adhering dots used for color-coding purposes, or tiny character stickers), or giving them a toy that typically costs less than a buck. You can even ask your family and friends to donate their discarded fast-food toys, or load up your basket at your local dollar store. Prizes are particularly helpful when you're running five minutes over and a fidgety child needs a strong incentive to refrain from catapulting out of the chair.

REMEMBER

Before the awards ceremony, make sure their "prize" is either sealed in the original packaging or sanitized, disinfected, and thoroughly rinsed and dried.

Chapter **23**

Ten Hair Fails and Fixes

When Alexander Pope wrote, "To err is human, to forgive is divine," he couldn't have been talking about hair. When going out in the world, a person's self-confidence heavily relies on having a good hair day. Every time you cut or style someone's hair, there's a risk — albeit a small one — that something could go wrong. This chapter shares insights into ten common hair fails and how to fix or avoid them the next time you dabble in hair.

REMEMBER

Turn every hair fail into a valuable lesson by studying what you did wrong, what you failed to do, and how to never repeat that same mistake again. I can say with certainty that you have more mistakes in your future because we all do. It's what you learn from them that will improve your haircutting skills over time.

Embracing the Good Times

If you're rushing because you're tight on time, rethink how you can better manage your day. Calculate how long it will take for you to prep and cut the hair — and then add 15 minutes for good measure. If you don't have enough time, cut or style the hair on another day when you do have enough time to get the job done right. If you're feeling pressure to please someone who is really pushing to get a haircut regardless of your schedule, always resist. If you don't, you could find yourself in a situation that would be bad for you and the person you're trying to please.

Multitasking with Scissors

Gardening shears are for trimming bushes; kitchen scissors are for opening packaged foods; and craft scissors are for cutting paper. Using any of these types of scissors to cut hair is like trying to use a chisel to split wood. The moment you commit to cutting hair — even if it's just your own bangs — I strongly recommend that you purchase a pair of dedicated haircutting scissors. Doing so will make your job much easier, and the results will be 100 times better.

WARNING

One last piece of advice: Never cut anything but human hair with your haircutting scissors. If you weaken your resolve and reach for your hair scissors to open a box or cut cardboard, for instance, you will immediately or eventually (depending on the offending material) ruin the cutting edge of the blades.

Playing by the Rules

Not learning the basic rules of haircutting can create spectacular hair fails. Do you remember reading (or at least trying to read) Chapter 5, the ponderous chapter that talks about head shapes, elevations, angles, and guides? Although it may not be the most fun-filled reading material, it is the most important chapter in this book. Seriously studying the information in Chapter 5 will allow you to successfully unleash your cutting creativity on family and friends.

TIP

If you've read this book in order, you were pretty new to the cutting game when you reached Chapter 5. If that's the case, I suggest that you re-read this information-filled chapter now. I promise that it will be much more relatable the second time around.

Going Overbold

Being overly confident is a human failing that bites all of us from time to time. When it happens to you, you need to put your ego in check. Being keenly aware of what you know and don't know is an important step in preventing hair fails. Instead of pushing your skills without training, know what you want to learn in order to do certain cuts and cutting techniques. I also recommend having a firm understanding of haircutting basics before expanding your skills because no matter how advanced a haircut might be, the basic rules of haircutting will still make up 95 percent of the overall design. Also, remember to always practice advanced skills on mannequin heads rather than actual people.

Disorderly Cutting Conduct

Being sloppy happens to the best of us, but that doesn't mean it's not a serious mistake. When you allow your haircutting habits to devolve, your work will become unpredictable — sometimes so-so and sometimes bad. Sloppy habits are easy to form and hard to break, whether you're cutting hair or following a recipe. Sloppiness also makes most of us forget what we learned in the first place. Taking thick cutting sections, failing to thoroughly comb the hair before cutting, not checking your haircut, or losing track of the head shape or your guide will always compromise your results.

Taking a Leave of Absence

Taking a mental vacation happens to everyone. It goes something like this: You're cutting along when suddenly your mind takes off and lands in the Bahamas. There's no magic pill that will fix this problem because staying focused takes discipline and practice. To aid in your effort to maintain concentration, avoid as many distractions as possible. Never eat a heavy meal before cutting hair, avoid being "fuzzy-brained" by snacking on proteins, and clear your head by drinking a glass of water before picking up your scissors. It also helps to "peace out" by taking a walk prior to cutting hair, doing a few mild exercises, or meditating to sharpen your concentration.

Keeping It Straight

Clients' body positions affect every haircut that you do. Scrunched-up shoulders, twisted torsos, crossed legs, moving heads, and other position fails will skew your haircuts. This is why it's important for all people in your chair to sit up straight, relax their shoulders, uncross their legs, and look straight ahead (until you move their noggin elsewhere). You also need to check their position throughout the haircut because most people will lose their concentration and revert back to their favorite (unfavorable) body position.

Reaching the Breaking Point

Hair that just snaps off is caused by dehydration (water), lack of moisture (oil), and/or damage.

>> **Hair broken off around the crown area** can be caused by brushing or detangling the hair from the top down, as opposed to starting at the ends; wearing uncovered rubber bands or overly tight hair elastics; or wearing hats, helmets or headphones that catch on the hair at the top of the head.

You can prevent most future "snap-fus" by always being gentle with hair, wearing a headscarf underneath a hat or helmet to avoid snagging the hair, and keeping the hair hydrated and moist.

>> **Hair breaking off along the midshafts and ends** can be caused by dehydrated, moisture-starved, or damaged hair. Dry or moisture-hungry hair is unhealthy hair that can be replenished to a balanced state. Damaged hair cannot be restored to a healthy state, although several bond-strengthening products and conditioners do a pretty good job of temporarily making damaged hair look healthy.

To maintain hair health, keep it hydrated and moisturized, have regular trims, don't play with the hair (twirling it or even chewing on it), avoid overexposure to UV rays (sun) and high-velocity winds, and use high-quality brushes and combs that are specifically designed to do what you want to do with the hair.

Exceeding Hair Capabilities

All hair has a range of specific abilities. As long as you stay within the boundaries of what it can do best, the odds of creating long-lasting styles grow exponentially. Using appropriate styling techniques and styling aids can help maximize the abilities of all hair types. But when you try to actually move — as opposed to push — the boundaries of different hair types, you're flirting with failure. You're also risking hair damage caused by the too-hot or too-frequent use of heat-styling tools. Using well-chosen styling aids will help, but overuse of them will also damage the hair. For the most reliable results, remain within the boundaries of what a particular hair type does best, at least most of the time.

Conquering Curl Rebellions

Wearing your hair naturally curly and loving it is the best example of making the most out of its natural capabilities. But even the best curly practices need a change-up now and then. Here's the best way to style curly hair when smooth hair is right in step with your current mood:

>> Always remember that when you're not controlling the hair, the hair is controlling you. You can be the one in charge by keeping the hair that you aren't immediately working on in pinned sections (ends tucked inside the hair), using a styling brush that grips the hair, working with an air concentrator nozzle attached to your blow-dryer, and always pointing the blow-dryer toward the ends of the hair.

>> Blow-drying is the first step in most styling processes. Use elevation to increase or decrease volume; apply the proper amount of tension to smooth the hair; and always be aware of the direction you're holding each hair subsection.

>> Hair doesn't have a say in how hot you style it, but you do. Always use the minimum amount of heat needed to create a long-lasting style.

>> Only use products that contain heat protectant and smoothing agents and are a perfect match for the hair type and style you want to create. Always apply styling aids and finishing products in layers to prevent re-saturating or causing buildup on the hair.

REMEMBER

Curl reversion is caused by a lot of factors, but chief among them are failing to completely dry the hair, using the wrong styling aids, and not using heat-styling tools properly.

» **Mastering cutting techniques to create the illusion of thicker hair**

» **Using styling tricks and products to camouflage mild hair loss**

Chapter **24**

Ten Bits of Advice for Thinning Hair

Unless you're only cutting children's hair, you will encounter hair loss, whether you're cutting your family's hair or even your own crowning glory. This chapter is focused on sharing many great tips and techniques on how to cut and style thinning hair. It also lightly touches on the emotional impact of hair loss.

What I don't cover in this chapter are hair loss supplements and drugs. Because supplements generally don't have in-depth studies to verify their claims, most of these types of products provide little more than hope in a bottle. On the other hand, while drugs that have been approved by the FDA for hair loss can help many people stop or slow the progression of thinning, they rarely regrow robust terminal (mature) hair. I strongly recommend that before you begin any oral hair loss program, consult with your doctor and, in the case of hair loss drugs, carefully study the potential side effects that must be included in the literature accompanying these medications.

TIP

If you're a hair geek like I am, you can continue expanding your knowledge of hair loss by visiting www.mayoclinic.org and www.americanhairloss.org.

Understanding How You Can Help Those Dealing with Hair Loss

Whether a person is finding too much hair in their brush or their hair part appears to be widening, hair loss could be underway. Although it isn't within your realm of expertise to advise others how to treat their disappearing strands, it's still important to know what to do when you notice that you or one of your family members appears to be losing their hair.

Here are some ways you can help those who are experiencing hair loss:

» Assess the severity of the hair loss. For the purposes of this chapter, mild pattern hair loss refers to the early stages of hair thinning along the front hairline, and on the top and crown of the head. Profound pattern hair loss involves the significant loss of hair in these same areas, and also potentially extends as far back as the occipital bone.

» Refer anyone showing signs of hair loss to a dermatologist for a medical diagnosis.

» Become a camouflage expert to help those with minor thinning issues keep their scalp covered and their self-esteem intact.

» Once medically diagnosed and cosmetic services or procedures are approved, refer advanced cases to hair augmentation specialists who devote their entire career to camouflaging profound hair loss.

Communicating with Care

Because most men with balding issues likely watched their fathers or uncles lose their hair, it's less of a shock when their own hair starts to thin. However, knowing this usually doesn't make them feel any better about their situation. In fact, while many men act blasé about losing their hair, don't let their demeanor or words fool you. Any time men joke about their hair loss — such as asking if you also polish scalps — it bothers them. It's always best to respond to bald jokes by changing the conversation to things like, "I'm checking out your current haircut. Were you happy with it?" Or switch immediately to helpful comments such as, "Are you comfortable with a slightly longer length on top? It will make your hair look noticeably thicker."

On the flip side, in all my years of working behind the chair I never had one female client joke about their hair loss. The grief is too deep; the perceived loss of their femininity is too profound. Always tread lightly when you encounter these situations. No matter how much the person you are caring for speaks about how severe their hair loss is, never agree with them. Instead, study their hair and tell them how you can make their hair appear thicker by doing this or that, or let them know about hair augmentation experts (a more positive way to say "hair loss specialists" for women) who use different techniques to visibly restore the thickness of their hair.

Terms of Concealment

While some haircuts work better than others to conceal hair loss, there isn't a one-size-fits-all technique that solves everything. Some hair thinning is more noticeable due to the hair type, the contrast between the color of the hair and the scalp, or the natural growth direction (cowlicks are the worst betrayers of thinning hair). Thinning Type 1 hair (fine, straight), for instance, is much more noticeable than thinning Type 4 hair (coily), because the former lies flat on the scalp. Because there are so many variables, you really need to define the texture and look at different areas of the hair before deciding on what you need to do to help fill in the empty spaces. (See Chapter 4 for more information on hair types.)

TIP

If you or a family member is experiencing hair loss, you should always provide coverage in such a way that it blends with normal, everyday haircuts and hairstyles. This means no combovers (super deep parts) or other odd hair placements that aren't part of any hairstyle, ever.

Techniques for Hiding Hair Loss

Depending on the location and severity of the hair thinning, cutting techniques generally focus on adding lift, length, and/or bulk.

>> **Lift** is used for mild to moderate thinning where the hair flattens against the crown and at the top of the head.

>> **Length** is helpful when covering a mild thinning condition at the crown, as well as the recession areas along the front hairline (see Chapter 5).

>> **Bulk** is used to create more natural-looking hair density, especially in cases of diffuse thinning.

Haircutting Tips for Pattern Baldness

Male and female pattern baldness generally starts at the recession points along the front hairline, followed by the crown.

TIP

>> When addressing the front hairline, separate the hair around the recession points and cut them separately. The hair in these areas not only needs to be long enough to bridge the gap where the regular front hairline is missing, but also to blend with the hair on the other side of the bare area.

   To ensure that you never cut the hair too short or leave it too long, cut these areas after the balance of the front area is complete and the hair is only slightly damp.

>> Addressing the crown area, leave the hair above the crown long enough to not only cascade over the crown area, but also to be an inch (2.5 centimeters) or more below this area to blend the hair.

>> Cut the hair so that it's shorter on the sides and longer on top. The added length will provide better coverage while still being an integral part of the haircut.

>> Create a short, tousled style with layers that are long enough to casually cover receding and thinning areas.

Haircutting Tips for Diffuse Hair Thinning

Diffuse hair thinning — uniform hair loss in the same areas as pattern hair loss — is treated differently when cutting masculine or feminine styles. Either way, minimizing the appearance of mild diffuse hair loss is much easier to do than pattern hair loss.

Masculine haircutting tips for diffuse hair thinning:

>> Cut a short, uniform length buzz cut using clippers and a No. 2 clipper guard.

>> Clipper cut a high fade with long layers on top.

>> Clipper cut a taper cut starting with a No. 1 clipper guard at the back hairline and gradually lengthening to a No. 4 clipper guard for the entire top section.

Refer to Chapter 8 and Chapter 15 for tips on how to accomplish these cuts.

Feminine haircutting tips for diffuse hair thinning:

>> Cut longer layers and tease the root area to create bulk at the scalp (see Chapter 20).

>> Cut a short, blunt bob with a wispy fringe (see Chapters 9 and 13). If only mild diffuse thinning is present, cut some long layers to give the hair a natural lift.

>> Get edgy with shaved sides, a slightly deeper side part to create more bulk on top, and long layers for even greater coverage (see Chapter 12).

Styling Tips for Male Hair Loss

Creating unnaturally deep parts or combing the hair forward where it would normally lie down the sides or back of the head areas only brings attention to hair loss. Instead, always focus on creating natural, subtle coverage.

>> For hair thinning on the top of the head, blow-dry the hair in the opposite direction that it will ultimately be styled to create lift at the scalp.

>> When camouflaging front recession areas create a less structured, casually placed style.

>> For mild thinning at the crown, place the bristles of a styling brush (see Chapter 19) in the middle of the balding area and move the brush forward and back a couple of times to get a better grip on the hair. Then, while applying tension, blow-dry the thinning area — as well as the hair right above it — straight back and down. If a strong cowlick is involved — and it usually is — this action also disrupts the natural growth pattern and discourages flattening at the scalp.

>> Use the recommended styling aids and hair thickening products covered in "Styling Aids and Thickening Hair Products" in this chapter.

All styling products are covered in Chapter 18. More styling tips are included in Chapter 20.

Styling Tips for Female Hair Loss

Camouflaging mild hair loss on short, feminine hairstyles involves encouraging natural lift, adding bulk at the scalp, and directing the hair so that thinning areas have more coverage.

» Natural lift is good but adding too much volume will expose the scalp and create a see-through hairstyle that only makes hair thinning more obvious.

» If you can see the scalp through the hair, lightly brush tease the base of the hair to create more density at the scalp (see Chapter 20).

» Brush tease the crown area to prevent the hair from separating and putting hair loss on display.

» Thinning sides can be camouflaged by creating a hairstyle that includes curling and combing the hair forward. This enables you to borrow some hair from behind the ears, which is significantly thicker.

» The top of the hair can appear thicker by creating a tousled hairstyle that is seemingly curled in random directions. This, of course, is a sleight of hand for those with thinning hair, as you can move the hair near the top up and do the same for pieces of hair at the back nearest the top area of the head.

» Create a fairly thin but fluffy fringe by lightly teasing the base of the hair and then fanning the fringe across the forehead.

» Use the recommended styling aids and hair thickening products covered later this chapter.

Styling Aids and Thickening Hair Products

Thickening shampoos and conditioners can temporarily thicken individual hair strands. Styling aids can do this same thing, with some even creating pronounced density at the scalp. The most effective approach to improving the appearance of mild hair loss is by using a volumizing shampoo and conditioner, followed by lightly layering thickening products during the styling process.

» Thickening hair care products are sold in beauty stores, mass-merchandise outlets and beauty-related websites. Because hair strands shrink in diameter as part of the thinning process, thickening products give them a more robust appearance. You may want to alternate with general haircare products to avoid over-coating the hair.

>> Styling aids for thinning hair are also labeled as thickening products. Among this subcategory of styling aids, choose the ones you want to use by matching the specific styling needs of the hair and your haircut with the products at hand.

>> Thickening powders dramatically thicken the appearance of hair. The one drawback is they can seriously dry the hair. Apply them sparingly and avoid daily use. Also tease the base of the hair before applying the thickening powder for maximum scalp coverage.

>> Keratin hair fibers create much thicker looking hair. They're applied at the scalp where they tenaciously cling to even the tiniest strands. The best brands don't shed onto clothing or lose their staying power, even after hours of wear. My personal choice is Top Secret because it has an easy-to-apply applicator and a respectable selection of colors. Always finish the application of fibers with a light application of hairspray to make them super-secure.

Seeing Neither Hide nor Hair

When cutting and styling thinning hair becomes less effective, you may conclude that you're not only losing the battle but also the war. This is more common with men's hair thinning issues, but some women must face this reality as well.

While profound male hair loss has limited haircut solutions, there are a wealth of options regarding custom hairpieces.

>> A conservative solution to profound male hair loss is to use clippers (without a guard) to cut the random strands that are still present on the top area of the head and use a No. 2 clipper guard for the bottom and sides where denser hair is still present. Take care to shape and finish the neckline area and shorten and shape the sideburns.

>> An edgier solution for profound male hair loss is a balding cut (see Chapter 8 for instructions). Before doing this, make sure to check the scalp for shape irregularities, scars, and bulging veins. If one or more of these things are present, share your findings first and then only proceed if you are given permission to completely bare the scalp.

>> Modern toupees look so natural that if a man still wants to have the appearance of a full head of hair, they can wear a believable, custom hairpiece. Many barbers and stylists offer this service, as well as all hair replacement centers.

Profound female baldness needs to be addressed with undetectable hair coverings.

» Although you aren't a hair replacement specialist, you should be familiar with hair loss experts in your area. Providing a referral list of specialists for women with profound hair loss can be life-changing in terms of their self-confidence and appearance.

» Toppers (hairpieces that cover the top portion of the head) and full wigs are often the most effective options for women with profound hair loss. When fitted, cut, and colored professionally, they look 100 percent natural. These services should be done by wig or hair loss specialists.

» When complete hair loss is present, a special prosthetic wig can be worn that grips the scalp so efficiently that it will stay snugly attached to the scalp through everything from roller coaster rides to performing triple somersault high dives. These wigs can be quite expensive and require a special fitting process. Even though total hair loss is not always associated with medical treatments for cancer, your nearest cancer center is a good place to start when looking for referrals.

Index

About the Author

Jeryl E. Spear was a successful stylist, makeup artist, and salon owner for several years. Using her beauty and business expertise, she has pivoted to build a successful literary career and become a marketing guru for beauty corporations. Her passion, though, is her platform on social media that allows her to support fellow stylists who are making their mark in the beauty business. Jeryl currently has a total of 1 million followers, and that number continues to grow exponentially. Her primary accounts are Instagram (@hotonbeauty) and Facebook (@Hot Beauty Magazine).

Besides her relaxed, humorous approach to life, Jeryl's philosophy about all forms of beauty is easy: Keep it simple and you'll never go wrong. This is also her approach to the wealth of haircutting information, plus more than a few funny "snip-and-tell" stories, that she shares in *Haircutting For Dummies.*

Dedication

For my son Cody, who has grown from a young child filled with wonder to a man who professionally gives aid to others who are in trouble or distress. Your presence makes my life complete. To Jay, my companion in life, who was banished to our travel trailer for weeks without a single complaint while I wrote this book. And to all those who have nurtured my second career as a writer and given me countless opportunities to develop my skills and achieve success, I find your support and belief in me humbling.

Author's Acknowledgments

No man is an island, and no author can put a book together by herself. I feel honored to have had such wonderful support from people who offered their expert opinions, time, and caring to make *Haircutting for Dummies* a reality.

First on my list is Tom Carson, owner of Tom Carson Photography (www.tomcarsonphoto.com). As the primary photographer for this book, Tom spent endless hours sorting and sending me hundreds of pictures — every one being beautiful in its own way — to review. Due to his generosity and professional expertise, *Haircutting For Dummies* has a beautiful series of contemporary beauty photos that both inspire and teach you about haircutting.

Much gratitude also goes to content editors Dwight Miller (www.facebook.com/dwight.miller) and Brendnetta Ashley (www.instragram.com/edgybgirl). Dwight is a world-renowned hairstylist and a living legend in the beauty industry. He's also a treasured friend who has generously given his time and expertise to ensure this haircutting book is the best consumer guide for haircutting. Brendnetta is a rising hair educator and hair artist who is expert in all hair types, including natural haircuts and styles. You should check out her Instagram page, which is filled with posts of her work and short video tutorials.

Lastly, my Acknowledgments page wouldn't be complete without giving a special thank you to the Dummies editorial team. All involved were a dream to work with throughout this long book project. While writing any book, the editorial team can either create a happy or unhappy work experience for the author. Rest assured that I am finishing this project wearing a smile.

Publisher's Acknowledgments

Acquisitions Editor: Kelsey Baird
Project Editor: Tim Gallan
Development Editor: Christina Guthrie
Technical Reviewer: Kate Tully
Illustrators: Lisa Reed, Rashell Smith
Photographer: Tom Carson
Proofreader: Debbye Butler

Production Editor: Mohammed Zafar Ali
Cover Image: © MilanMarkovic/iStock/ Getty Images

Dummies is the global leader in the reference category and one of the most trusted and highly regarded brands in the world. No longer just focused on books, customers now have access to the dummies content they need in the format they want. Together we'll craft a solution that engages your customers, stands out from the competition, and helps you meet your goals.

Advertising & Sponsorships

Connect with an engaged audience on a powerful multimedia site, and position your message alongside expert how-to content. Dummies.com is a one-stop shop for free, online information and know-how curated by a team of experts.

- Targeted ads
- Video
- Email Marketing

- Microsites
- Sweepstakes sponsorship

20 MILLION PAGE VIEWS
EVERY SINGLE MONTH

15 MILLION UNIQUE
VISITORS PER MONTH

43% OF ALL VISITORS ACCESS THE SITE **VIA THEIR MOBILE DEVICES**

700,000 NEWSLETTER SUBSCRIPTIONS
TO THE INBOXES OF

300,000 UNIQUE INDIVIDUALS EVERY WEEK

# of dummies

Custom Publishing

Reach a global audience in any language by creating a solution that will differentiate you from competitors, amplify your message, and encourage customers to make a buying decision.

- Apps
- Books
- eBooks
- Video
- Audio
- Webinars

Brand Licensing & Content

Leverage the strength of the world's most popular reference brand to reach new audiences and channels of distribution.

For more information, visit dummies.com/biz

Learning Made Easy

ACADEMIC

Algebra I dummies

Mary Jane Sterling

9781119293576
USA $19.99
CAN $23.99
UK £15.99

Basic Math & Pre-Algebra dummies

Mark Zegarelli

9781119293637
USA $19.99
CAN $23.99
UK £15.99

Calculus dummies

Mark Ryan

9781119293491
USA $19.99
CAN $23.99
UK £15.99

Chemistry dummies

John T. Moore, EdD

9781119293460
USA $19.99
CAN $23.99
UK £15.99

Physics I dummies

Steven Holzner, PhD

9781119293590
USA $19.99
CAN $23.99
UK £15.99

1,001 Practice Questions
SAT dummies

Ron Woldoff

9781119215844
USA $26.99
CAN $31.99
UK £19.99

Organic Chemistry I dummies

Arthur Winter

9781119293378
USA $22.99
CAN $27.99
UK £16.99

Statistics dummies

Deborah J. Rumsey, PhD

9781119293521
USA $19.99
CAN $23.99
UK £15.99

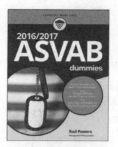

2016/2017
ASVAB dummies

Rod Powers

9781119239178
USA $18.99
CAN $22.99
UK £14.99

Includes Online Practice Tests
1,001 Practice Questions
Praxis Core dummies

Carla Kirkland
Chan Cleveland

9781119263883
USA $26.99
CAN $31.99
UK £19.99

Available Everywhere Books Are Sold

dummies.com

dummies
A Wiley Brand

Small books for big imaginations

GETTING STARTED WITH Coding

Get Creative with Code!

Camille McCue, PhD

9781119177173
USA $9.99
CAN $9.99
UK £8.99

MODDING Minecraft™

Build Your Own Minecraft Mods!

Sarah Guthals, PhD
Stephen Foster, PhD
Lindsey Handley, PhD

9781119177272
USA $9.99
CAN $9.99
UK £8.99

MAKING YouTube® VIDEOS

Star in Your Own Video!

Nick Willoughby

9781119177241
USA $9.99
CAN $9.99
UK £8.99

DESIGNING Digital Games

Create Games with Scratch™!

Derek Breen

9781119177210
USA $9.99
CAN $9.99
UK £8.99

GETTING STARTED WITH Raspberry Pi®

Program Your Raspberry Pi!

Richard Wentk

9781119262657
USA $9.99
CAN $9.99
UK £6.99

EXPERIMENTING WITH Science

Think. Test. and Learn!

Chris J. Mullins, PhD

9781119291336
USA $9.99
CAN $9.99
UK £6.99

CREATING Digital Animations

Animate Stories with Scratch™!

Derek Breen

9781119233527
USA $9.99
CAN $9.99
UK £6.99

GETTING STARTED WITH Engineering

Think Like an Engineer!

Camille McCue, PhD

9781119291220
USA $9.99
CAN $9.99
UK £6.99

WRITING Computer Code

Learn the Language of Computers!

Chris Minnick and Eva Holland

9781119177302
USA $9.99
CAN $9.99
UK £8.99

Unleash Their Creativity

dummies.com

dummies®
A Wiley Brand